Applied Positive Psychology

Improving Everyday Life, Health, Schools, Work, and Society

Series in applied psychology
Edwin A. Fleishman, George Mason University
Jeanette N. Cleveland, Pennsylvania State University
Series Editors

Applied Positive Psychology

Improving Everyday Life, Health, Schools, Work, and Society

Edited by

Stewart I. Donaldson
Claremont Graduate University

Mihaly Csikszentmihalyi
Claremont Graduate University

and

Jeanne Nakamura
Claremont Graduate University

Psychology Press
Taylor & Francis Group
NEW YORK AND HOVE

Published in 2011
by Routledge
711 Third Avenue
New York, NY 10017
www.psypress.com

Published in Great Britain
by Routledge
2 Park Square, Milton Park
Abingdon, Oxon, OX14 4RN

Routledge is an imprint of the Taylor & Francis Group, an Informa business

Typeset by RefineCatch Limited, Bungay, Suffolk, UK

Library of Congress Cataloging-in-Publication Data
Applied positive psychology : improving everyday life, health, schools, work, and society/edited by Stewart I. Donaldson, Mihaly Csikszentmihalyi, Jeanne Nakamura.
    p. cm. – (Applied psychology; 40)
    Includes bibliographical references and index.
    ISBN 978–0–415–87781–7 – ISBN 978–0–415–87782–4 1. Psychology, Applied. I. Donaldson, Stewart I. (Stewart Ian) II. Csikszentmihalyi, Mihaly. III. Nakamura, Jeanne.
    BF636.A597 2011
    158'.9–dc22

ISBN: 978–0–415–87781–7 (hbk)
ISBN: 978–0–415–87782–4 (pbk)

A gift for our students past, present, and future, and for those bold enough to look at the world through positive lenses with scientific discipline and rigor.

Contents

About the Editors

Stewart I. Donaldson is Professor and Chair of Psychology, Director of the Institute of Organizational and Program Evaluation Research, and Dean of the School of Behavioral and Organizational Sciences at Claremont Graduate University. Dean Donaldson continues to develop and lead one of the most extensive and rigorous graduate programs specializing in applied psychology, positive psychology, and evaluation science. He has taught numerous university courses, professional development workshops, and has mentored and coached more than 100 graduate students and working professionals during the past two decades. Dr. Donaldson has also provided organizational consulting, applied research, or program evaluation services to more than 100 different organizations. He has been Principal Investigator on more than 30 extramural grants and contracts to support research, evaluations, scholarship, and graduate students at Claremont Graduate University.

Dr. Donaldson is a fellow of the Western Psychological Association, is serving a three-year elected term on the Board of the American Evaluation Association, and is on the Editorial Boards of the *American Journal of Evaluation*, *New Directions for Evaluation*, and the *SAGE Research Methods Online*. He has authored or co-authored more than 200 evaluation reports, scientific journal articles, and chapters, including his latest article in the *Journal of Positive Psychology* (2010; with Ia Ko) entitled "Positive organizational psychology, behavior, and scholarship: A review of the emerging literature and evidence base." His recent books include: *Applied Positive Psychology: Improving Everyday Life, Health, Schools, Work, and Society* (this volume; with Mihaly Csikszentmihalyi and Jeanne Nakamura); *Social Psychology and Evaluation* (forthcoming; with Melvin M. Mark and Bernadette Campbell); *What Counts as Credible Evidence in Applied Research and Contemporary Evaluation Practice?* (2008; with Christina A. Christie and Melvin M. Mark); *Program Theory-Driven Evaluation Science: Strategies and Applications* (2007); *Applied Psychology: New Frontiers and Rewarding Careers* (2006; with Dale E. Berger and Kathy Pezdek); and *Evaluating Social Programs and Problems: Visions for the New Millennium* (2003; with Michael Scriven). Dr. Donaldson has been honored with Early Career Achievement Awards from the Western Psychological Association and the American Evaluation Association.

Mihaly Csikszentmihalyi (CHEEK sent me high ee) was born in Italy where his father was serving as a consul for the Hungarian government. During World War II as a pre-teen child, he witnessed the crash of European society and wondered why grown-ups had not found a better way to live. While one older brother was killed and the other taken prisoner for many years in the Russian *gulags*, he was lucky to escape from the war relatively unscathed. He had to work, however, at many jobs instead of finishing high school. The quest to understand how to improve life led him through religion, philosophy, literature, and art, before coming to rest on psychology, which promised more empirically based answers to his questions.

He came to the USA in 1956, with $1.25 to his name and almost no English. While working at night (11pm–7am) as a hotel auditor, he enrolled at the University of Illinois in Chicago. For his ESL class he wrote the first of two autobiographical short stories that were published in the *New Yorker*. He then transferred to the University of Chicago, where he received his PhD in Human Development in 1965, with a thesis on artistic creativity. After graduation he started teaching at Lake Forest College, where he became Chair of the Department of Sociology and Anthropology; here he wrote his first papers on what later became known as the flow experience. After five years he returned to the University of Chicago in a faculty position; he taught there for 30 years, eventually becoming Chair of the Psychology Department. He wrote several books and over 200 articles while at Chicago. In 1999 he accepted a Chair in the Drucker School of Management in Claremont, California, where he taught for eight years before transferring to the Psychology Department in the same University. Besides writing numerous books and articles on the topics of creativity and flow, Csikszentmihalyi has developed the Experience Sampling Method as a way to measure people's activities and experiences in their natural environment.

Jeanne Nakamura is Assistant Professor of Psychology, Co-Director of the Positive Psychology concentration, and Co-Director of the Quality of Life Research Center in the School of Behavioral and Organizational Sciences at Claremont Graduate University. She received her BA and PhD from the University of Chicago. She helped direct the GoodWork Project, a series of studies of excellence and social responsibility in professional life, including the Study of the Transmission of Excellence. She investigates positive psychology in a developmental context, including engagement and creativity, mentoring and good work, and aging well. She is the co-author of *Good Mentoring* and *Creativity and Development*, and co-editor of *Supportive Frameworks for Youth Engagement*.

About the Contributors

Jeff Bednar is a doctoral candidate at the University of Michigan in the Management and Organizations Department of the Ross School of Business. His current research explores how individuals construct work-related identities that are sources of life-giving and sustaining meaning. Jeff is also a graduate of the Marriott School of Management at Brigham Young University, where he earned a bachelor's and a master's degree in accounting.

Valerie J. Calderon is a consultant with Gallup. She is responsible for providing strategic and tactical consulting to internal and client teams for research project execution. She advises enterprise, education, non-profit sector, and faith-based clients.

Dr. Calderon is the managing consultant for the Gallup Student Poll, an assessment and solutions initiative measuring the hope, engagement, and well-being of America's students in grades 5–12. She leads internal teams in project development and advises schools, districts, state departments of education, and partner organizations in survey administration, data interpretation, and application.

Prior to joining Gallup, Dr. Calderon was a freelance writer and editor, publishing dozens of popular articles, curriculum, and scholarly work for both Web and print media. She has worked extensively with youth and parents as a minister, substitute teacher, program adviser, and coach.

Dr. Calderon received a bachelor's degree from Miami University (Ohio) in zoology. She received master of divinity and doctorate degrees in theology from Southwestern Baptist Theological Seminary.

Kim S. Cameron is William Russell Kelly Professor of Management and Organization at the Ross School of Business and Professor of Higher Education in the School of Education at the University of Michigan. He served as Dean of the Weatherhead School of Management at Case Western Reserve University, Associate Dean in the Marriott School of Management at Brigham Young University, and as department chair and director of several executive education programs at the University of Michigan. He also served on the faculties of the University of Wisconsin-Madison and Ricks College. He organized and directed the Organizational Studies Division of the National Center for Higher Education Management Systems in Boulder, Colorado.

Dr. Cameron's past research on organizational downsizing, effectiveness, quality culture, and the development of management skills has been published in more than 120 academic articles and 13 scholarly books. His current research focuses on the virtuousness of and in organizations and their relationships to organizational performance. He is one of the co-founders of the Center for Positive Organizational Scholarship at the University of Michigan, and consults with organizations throughout the United States, Europe, Asia, South America, and Africa.

He received BS and MS degrees from Brigham Young University and MA and PhD degrees from Yale University. He is married to the former Melinda Cummings and has seven children.

Matthew D. Della Porta is a doctoral candidate at the University of California, Riverside and is a member of Dr. Sonja Lyubomirsky's Positive Psychology Laboratory. He received his BA from the University of Rochester (2006) with high honors in research in psychology and his MA from the University of California, Riverside (2009).

Della Porta currently works as a researcher and teaching assistant. His primary interests include individual differences in practicing happiness-boosting activities, the implementation of positive interventions in applied settings, and the relationship between mindfulness and well-being.

Ed Diener is the Joseph R. Smiley Distinguished Professor of Psychology at the University of Illinois. He received his doctorate at the University of Washington in 1974 and has been a faculty member at the University of Illinois for the past 34 years. Dr. Diener was the president of both the International Society of Quality of Life Studies and the Society of Personality and Social Psychology. Currently he is the president of the International Positive Psychology Association. Dr. Diener was the editor of the *Journal of Personality and Social Psychology* and the *Journal of Happiness Studies*, and he is the founding editor of *Perspectives on Psychological Science*. Diener has over 260 publications, with about 200 being in the area of the psychology of well-being, and is listed as one of the most highly cited psychologists by the Institute of Scientific Information, with over 15,000 citations to his credit. He won the Distinguished Researcher Award from the International Society of Quality of Life Studies, the first Gallup Academic Leadership Award, and the Block Award for Personality Psychology. Dr. Diener also won several teaching awards, including the Oakley-Kundee Award for Undergraduate Teaching at the University of Illinois.

Jane E. Dutton is the Robert L. Kahn Distinguished University Professor of Business Administration and Psychology at the University of Michigan. Jane received her PhD in Organizational Behavior from Northwestern University. She co-directs the Center for Positive Organizational Scholarship at the Ross School of Business (see http://www.bus.umich.edu/Positive/). Her research interests include positive identities at work, compassion and work organizations, positive work relationships, and job crafting at work. She has co-edited a series of books that link positive psychology to work organizations: *Positive Organizational Scholarship: Foundations of a New Discipline*, K. Cameron, J. Dutton and R. E. Quinn (Eds.),

2003; *Exploring Positive Relationships at Work*, J. Dutton and B. Ragins (Eds.), 2007; and *Exploring Positive Identities and Organizations*, L. Roberts and J. Dutton (Eds.), 2009. She is currently working on a forthcoming edited book on *Positive Social Change and Organizations*, by K. Golden-Biddle and J. Dutton (Eds.). Her research articles and chapters written in the last 10 years all try to establish how work organizations contribute to human flourishing.

Barbara L. Fredrickson is Kenan Distinguished Professor of Psychology and principal investigator of the Positive Emotions and Psychophysiology Laboratory at the University of North Carolina at Chapel Hill. She has published widely in social psychology, affective science, and positive psychology. Dr. Fredrickson has won numerous awards for her teaching and research, including the American Psychological Association's Templeton Prize in Positive Psychology and the Society of Experimental Social Psychology's Career Trajectory Award, and is regularly invited to give keynote addresses nationally and internationally. Her book, *Positivity* (2009), shares the science of positive emotions with a general readership, with an emphasis on how to apply it to overcome negativity and thrive.

Hans Henrik Knoop is Associate Professor of Educational Psychology at the Danish School of Education, University of Aarhus, Denmark, and Director of the Universe Research Laboratory – an international research center focused on learning and creativity.

Hans Henrik Knoop has been involved in research cooperation with colleagues at Harvard University, Stanford University, and at Claremont Graduate University in the GoodWork® Project (1996–), and as researcher he has participated in development projects for LEGO (1998–2004), Danfoss Universe (2005–), SIS Akademi (2004–), and Royal Greenland Academy (2006), among others. In 2006–2007 he contributed to the Danish DR2's programs on talent development in schools, and he was the scholarly anchor of the Danish TV2's reality documentary series "Plan B" (2006–2007) and "SKOLEN – verdensklasse på 100 dage" (2008) concerning efficient education. "Plan B" received international attention in being nominated for the prestigious television award Golden Rose of Montreux in 2007. More than 12,000 pupils and 2000 teachers are currently collaborating with the Universe Research Laboratory.

Hans Henrik Knoop is a member of the Board of Directors of the International Positive Psychology Association (IPPA, 2007–), a member of the Executive Committee of the European Network for Positive Psychology (2008–), and Chair of the 5th European Conference on Positive Psychology in Copenhagen in 2010.

Hans Henrik Knoop has presented his work through more than 900 invited keynotes and lectures in Denmark and conferences in China, Finland, France, Germany, Iceland, Norway, Spain, The Philippines, the UK, and the USA.

Ia Ko is a doctoral student in the School of Behavioral and Organizational Sciences at Claremont Graduate University. She received her BA and BAA from Ewha Women's University, an MOD from Bowling Green University, and an MA from Claremont Graduate University.

The research of Ia Ko focuses on people's optimal experiences at work and their relations to the work. Specifically, she is interested in flow, job crafting, engagement, meaning, and happiness in the workplace. Ia Ko is currently involved with the study of sources of good mentoring and another study on positive organizational psychology.

Laura E. Kurtz received her bachelor's degree in psychology with highest honors from the University of North Carolina at Chapel Hill. During her undergraduate career, Laura completed her honors thesis on the interpersonal effects of shared laughter in friendship pairs in Dr. Fredrickson's Positive Emotions and Psychophysiology Laboratory. She is currently working at Duke University as the coordinator for the Wilbourn Infant Laboratory, assisting in research on early language acquisition and cognitive development. Laura plans to pursue her doctorate in either clinical or social psychology, further her research on the importance of shared laughter, and ultimately aspires to be a professor of psychology.

Shane J. Lopez, Senior Scientist in Residence, is an architect of the Gallup Student Poll. A measure of hope, engagement, and well-being, the Student Poll taps into the hearts and minds of American students to determine what drives achievement. Dr. Lopez is the director of the annual Gallup Well-Being Forum, which convenes scholars, leaders, and decision-makers to discuss healthcare and global well-being. He also serves as the Research Director for the Clifton Strengths School.

Dr. Lopez has published more than 100 articles and chapters and seven books, including *Positive Psychology: Exploring the Best in People* and *The Encyclopedia of Positive Psychology*. With C. R. Snyder, he published *Positive Psychology: The Scientific and Practical Explorations of Human Strengths*, which won the Sage Press Book of the Year Award; *Positive Psychological Assessment: A Handbook of Models and Measures*; and *The Handbook of Positive Psychology*.

Sonja Lyubomirsky is Professor of Psychology at the University of California, Riverside. She received her AB, *summa cum laude*, from Harvard University (1989) and her PhD in Social/Personality Psychology from Stanford University (1994). Lyubomirsky currently teaches courses in social psychology and positive psychology and serves as graduate advisor. Her teaching and mentoring of students have been recognized with the Faculty of the Year and Faculty Mentor of the Year Awards.

In her work, Lyubomirsky has focused on developing a science of human happiness. To this end, her research addresses three critical questions: (1) What makes people happy?; (2) Is happiness a good thing?; and (3) How can we make people happier still? She is currently testing the potential of happiness-sustaining activities – for example, expressing gratitude, practicing altruism, and visualizing a positive future – to durably increase a person's happiness level higher than his or her "set point" and to thwart adaptation to positive experiences. In 2002, Lyubomirsky's research was recognized with a Templeton Positive Psychology Prize. Her research has been written up in hundreds of magazines and newspaper articles and she has appeared in multiple TV shows, radio shows, and feature documentaries in North America, Asia, South America, Australia, and Europe. Her book, *The How of Happiness*, was released in January 2008 by Penguin Press (North America) and translated into 18 languages.

Nansook Park is Associate Professor of Psychology at the University of Michigan and a nationally certified school psychologist (NCSP). She did her graduate work both in Korea and the USA and has a research and practice background in clinical and school psychology. Her work in studying character strengths and virtues is considered groundbreaking. Dr. Park took the lead in developing ways to assess character strengths for children and youth and for conducting cross-cultural investigations. Her main research interest is the promotion of positive development and well-being. Using cross-cultural and lifespan developmental perspectives, she is interested in the development, correlates, mechanisms, and consequences of character strengths and virtues, positive experiences, happiness, and positive relationships, and especially their role in resiliency, well-being, health, family functioning, education, and work. She is also interested in character education and strength-based practice. Her studies of children and youth well-being have been recognized by several national and international honors. She is a member of the Annenberg/Sunnylands Commission on Positive Youth Development and the International Positive Psychology Association Board of Directors, a Research Fellow at the Positive Psychology Center of the University of Pennsylvania, and an Associate Editor of *Applied Psychology: Health and Well-Being* and a Consulting Editor of the *Journal of Positive Psychology*.

Christopher Peterson is Professor of Psychology and Organizational Studies and former Director of Clinical Training at the University of Michigan. He also holds an appointment as an Arthur F. Thurnau Professor, in recognition of his excellence in undergraduate teaching. He was the recipient of a Rackham Distinguished Faculty Achievement Award at the University of Michigan. In 2003, Dr. Peterson was named by the Institute for Scientific Information (ISI) as among the world's 100 most widely cited psychologists over the past 20 years. He is author of more than 300 scholarly publications.

He is the research director of the Values in Action (VIA) Project, which is arguably the most ambitious research project to date within positive psychology. He has created a coherent classification of human strengths and virtues and reliable and valid strategies for assessing these aspects of excellence. He is also well-known for his pioneering studies on optimism and health. He developed the CAVE technique – an acronym for Content Analysis of Verbatim Explanations – that allows optimism to be assessed from how individuals explain the causes of events. He is a member of the Positive Psychology Steering Committee and the International Positive Psychology Association board of directors, a senior fellow at the Positive Psychology Center, and a lecturer for the Master of Applied Positive Psychology program at the University of Pennsylvania. He is a Co-Editor of *Applied Psychology: Health and Well-Being* and the Positive Psychology Book Series Editor for Oxford University Press. His most recent books are *Character Strengths and Virtues* (2004) and *A Primer in Positive Psychology* (2006).

Laura Morgan Roberts is Professor of Psychology, Culture and Organization Studies in Antioch University's PhD in Leadership and Change Program. She has also served on the faculties of the Harvard Business School, University of Michigan, Wharton School, Simmons School of Management, Georgia State University, and AVT Business School in Denmark. Laura's research and consulting focuses on unlocking the pathways for increasing personal and professional alignment, by constructing, sustaining, and restoring positive identities at work. She has published her work on authenticity, identity, image management, diversity, strengths, and value creation in her edited book, *Exploring Positive Identities and Organizations* (Roberts and Dutton, Eds.), and in numerous articles, book chapters, and case studies. Laura earned her BA in Psychology from the University of Virginia and her MA and PhD in Organizational Psychology from the University of Michigan.

Katherine Ryan received a BS in Psychology and English from the University of Illinois before joining *Perspectives on Psychological Science* as Editorial Assistant. She is currently a PhD student in English at the University of California, Irvine.

Nancy L. Sin is a graduate student in the Department of Psychology at the University of California, Riverside. She received her BA in Psychology with honors from UCLA and her MA in Social/Personality Psychology from the University of California, Riverside.

Sin is interested in how positive states influence mental and physical health. In her work, Sin has explored the efficacy of positive psychology interventions for ameliorating depression and improving well-being. She is currently conducting research on the relationships between positive emotions and health behaviors, including adherence to medical treatment and doctor–patient interactions.

Shelley E. Taylor studies social relationships and how they are protective against stress. Her tend-and-befriend model, which was developed in response to the fight-or-flight metaphor that usually guides stress research, builds on the fact that, in response to stress, people come together with others for joint protection of self and offspring. Professor Taylor also studies self-regulation, stress, and coping, and explores the skills that people develop and use for anticipating stressful events and for minimizing their adverse effects when they do occur. Finally, Taylor studies how positive beliefs are protective of mental and physical health. She shows that optimism, self-enhancement, a perception of control, and social support can protect against threats or traumas, not only psychologically but also in terms of physical health.

Dr. Taylor received her doctorate from Yale University. She is the author of more than 350 publications in journals and books and is the author of *Social Cognition, Positive Illusions, Health Psychology*, and *The Tending Instinct*. Professor Taylor is the recipient of a number of awards, including the American Psychological Association's Distinguished Scientific Contribution to Psychology Award. She is a member of the American Academy of Arts and Sciences, the Institute of Medicine, and the National Academy of Sciences.

Series Foreword

There is a compelling need for innovative approaches to the solution of many pressing problems involving human relationships in today's society. Such approaches are more likely to be successful when they are based on sound research and applications. Our *Series in Applied Psychology* offers publications that emphasize state-of-the-art research and its application to important issues of human behavior in a variety of social settings. The objective is to bridge both academic and applied interests.

We are pleased to have *Applied Positive Psychology: Improving Everyday Life, Health, Schools, Work, and Society*, edited by Stewart I. Donaldson, Mihaly Csikszentmihalyi, and Jeanne Nakamura, join our Series. The volume is the outcome of the Stauffer Symposium held at the Claremont Graduate University in 2009. The most prolific scholars and researchers in positive psychology were invited to discuss and develop new strategies for improving (1) everyday life, and healthcare, (2) schools and education systems, and (3) organizations, work life, and societies globally.

Along with Dr. Seligman, who provides opening remarks in the preface of this volume, the editors are instrumental founders of the science of positive psychology. Dr. Donaldson is Professor and Chair of Psychology, Director of the Institute of Organizational and Program Evaluation Research, and Dean of the School of Behavioral and Organizational Sciences at Claremont Graduate University. He has co-authored more than 200 evaluation reports, scientific journal articles, and chapters, and has provided organizational, consulting, or program evaluation to more than 100 different organizations. He has numerous texts and was honored with Early Career Achievement Awards from the Western Psychological Association and the American Evaluation Association. Dr. Csikszentmihalyi is a Distinguished Professor of Psychology at Claremont Graduate University, and one of the pre-eminent researchers and thinkers in this extraordinary field of positive psychology. He is best known for his research on creativity, innovation, and the concept of flow. He is the Founder of the Quality of Life Research Center (QLRC), which is a non-profit research institute that studies "positive psychology," specifically, human strengths such as optimism, creativity, intrinsic motivation, and responsibility. Dr. Nakamura is an Assistant Professor in the School of Behavioral and Organizational Sciences at Claremont Graduate University and co-directs the positive psychology concentration and the QLRC.

The present volume is an ambitious and strategic discussion of a growing field. Further, it is a constructive and timely approach to reframing the challenges we face both at work and in schools. Over the last 45 years, through legal and government mandates, individuals, institutions, and workplaces are often told what they cannot do. However, it is often not clear what they should or can do. This book is a refreshing reaffirmation of the strengths of healthy, positive human interactions. The lead editor begins with an articulation of what positive psychology involves, the subfield's short history, and the rapid expansion of positive scholarship. The remaining 13 chapters are organized into four major sections: (1) core areas in applied positive psychology, (2) improving health, education, and human development, (3) improving institutions, organizations, and work, and (4) future directions for the application of positive psychology.

Three chapters identify and elaborate on the core areas of positive psychology. First, the distinguishing feature of this emerging field is the enhancement of human well-being, and going beyond simply the elimination of dysfunctional behaviors or illness (Chapter 2). Further, two core correlates of well-being are presented in separate chapters: positive emotions (Chapter 3) and character strengths and virtues (Chapter 4). Each chapter defines a core construct, how it is measured, and the scientific evidence linking the benefits or outcomes of developing and promoting each. Consistent with the theme of this Series, each chapter identifies ways based on scientific research to develop innovative approaches to apply each construct. For example, in Chapter 2 the case to assess well-being at the national level is made, linking such applications as commuting, green space, and air pollution. Each author emphasizes the need to focus on ways in which individuals, organizations, and institutions can cultivate and enhance our well-being, positive emotions, and character/virtues.

In the next section, four chapters incorporate the core areas and articulate how positive psychology can enhance individual health and well-being, help depressed individuals, redirect educational practices, and recalibrate our focus on student assessment to measure what is achieved in relation to positive behaviors rather than a focus on deficiencies. For example, Chapter 5 on enhancing health and well-being focuses on the development of positive characteristics and skills such as optimism, mastery, self-esteem, and social support rather than on the antecedents of mental or physical illness. Further, Chapter 6 describes why and how positive psychology can be used not only to treat depressed individuals but to enrich the lives of non-depressed persons. Similarly, Chapters 7 and 8 underscore the important role that positive psychology can have in the redesign of our schools, institutions, and societies, as well as the evaluation of these changes. Affirmative assessment measures include tracking students' hopes, engagement levels, and well-being over a 10-year period and linking these with grade point average (GPA), achievement scores, retention rates, and employment.

In the third section of the text, three chapters describe the application of positive psychology to work contexts, including the growth and importance of positive organizational psychology (POP; Chapter 9), prosocial organizational practices and the development of positive identity at work (Chapter 10), and effects of virtuous leadership on work performance (Chapter 11). Again, the message throughout these chapters is that organizations can design an environment that will enhance employees' subjective experiences and quality of life at work and cultivate employee flourishing by shaping his/her identity constructed at work and by studying "positive deviance" (or the best of the human condition) at work in order to understand its relation to performance. Finally, Chapter 12 discusses mentoring within the framework of positive psychology as a method for enhancing adult development at work.

In the final section, Chapter 13 and the Epilog chart the philosophical, virtue-guided, application of positive psychology to individual health, education, work, and society. Between these two final chapters, the balance between an ideal state to strive for in enhancing the human experience and practical concrete steps to move us in that direction is achieved. Further, the senior editors acknowledge critiques of the field and encourage both scholars and practitioners to either track intervention effectiveness or ensure that applications demonstrate effectiveness through systematic evaluation.

Applied Positive Psychology: Improving Everyday Life, Health, Schools, Work, and Society is an appropriate text for senior undergraduate and graduate students in clinical and counseling psychology, occupational health psychology, child and school psychology, organizational psychology, management and organization, sociology of work, and organizational change. Both scholars and practitioners alike will find this text useful. The book is a solid collection of theory and science-based reviews and recommendations for practice. Finally, for teachers and practitioners who want to know what they can do rather than what they cannot, this book is one that should be in your library.

Jeanette N. Cleveland and Edwin A. Fleishman
Series Editors

Preface

Positive psychology has experienced extraordinary growth in the past decade. Emerging research in this area is suggesting new strategies for improving everyday life, healthcare, schools and education systems, organizations and work life, and societies across the globe. In an effort to learn more about this thriving movement within psychology and the social sciences more generally, we invited some of the most prolific scholars and researchers in these areas to the Claremont Colleges to help us understand how best to apply the science of psychology to better the human condition. One of the founders of the positive psychology movement, Professor Martin Seligman, offered to kick off this amazingly well-attended event. There were more than 850 participants onsite or online for our day-long Stauffer Symposium. He offered up some opening remarks to set the stage that were projected onto a big screen in the front of the newly remodeled Garrison Theater.

MARTIN SELIGMAN – PAST, PRESENT, AND FUTURE OF POSITIVE PSYCHOLOGY

Welcome to this auspicious occasion. It is a privilege to be among you to help celebrate Claremont Graduate University's honoring the burgeoning science of positive psychology. I'm sorry I can't be among you in person, and in my last 30 seconds you'll find out why I can't be among you. I want to talk about the past, the present, and my vision of the future of positive psychology. The past begins, in many ways, with someone you are probably looking at right now, Mike Csikszentmihalyi. Ten years ago, when I was president of the American Psychological Association, I called Mike up and said: "Mike, it's time to found a field together. It's time to legitimize what you and Jeanne Nakamura and Ed Diener and so many other fine scientists have been doing." And that legitimization became known as positive psychology. Mike has been my co-conspirator every step of the way and it has culminated at the present. And what I want to say about the present is: "Where does one go to learn positive psychology?" Well, there are several Masters of Applied Positive Psychology programs in the world. There's one that's been going for four years at the University of Pennsylvania under the direction of James Pawelski and Debbie Swick, with my help. There's a fine one at the University of East London run by Ilona Boniwell. And graduate degrees and certificate programs are springing up in Milan, in Mexico City, in Australia, and elsewhere. But Claremont Graduate University has founded the first fully fledged doctoral programs in positive psychology and I want to commend the vision of Claremont in doing this. So that's the present.

The future: What does the future hold for positive psychology and the contribution it can make to society? Well, my vision of the future has four different endeavors. The first endeavor I call "positive physical health." If you think about positive psychology as having argued that positive mental health is something over and above the absence of mental illness – that is, the presence of positive emotion, the presence of flow, the presence of engagement, the presence of meaning, the presence of positive relationships – can the same thing be said for physical health? Is there a real entity, "physical health," over and above the absence of physical illness? Well, many of us think this is so, and the Robert Wood Johnson Foundation is putting this to the test now. Is there a set of subjective indicators (such as optimism and a sense of control over health), biological indicators (not in the usual bottom illness part, but the top part, the upper 5% of cholesterol), and functional indicators (excellent marriage, excellent fit to work, excellent physical shape) that constitute a latent variable that we could call "positive physical health?" And does this variable predict longer life, higher quality of life, better prognosis when illness strikes, and lower healthcare expenditures? So, over the next decade, I think positive physical health may arise as a science.

The second endeavor is positive neuroscience, and I'm pleased to tell you that the Templeton Foundation has decided to support positive neuroscience. Over the next year and a half, we will be giving roughly twenty $200,000 grants to people who want to do breakthrough research in positive neuroscience. So we want to do for neuroscience what we did with Mike Csikszentmihalyi and Ray Fowler 10 years ago for positive psychology.

The third endeavor is positive social science, and in many ways this is the theme that brings you together. It is my hope that considerations of what makes life worth living (of meaning, of engagement, of virtue and strength) can be at the heart of a revivified political science, economics, and philosophy. And to that end, it is my hope that we will be supporting and rewarding the leaders in the field of what I will call the social science of thriving.

And finally, the reason why I can't be here today – the fourth endeavor – is positive education. Education as usual consists of taking young people and teaching them workplace skills. But there's an epidemic of depression, with low life satisfaction in addition. Would it be possible to have positive education? That is, without sacrificing any of the usual skills of discipline, reading, literacy, numeracy, can we build engagement, meaning, positive emotion, and good relations at schools? And to this end, we've been running programs in the United States with the Kipp Schools in Riverdale, in the United Kingdom, and where I am right now, and why I can't be with you, in Australia. A year ago we began our training of the entire faculty of the Geelong Grammar School, one of the great schools of Australia, south of Melbourne. We've come back again this January to give booster training to the faculty and to train 200 state school teachers from all of Australia to spread the notion of positive education. So that, I think, is part of our future that gleams in my eye: positive health, positive neuroscience, a positive social science of thriving, and positive education. Well, you are in the presence of all the leaders of the field of positive psychology, and I wish you a fruitful, stimulating celebration of positive psychology. Thank you for coming.

THE STAUFFER SYMPOSIUM PRESENTATIONS AND VOLUME

Professor Seligman's remarks were followed by a full day of presentations, panel discussions, questions from the audience, and responses from thought leaders in the emerging positive social sciences. Each presenter was also asked to provide a chapter for this volume, and we invited Sonja Lyubomirsky of the University of California, Riverside, and her lab, and Shane Lopez of Gallup University and his colleagues to provide additional chapters to round out this volume. It turned out that David Cooperider was not able to deliver a chapter on the timeline of this volume, so Ia Ko and Stewart Donaldson provided a chapter on applied positive organizational psychology to extend coverage on improving work and organizations. Each chapter in this volume addresses how the science of positive psychology can be used to promote human betterment and societal well-being. The authors take on the challenges of improving nations, governments and their public policies, health and healthcare issues, education, organizational effectiveness, and quality of work life. Furthermore, Professor Mihaly Csikszentmihalyi leaves us with a new vision of the human condition. He believes that our understanding of human nature is now changing from one of dismal pessimism to a vision that foregrounds what is good about women and men, and that provides ideas and processes that will nurture, cultivate, and increase what is good about us and about our actions. He also outlines the opportunities that this new image of humanity presents to applied positive psychologists, and inspires us by declaring that this new perspective in psychology should guarantee a rewarding life to those who choose to pursue it. It is my hope that this volume both informs and inspires you to pursue ways in which you can make societal contributions by applying the science of positive psychology.

ACKNOWLEDGMENTS

The editors of this volume would like to express much gratitude to and admiration of our research associate, Ia Ko, for her outstanding leadership, contributions to positive psychology, and stellar editorial work on the production of this manuscript. Special thanks go out to the School of Behavioral and Organizational Sciences (SBOS), Director of External Affairs, Paul Thomas, and his wonderful team of graduate student volunteers for making sure that the Stauffer Symposium was successful beyond expectations. And much appreciation must go out to Shabnam Ozlati and Scott Donaldson for running a flawless interactive online broadcast.

We are also very thankful to the chapter authors for providing engaging chapters and for their best work in thinking about applications of positive psychology. We sincerely appreciate the helpful reviews and suggestions for improvement given by the reviewers: Lois Tetrick, George Mason University; Cary Cherniss, Rutgers University; Karen Golden-Biddle, Boston University; Joe Hatcher, Ripon College; Mary Devitt, Jamestown College; Mark Hopper, Loras College; and the Routledge Editorial Team.

Finally, this project would not have been possible without a generous gift shepherded by SBOS Board of Advisor Member, Michael Whalen, and provided by the John Stauffer Charitable Trust to SBOS, Claremont Graduate University. You will never know how much your financial support has advanced the mission of SBOS.

Stewart I. Donaldson
Claremont Graduate University

Part I

Introduction

1

Determining What Works, if Anything, in Positive Psychology

STEWART I. DONALDSON

*M*any have claimed that the emerging area within psychology known as positive psychology holds great promise for advancing knowledge about optimal human functioning and improving the quality of life in modern societies. Curious about these claims, we invited some of the most prominent leaders in this new area of scholarship to the Claremont Colleges to discuss the implications of scientific findings from positive psychology for improving human welfare and performance. The chapters in this volume explore the potential applications of the science of positive psychology for improving everyday life, health, schools, work, and society at large.

WHAT IS POSITIVE PSYCHOLOGY?

You will learn more about this question throughout the pages of this volume. But, let me start with a bit of folklore or perhaps informal history about the inception of positive psychology as we know it today. It all began on a beautiful beach in Hawaii. I've long discovered that many of the best things in life as we know it originate from the ocean and beautiful beaches across the planet. In this case, an adventurous Mihaly Csikszentmihalyi was swimming off the volcanic coast of the Big Island of Hawaii, Kona. Underestimating the force of swell he found himself being smashed against the volcanic rock and struggling for his survival. Beaten and bloodied, he was barely able to struggle his way back to the beach. A man on the beach had been watching this frightening incident, and had made his way down to the beach to help Dr. Csikszentmihalyi. The man guided Mihaly back to the life-guard station near the resort where they both were staying. As fate would have it the helpful bystander was President-elect of the American Psychological Association – Professor Martin Seligman from the University of Pennsylvania. Mihaly and Marty began what would become a special relationship as they walked along that beach. The rest of their Hawaiian vacation was filled with breakfasts and dinners together and serious conversations about what was missing from the discipline and profession of psychology.

They became increasingly concerned about the kind of legacy that should be left for future generations of psychologists. After returning to the mainland, Marty telephoned Mihaly and began a new series of discussions focused on how best to create a field of positive psychology.

One of the creative ideas they developed addressed how to build the domain and people for this new endeavor. They identified 50 of the most widely cited psychologists and asked them to nominate their most promising students, students who they thought had what it takes to become chairs of psychology departments (or leaders) by age 50. Approximately 20 young psychologists were given an all-expenses-paid trip with Mihaly, Marty, and a few colleagues to spend a week on another beautiful beach near a remote fishing village in Akumal, Mexico. So the next set of foundational discussions about building a "field of dreams" called positive psychology were conducted in swimsuits and flip flops on beautiful beaches, while staying at a wonderful beach house owned by Jerry Garcia of the Grateful Dead.

One might raise eyebrows or question the creative process used to establish what we now know as positive psychology, but the evidence suggests it has paid off handsomely. The positive psychology theme of the 1998 American Psychological Association Convention was a huge success. The first positive psychology summit was held in 1999, followed by the first international conference on positive psychology in 2002. Positive psychology conferences have now been held all over the world, and in June 2009 the first World Congress on positive psychology took place in Philadelphia (see Ruark, 2009).

On the scholarly front, the January 2000 special issue of the *American Psychologist* on happiness, excellence, and optimal human functioning helped to ignite a wide range of research and scholarly pursuits that have supported the development of a science of positive psychology (Seligman & Csikszentmihalyi, 2000). This new activity was further fueled by generous prizes to honor stellar research and achievement, and a wealth of research funding from major philanthropic foundations and from a range of government funders, including the National Institutes of Health. A plethora of books and research articles have also been written to disseminate the ideas and findings from this new science of positive psychology (see Donaldson & Ko, 2010). University courses and graduate programs in positive psychology are now thriving, including a highly visible professional masters program at the University of Pennsylvania under the leadership of Professor Seligman, and the first doctoral programs in positive psychology at Claremont Graduate University under the leadership of Professor Csikszentmihalyi. The scholarly *Journal of Positive Psychology* was established in 2006, and most recently the International Positive Psychology Association (IPPA) was formed as a professional home for more than 3000 professionals worldwide who are interested in positive psychology.

THE RAPID EXPANSION OF POSITIVE SCHOLARSHIP

Positive psychology seems to have become an umbrella term for studies on strengths, virtues, excellence, thriving, flourishing, resilience, optimal functioning in general, and the like. Some have called it a fresh lens or a new way of focusing research on human and organizational behavior. This organized positive orientation to research, application, and scholarship has quickly escaped the disciplinary confinement of psychology, and has spread rapidly across a wide range of disciplines and professions (Donaldson & Ko, 2010). For example, research and scholarship adopting a positive psychology perspective can be found in the areas of education (Clonan, Chafouleas, McDougal, & Riley-Tillman, 2004; Gilman, Furlong, & Huebner, 2009; Liesveld & Miller, 2005), public health (Post, 2005; Quick & Quick, 2004; Taylor & Sherman, 2004), healthcare (Houston, 2006), social and human services (Radey & Figley, 2007; Ronel, 2006), economics (Frey & Stutzer, 2002; Marks, Shah, & Westall, 2004), political science (Linley & Joseph, 2004), neuroscience (Burgdorf, 2001), leadership (Avolio, Gardner, Walumbwa, Luthans, & May, 2004; Gardner & Schermerhorn, 2004; Luthans & Avolio, 2003), management (Ghoshal, 2005), and the organizational sciences (Cameron, Dutton, & Quinn, 2003; Dutton, 2003; Luthans 2002a, 2002b), among others. This new focus on the science of thriving or optimal functioning seems to be fully energized across the social and human sciences and is suggesting new ways to address some of the most pressing issues facing modern societies.

The participants in the volume were asked to help us understand how this new focus, body of knowledge, methods of inquiry, and broad movement within the social sciences can contribute to social betterment. We organized our symposium and this volume to help us discover what works, if anything, when we apply scientific knowledge based on positive psychology toward improving many important aspects of modern life. We were specifically interested in how positive psychology can be applied to improve:

- Nations, governments, and public policies
- Healthcare
- Education
- Communities
- Work life and organizations
- Everyday life.

In the chapters that follow, leading scientists working on topics related to positive psychology will share with us their views on how we should apply the science of positive psychology to improve society.

CORE TOPICS IN POSITIVE PSYCHOLOGY

Chapters 2, 3, and 4 address the practical implications of research on some of the core topics in positive psychology. These core areas include well-being and happiness, positive emotions, and character strengths. First, in Chapter 2, Ed Diener and Katherine Ryan discuss how to move toward national accounts of well-being for public policy. They argue that societies need to utilize national accounts of well-being in the same way they use other indicators, such as the gross national product (GNP), savings rates, and consumer confidence, to monitor and increase well-being within nations and thus improve societal conditions. Throughout their chapter you will learn (1) why they think it is important to measure well-being, (2) about the latest scientific findings on the benefits of subjective well-being (e.g., benefits for our social relationships, work and income, and health and longevity), and (3) about the societal benefits of happiness. Diener and Ryan also discuss scientific findings that illuminate the societal causes of well-being, and conclude that because well-being is good for individuals and for societies their approach to public policy will enormously aid the positive behavioral sciences and will continue to improve the human condition.

Next, in Chapter 3, Barbara Fredrickson and Laura Kurtz discuss how to cultivate positive emotions to enhance human flourishing. They claim that science now confirms that positive emotions do far more than simply feel good: they have wide-reaching implications for psychological, social, and physical well-being in ways that fuel human flourishing. In this chapter, they present an overview of research stemming from Fredrickson's broaden-and-build theory of positive emotions that reveals that positive emotions expand awareness, undo lingering negative emotions, fuel resilience, promote personal growth, produce relational intimacy, and transform people. They also discuss research suggesting that, for every negative emotion that weighs us down, we should aim to cultivate at least three positive emotions to lift us up. Three-to-one is the ratio that they have found to be the tipping point beyond which the full impact of positive emotions becomes unleashed. The individual and societal implications for cultivating positive emotions, by increasing the numerator and decreasing the denominator of the positivity ratio, are discussed. Fredrickson and Kurtz conclude their chapter by pointing out that the science of emotions reveals that people have far more control over what emotions they experience than they typically give themselves credit for. In fact, they claim that opportunities to experience positive emotions abound, waiting to be noticed, explored, and amplified, and provide another route for applying positive psychology to improve society.

Finally, in Chapter 4, Christopher Peterson and Nansook Park complete this first section of the volume by exploring the applied value of research on character strengths and virtues. They demonstrate how positive traits enable positive experiences and close relationships with others, which in turn have important consequences in the contexts of families, schools, workplaces, and communities. They point out that good character is what we look for in our leaders, what we look for in our teachers and students in classrooms, what we look for in our colleagues at work, what parents look for in their children, and what friends look for in each other. Positive psychology specifically emphasizes building individual and societal well-being by identifying and fostering these strengths of character. Peterson and Park go on to discuss their Values in Action (VIA) Project and to provide a range of empirical findings shedding light on the distribution and demographics of character strengths, the correlates and consequences of character, and the origins and development of character strengths. They conclude by arguing that their research supports the premise of positive psychology – that attention to good character sheds light on what makes life worth living and how to build a thriving society.

CONTEXTS FOR APPLYING THE SCIENCE OF POSITIVE PSYCHOLOGY

This section of the volume shows how the science of positive psychology can be applied across the lifespan in contexts such as health, education, and working life. Each of the chapters below discusses how the science of positive psychology is currently being applied and suggests future directions for improving the quality of healthcare, education, organizational effectiveness, and work life.

Health

In Chapter 5, Shelley Taylor demonstrates how psychosocial resources such as social support, optimism, a sense of mastery, self-esteem, and active coping skills enhance health and well-being. She discusses the implications of 30 years of empirical research illuminating the pathways between psychosocial resources and health. Taylor makes it clear that positive psychology interventions hold great promise for engineering positive social environments that can improve health and well-being throughout society. In Chapter 6, Nancy Sin, Matthew Della Porta, and Sonja Lyubomirsky provide the second application of positive psychology in the context of health. They describe an approach for tailoring positive psychology interventions to treat depressed individuals. They demonstrate that positive psychology interventions have been successful in reducing depressive symptoms and enhancing well-being. However, their research provides a caution that not all previous findings from happiness interventions with healthy individuals will generalize to depressed or dysphoric samples, because the motivational, affective, and cognitive deficits characteristic of depression can limit or even reverse the beneficial effects of effortful happiness-promoting activities. They conclude by summarizing the body of evidence that demonstrates how positive psychology interventions show great promise for enhancing well-being, whether it be for making euthymic individuals happier or as a complement to traditional treatments for depression. Taken together, these chapters provide a wide range of research studies and examples of how the science of positive psychology can be used to improve health and well-being in modern societies.

Education

In Chapter 7, Hans Henrik Knoop provides a vision for how positive psychology can revitalize our schools and educational systems. He reviews evidence-based principles of positive psychology and suggests how they can be used to reform how we educate future generations. He provides scenarios for a better future for education by 2025, which would include that all over the world political leaders will face the conclusion of positive psychology, namely, that the single most important source for human happiness is for people to live in circumstances enabling them to be wholeheartedly engaged in both their immediate goals and a greater purpose. In Chapter 8, Shane Lopez and Valerie Calderon provide a concrete example of positive psychology being applied in the American educational context. They discuss the Gallup Student Poll, a landmark new measure that will track for 10 years the hope, engagement, and well-being of students across the United States, as a way to measure and promote what is right with students. Lopez and Calderon describe the results of the inaugural poll in some detail and discuss the policy implications associated with the data. They are hopeful that this new work will eventually bring psychological reform to our schools and more vitality to our communities, and that by doubling hope, building engaged schools, and boosting well-being they could turn every school into a magic kingdom and every neighborhood into a great place to grow up.

Work and Organizations

Ia Ko and Stewart Donaldson review the emerging empirical research on positive organizational psychology, behavior, and scholarship in Chapter 9. They show how the science of positive psychology is being applied to improve workplace coaching practices, leadership and organizational development efforts, organizational virtuousness, psychological capital, and flow at work. They provide a theory-driven perspective on how to improve research in this area and to develop and evaluate positive interventions to improve organizational effectiveness and the quality of work life. In Chapter 10, Jane Dutton, Laura Morgan Roberts, and Jeff Bednar explore how work contexts cultivate employee flourishing through the way they shape the identities that employees construct at work. Their focus on the impacts of prosocial practices illuminates relationships between the three pillars of positive psychology – positive subjective experiences of the past, present, and future, positive individuals (i.e., a strengths-based conception of human nature), and positive institutions (Seligman, 2002; Seligman & Csikszentmihalyi, 2000). They note that the third pillar – positive institutions – has received relatively less attention in the field of positive psychology compared to the study of positive emotion and individual strengths. The work presented in this chapter illuminates one way in which positive institutions (prosocial practices) help to create more positive individuals (by facilitating positive identity construction), leading to more positive subjective experiences (employees flourishing at work).

Next, in Chapter 11, Kim Cameron examines research on the effects of virtuous leadership and organizational practices on organizational performance. He summarizes several of his investigations across a variety of industries – from airlines to financial services – and a variety of sectors – including government, not-for-profit, and private sector organizations. He concludes that the body of evidence in this area has become quite compelling: Virtuous practices in organizations are associated with, and may even produce, desired performance in organizations, even when the outcomes are traditional performance indicators such as profitability, productivity, quality, customer satisfaction, and employee engagement. Finally, in Chapter 12, Jeanne Nakamura describes contexts for positive adult development. She uses an extended example of good mentoring to focus on the study of positive adult development and, through it, has made a case for a positive psychology that integrates positive with negative, and agency with context. She discusses why good mentoring is recognized as a rich context of adult development for both of the individuals involved: it facilitates the young person's navigation of the transition to adulthood and it allows the more experienced adult to contribute to the welfare of rising generations by sharing the lessons of longer experience. The results of the GoodWork Project highlight the contribution of good mentoring to the well-being of the profession in which younger and older adults work, and thus indirectly to the flourishing of those served by the profession and those who may work in it in the future.

THE FUTURE FOR APPLYING THE SCIENCE OF POSITIVE PSYCHOLOGY

In Chapter 13, Mihaly Csikszentmihalyi focuses on the intangible and almost invisible difference that positive psychology is likely to make to our understanding of what it means to be human. He argues that we are about to change our vision of the human condition from one of dismal pessimism to one that foregrounds what is good about women and men and provides ideas and processes that will nurture, cultivate, and increase what is good about us and about our actions. And he believes that this change is likely to pay dividends in many areas of life, from the economy to the arts, and from politics to religion. He points out that it is rather strange that, with the enormous accumulation of knowledge in the past centuries, humanity has not attempted to do what positive psychology has now begun to envision: a way to integrate systematically, scientifically, what has been found across time and space to be best about men and women, and what constitutes a good life. He outlines the opportunities that this new image of humanity presents to applied positive psychologists, and inspires us by declaring that this new perspective in psychology should guarantee a rewarding life to those who choose to pursue it.

In the Epilog, Stewart Donaldson summarizes some of the main lessons and insights that he has gleaned from asking this distinguished group of positive psychologists the question: "What works in positive psychology?" Next, he presents and puts in context some of the scathing critiques of positive psychology. While remaining optimistic about the potential of the expanding science of positive psychology, he cautions practitioners and challenges them to think critically about the evidence that is presented in support of positive psychology interventions, and to think carefully about the challenges involved with moving from sound scientific research to applications of positive psychology-based principles, programs, and policies in "real-world" settings.

The chapters that lie ahead are written to engage and inspire you to think about what works, if anything, in positive psychology in relation to the areas and topics you care about. Our distinguished group of symposium presenters and chapter authors – leading experts in their respective fields – have provided us with cutting-edge research, theory, ideas, concepts, and applications of the science of positive psychology. May you become absorbed in the journey and find purpose and meaning, and eventually emerge with the passion to join efforts to apply the science of positive psychology to improve everyday life, health, schools, work, and society.

REFERENCES

Avolio, B. J., Gardner, W. L., Walumbwa, F. O., Luthans, F., & May, D. R. (2004). Unlocking the mask: A look at the process by which authentic leaders impact follower attitudes and behaviors. *Leadership Quarterly, 15,* 801–823.

Burgdorf, J. (2001, August). *The neurobiology of positive emotions.* Paper presented at the Positive Psychology Summer Institute, Sea Ranch, CA.

Cameron, K. S., Dutton, J. E., & Quinn, R. E. (2003). Foundations of positive organizational scholarship. In K. S. Cameron, J. E. Dutton, & R. E. Quinn (Eds.), *Positive organizational scholarship: Foundations of a new discipline* (pp. 3–13). San Francisco: Berrett-Koehler.

Clonan, S. M., Chafouleas, S. M., McDougal, J. L., & Riley-Tillman, T. C. (2004). Positive psychology goes to school: Are we there yet? *Psychology in the Schools, 41,* 101–110.

Donaldson, S. I., & Ko, I. (2010). Positive organizational psychology, behavior, and scholarship: A review of the emerging literature and evidence base. *Journal of Positive Psychology, 5,* 177–191.

Dutton, J. E. (2003). Breathing life into organizational studies. *Journal of Management Inquiry, 12,* 5–19.

Frey, B. S., & Stutzer, A. (2002). *Happiness and economics: How the economy and institutions affect human well-being.* Princeton, NJ: Princeton University Press.

Gardner, W. L., & Schermerhorn Jr., J. R. (2004). Unleashing individual potential performance gains through positive organizational behavior and authentic leadership. *Organizational Dynamics, 33,* 270–281.

Ghoshal, S. (2005). Bad management theories are destroying good management practices. *Academy of Management Learning and Education, 4,* 75–91.

Gilman, R., Furlong, M., & Huebner, E. S. (2009). *Handbook of positive psychology in schools.* New York: Taylor & Francis.

Houston, S. (2006). Making use of positive psychology in residential child care. In D. Iwaniec (Ed.), *The child's journey thorough care: Placement stability, care planning, and achieving permanency* (pp. 183–200). Hoboken, NJ: John Wiley & Sons.

Liesveld, R., & Miller J. (2005). *Teach your strengths: How great teachers inspire their students.* Omaha, NE: Gallup Press.

Linley, A., & Joseph, S. (2004). *Positive psychology in practice.* Hoboken, NJ: John Wiley & Sons.

Luthans, F. (2002a). Positive organizational behavior: Developing and managing psychological strengths. *Academy of Management Executive, 16,* 57–72.

Luthans, F. (2002b). The need for and meaning of positive organizational behavior. *Journal of Organizational Behavior, 23,* 695–706.

Luthans, F., & Avolio, B. J. (2003). Authentic leadership: A positive developmental approach. In K. S. Cameron, J. E. Dutton, & R. E. Quinn (Eds.), *Positive organizational scholarship: Foundations of a new discipline* (pp. 241–261). San Francisco: Berrett-Koehler.

Marks, N., Shah, H., & Westall, A. (2004). *The power and potential of well-being indicators: Measuring young people's well-being in Nottingham.* London: New Economics Foundation.

Post, S. G. (2005). Altruism, happiness, and health: It's good to be good. *International Journal of Behavioral Medicine, 12,* 66–77.

Quick, J. C., & Quick, J. D. (2004). Healthy, happy, productive work: A leadership challenge. *Organizational Dynamics, 33,* 329–337.

Radey, M., & Figley, C. (2007). Compassion in the context of positive social work: The role of human flourishing. *Clinical Social Work Journal, 36,* 207–214.

Ronel, N. (2006). When good overcomes bad: The impact of volunteers on those they help. *Human Relations, 59,* 1133–1153.

Ruark, J. (2009, August 3). An intellectual movement for the masses: 10 years after its founding, positive psychology struggles with its own success. *The Chronicles of Higher Education.* Retrieved June 14, 2010, from http://chronicle.com/article/An-Intellectual-Movement-for/47500/

Seligman, M. (2002). *Authentic happiness: Using the new positive psychology to realize your potential for lasting fulfillment.* New York: Free Press.

Seligman, M. E. P., & Csikszentmihalyi, M. (2000). Positive psychology: An introduction. *American Psychologist, 55,* 5–14.

Taylor, S. E., & Sherman, D. K. (2004). Positive psychology and health psychology: A fruitful liaison. In A. P. Linley & S. Joseph (Eds.), *Positive psychology in practice* (pp. 305–319). Hoboken, NJ: John Wiley & Sons.

Part II

Core Areas in Applied
Positive Psychology

2

National Accounts of Well-Being for Public Policy

ED DIENER and KATHERINE RYAN

B ecause modern industrialized societies possess the basic goods and services to satisfy the needs of citizenry, people today have the luxury of seeking a fulfilling life rather than mere economic sustenance. This shift in focus is justified due to the fact that increased levels of societal wealth have not eliminated social problems. Furthermore, economic measures do not necessarily reveal how a nation is performing in terms of fairness and justice, trust, and enjoyment of life.

Although the well-being of societies has hitherto been judged according to economic measures, economic indicators alone are not enough to reveal the quality of life within nations. While income has steadily climbed over the past 50 years, and the gross domestic product (GDP) has tripled, happiness has remained virtually flat (Diener & Seligman, 2004). Furthermore, a recent study utilizing the Gallup World Poll found that life satisfaction increased when national wealth increased, but enjoyment of life experienced little change (Diener, Kahneman, Tov, & Arora, 2009a). This discrepancy between happiness and economic growth is important when one considers that people rank happiness ahead of money as a life goal (Diener & Oishi, 2004). However, it is even more significant when one examines the large body of research suggesting that high levels of subjective well-being are not only good in and of themselves, but that they actually produce beneficial societal outcomes (Lyubomirsky, King, & Diener, 2005). Therefore, while monetary considerations are currently dominant in policy debates, other goals should be kept in mind.

Robert Kennedy described the basic premise underlying the need for national accounts of well-being in the following election speech at the University of Kansas on March 18, 1967:

> *Too much and too long, we seem to have surrendered community excellence and community values in the mere accumulation of material things . . . The Gross National Product includes air pollution and advertising for cigarettes, and ambulances to clear our highways of carnage. It counts special locks for*

our doors, and jails for the people who break them. The GNP includes the destruction of the redwoods and the death of Lake Superior. It grows with the production of napalm and missiles and nuclear warheads.

And if the GNP includes all this, there is much that it does not comprehend. It does not allow for the health of our families, the quality of their education, or the joy of their play. It is indifferent to the decency of our factories and the safety of our streets alike. It does not include the beauty of our poetry or the strength of our marriages, or the intelligence of our public debate or the integrity of our public officials.

GNP measures neither our wit nor our courage, neither our wisdom nor our learning, neither our compassion nor our devotion to our country. It measures everything, in short, except that which makes life worthwhile.

As Kennedy suggested, the economic measures could potentially be more useful when viewed alongside subjective measures of well-being, which take additional variables into account. Current economic indicators (e.g., GNP, savings rates, and consumer confidence) and other social indicators (e.g., crime rates, longevity, rates of infant mortality, and educational standards) bring attention to important areas, and when the measures show problems the public becomes concerned. Importantly, these measures also point to specific areas that require redress as well as policies that might best improve conditions. For example, education measures can reveal which schools are doing well or failing, in which grades, locations, and subjects. The measures also show which types of educational policies are succeeding. We suggest that societies need to utilize national accounts of well-being in the same way as these other indicators, to monitor and increase well-being within nations and thus to improve societal conditions.

WHAT IS WELL-BEING?

Subjective well-being refers to a variety of evaluations, both positive and negative, that people make about their lives. These evaluations include life satisfaction, interest and engagement, affective reactions to life events such as joy and sadness, and satisfaction with work, relationships, health, recreation, meaning and purpose, and other important domains. In this way, subjective well-being is in many ways an umbrella term that captures a variety of valuations that people make regarding their lives: the events happening to them, their bodies, and minds, and the circumstances in which they live. Although both well-being and ill-being are subjective in that they occur within a person's experience, manifestations of subjective well-being and ill-being can be observed objectively in verbal and non-verbal behavior, actions, biology, attention, and memory. In this way, subjective well-being encompasses a large number of the factors that constitute quality of life, and can provide much information that falls outside other indicators, such as economic, that only locate a person's well-being in the material realm of marketplace production and consumption.

POLICY AREAS

In the book *Well-Being for Public Policy* (Diener, Lucas, Schimmack, & Helliwell, 2009b), we discuss policies in four areas as they relate to well-being: the environment, health and longevity, the social context, and work and income. These areas serve as examples where we currently have well-being findings that are relevant to policy, although much better data are still needed in each area that would be provided by national accounts of well-being. These areas are not meant to include all the relevant domains. Moreover, we do not imply that other measures, such as economic indicators, are not also relevant.

COMMUTING

In the environmental domain, we review a number of places where the well-being data give us insights into how the environment affects quality of life, and the types of policies needed to enhance well-being. Specifically, we examine the impact of green space, air pollution, and commuting. There is now a large body of literature on the ill effects of commuting, and especially on long and traffic-heavy commutes. While commuting has many objective negative impacts such as monetary costs, natural resource waste, and lowered productivity for workers caught in traffic, there is growing evidence that commuting specifically lowers well-being.

   Commuting in crowded conditions and long commutes have been associated with lower levels of frustration tolerance, job stability, and health, and with work absences (Diener et al., 2009b), and commuting has generally been associated with lowered mood and life satisfaction (Novaco, 1992; Novaco, Kliewer, & Broquet, 1991; Novaco, Stokols, & Milanesi, 1990). A longitudinal study conducted by Stutzer and Frey (2008) found that life satisfaction was related to commuting time, and that those with longer commutes had significantly lower life satisfaction than those with shorter commutes. Similarly, other studies assessing moods during various activities in the day have found that the lowest moods of the day occur when one is commuting to and from work (Kahneman & Krueger, 2006; Schwarz, Kahneman, & Xu, 2009).

   Importantly, these subjective reports of lowered well-being are confirmed by a number of studies examining the biological and cognitive impacts of commuting. Those with longer commutes not only report higher stress, but also show higher cortisol on commuting days than on non-commuting days (Evans & Wener, 2006). Moreover, commuters also show lowered executive functioning, as shown by the fact that commuters in the above-mentioned study also showed poorer proof-reading performance, which is a measure of accuracy and motivation related to the length of their commute. Finally, studies of commuters show that they have worse task persistence after commuting (Koslowsky, Kluger, & Reich, 1995; White & Rotton, 1998). In this way, commuting has been shown not only to lower subjective well-being but, by doing so, to negatively impact the performance and abilities of workers. Because it is now estimated that over 100 million Americans commute to work each day, in our ever-growing urbanized environment, these findings on the link between commuting and well-being raise significant questions about what types of public policy might improve the health and well-being of people and thereby also improve worker productivity (Evans & Wener, 2006).

One often-suggested policy alternative to combat the ills of commuting is the promotion of public transportation or carpooling in order to reduce traffic. Because a substantial majority of the U.S. labor force commutes by private automobile (Novaco et al., 1990), and because a majority of these commuters travel alone (Collier & Christiansen, 1992; Liss, 1991), the number of vehicles has increased much faster than the number of people in most cities (Novaco & Collier, 1994). Inevitably this ratio has resulted in higher congestion for most roads and freeways (Novaco et al., 1990). Therefore, an important question for most policy-makers is whether promoting public transportation and carpooling mitigates the negative effects of commuting alone by car.

Importantly, Novaco and Collier (1994) found that carpooling attenuated some of the stress from commuting. Moreover, when Kahneman and Krueger (2006) found that the lowest moods of the day occurred during commuting times, they also found that the highest moods of the day occurred when participants were spending time with family and friends. Thus, commuting not only lowers subjective well-being in and of itself, but also exacerbates negative feelings by lessening the time available to spend with others. Long commutes can even lower the well-being of non-commuting family members, in what economists call an "externality" of market activity, because less time is ultimately spent together. Carpooling may counter this effect in some ways and could provide the basis for a policy of improving well-being during commuting.

If carpooling can attenuate negative feelings caused by commuting, perhaps public transportation will attenuate these drops in mood even further. Importantly, while studies examining those who commute alone by car have shown that commuting produces detrimental cardiovascular effects (Robinson, 1991), studies examining those who commute by public rail have yielded similar results (Singer, Lundberg, & Frankenhaeuser, 1978; White & Rotton, 1998). In addition, Stutzer and Frey (2008) found that in comparison to those who commute by car, or another means of transportation (motorcycle, bike, or on foot), those who commute by public transportation do not have lower levels of stress or higher life satisfaction. While the results of these studies may be disappointing, the information they provide is very important to the creation of appropriate policy measures. For example, Wener, Evans, Phillips, and Nadler (2003) found that improving the rail service to reduce the number of transfers and overall commute time resulted in decreases in passenger self-reported stress, as well as cortisol levels, and increases in proofreading ability. Thus, public transportation may, in fact, increase well-being and worker productivity provided that it operates as a more efficient and less stressful means of transportation.

While the above questions of public transportation or carpooling represent two of the most popularly discussed policy solutions to commuting, there are several other possibilities. Of course, it is also important to discuss how such policies might be implemented. In order to encourage the use of public transportation, governments might consider the construction of more light rail. Or, to encourage the use of both carpooling and public transportation, governments might discourage high-volume traffic from solo commuters by heavily taxing gas prices and tollways. Another policy alternative to reduce congestion and commuting stress is the construction of more freeways. In addition, more money could be spent on urban renewal in order to encourage workers to live downtown rather than commute from the suburbs. Likewise, a revision of zoning laws requiring residential and commercial districts to be separated would also lessen the need for commuting. And finally, companies and governments could avoid requiring their workers to commute to and from the office every day by encouraging more Internet-based infrastructure and working from home.

But which of these many possible solutions is the best choice? While building more freeways could reduce the lowered well-being and worker productivity resultant from high-stress commuting in heavy traffic, this solution is no doubt costly. Moreover, it would increase pollution levels by creating room for more vehicles, and it would certainly lessen the amount of green space, which has been shown to also significantly affect well-being. In a policy dilemma such as this, information provided by well-being measures could play a major role in helping policy-makers determine which outcome is more desirable after weighing all of the possible alternatives. Policy-makers may, in fact, decide that optimizing well-being produces the greatest gain for society, not only because it raises the happiness levels of citizenry, but also because it produces the most economic and health benefits. However, without the information provided by these measures, policy-makers will not have all the resources necessary to make the most informed decision for their citizenry.

GREEN SPACE

Another environmental area in which we have much information that could be used to inform public policy is the area concerning well-being and parks, or green space. Exposure to nature has been linked not only to higher subjective well-being, but also to better health and lower levels of stress, better work performance and concentration, and reduced crime and aggression (see Bird, 2007, for a review). In this way, policies concerning parks and green space may have far-reaching effects, and well-being measures would certainly add to the information available in this area.

In terms of well-being, subjects exposed to views of nature show more positive moods than those exposed to urban views (Rohde & Kendle, 1994; Ulrich, 1979). One study found that seniors with access to parks and green space had higher life satisfaction (Talbot & Kaplan, 1991), and even children with stressful lives report higher self-esteem if they are exposed to nature (Wells & Evans, 2003). While these studies show the baseline positive effects of green space, there are also a number of studies detailing the protective influence of the environment in sustaining well-being after and during stress. In studies where participants have been exposed to anxiety-provoking horror films, those who subsequently viewed nature scenes returned to baseline physiological measures faster than those exposed to urban scenes (Ulrich, Simons, Losito, Fiorito, Miles, & Zelson, 1991). Furthermore, participants who viewed nature scenes after a stressor were more protected from the negative physiological consequences of a subsequent stressor (Parsons, Tassinary, Ulrich, Hebl, & Grossman-Alexander, 1998). These results are replicated when participants who have just experienced a stressful event are asked to walk in a nature versus urban setting; for those who take the nature walk, anger decreases and positive emotions increase (Hartig, Evans, Jamner, Davis, & Garling, 2003).

Further studies reveal that exposure to nature can reduce a patient's need for painkillers (Ulrich, 1984), and it can decrease mortality among senior citizens, decrease recovery times for hospital patients, and cause fewer sick call visits for prisoners (Lavin, Higgins, Metcalfe, & Jordan, 2006; Maller, Townsend, Pryor, Brown, & St. Leger, 2006; Moore, 1981). In addition, one study revealed that patients showed less stress on days when the waiting room contained a mural of nature rather than a blank wall, as reflected in both self-ratings of stress and heart rate measurements (Heerwagen 1990; White & Heerwagen, 1998). Experimental studies have also found that subjects perform executive functioning tasks such as proofreading more competently when they are exposed to a natural versus an urban environment (Hartig, Mang, & Evans, 1991), and university students score higher on tests when they are given a view of nature (Tennessen & Cimprich, 1995). In addition, workplace views of nature have been linked to lower job stress, less likelihood of quitting, and higher job satisfaction (Kaplan & Kaplan, 1989; Leather, Pygras, Beale, & Lawrence, 1998). And finally, green space has also been tied to social domains, such as crime rates in neighborhoods. Kuo and Sullivan (2001a, 2001b), for instance, found that vegetation reduced crime in inner-city housing.

In an increasingly urbanized world, the data provided by well-being measures with regard to parks and green space again provide important information for policy decisions relevant to a wide variety of issues, such as healthcare or education settings and urban planning. However, this represents another area in which more well-being measures are needed to improve our ability to make better policy decisions.

AIR POLLUTION

The impact of air pollution on well-being is another important environmental domain that requires more study. However, initial evidence suggests that air pollution has significant influence on societal well-being. For instance, Welsch (2006) found that, over time, air pollution levels were related to life satisfaction in 10 European nations, and Jacobs, Evans, Catalano, and Dooley (1984) found that symptoms of depression were related to air quality in Los Angeles. In addition, a study by Luechinger (2007) examined areas in several nations that varied in smokestack pollution (specifically levels of sulfur dioxide), as well as longitudinal data across a period where air pollution decreased through the installation of industrial scrubbers. Importantly, greater levels of sulfur dioxide were found to negatively affect life satisfaction of areas. While this domain does not have as much data as commuting and green space, initial evidence shows that air pollution does have significant effects on well-being levels, and that the data should certainly be taken into consideration by policy-makers. However, it is important to note that the environmental issues are meant only to give examples of the usefulness of the well-being measures, which can be useful also in most other policy areas.

PROGRESS

While the data presented in this chapter on the links between the environment and subjective well-being reveal the importance of taking well-being measures into consideration for public policies, it is clear that more data are needed. Fortunately, there has been much progress over the past several years in promoting the adoption of well-being measures by organizations. For example, the Organization for Economic Cooperation and Development (OECD) is currently moving ahead with plans to include measures of well-being in their database. Because the OECD publishes a large number of statistics on approximately 30 of the world's most economically developed nations, the inclusion of well-being measures in their reports will provide a wealth of new information about the well-being of nations.

In addition, the health promotion and chronic disease prevention group within the United States Centers for Disease Control and Prevention (CDC) now plans to use measures of well-being in surveys. In a speech recently given to personnel working in these areas, we presented findings that people's average moods in nations are a better predictor of whether they report health problems than is their objective health as indicated by life expectancy. This finding suggests that unhappy people feel they have more health problems, regardless of their objective health. Another finding presented at the CDC is that Cantril's (1965) Ladder of Life scores for nations predict life expectancy to a better degree than either average income or healthcare expenditures. Importantly, this finding and others suggest not only that poor physical health can negatively impact well-being, but that poor life satisfaction can negatively impact physical health. Due to the rising, and perhaps unsustainable, cost of healthcare in the United States, prevention programs aimed at improving levels of subjective well-being at the societal level could play an important role in improving the health of citizenry and reducing the current monetary drain of healthcare. Statisticians and economists involved in the United Nations' Human Development Report have also recognized the possible benefits from collecting well-being data for nations, and are showing interest in the idea of including these measures in reports.

The use of national indicators of subjective well-being is also spreading at the international level as well. In the United Kingdom, a group of behavioral scientists led by Felicia Huppert designed survey questions for the European Union biennial survey, which measures both subjective well-being and psychological well-being, derived from the Self-Determination Theory of Ryan and Deci (2000) as well as the work of Carol Ryff (1989). Moreover, several groups in the UK have lobbied for the inclusion of well-being data in policy decisions. For example, economist Richard Layard is working to implement well-being surveys for adolescents, and the New Economics Foundation (NEF) offers the service of collecting well-being measures for various organizations. Statistics Canada has also routinely utilized measures of life satisfaction in their surveys.

ISSUES

Of course, a number of issues arise when the proposal for national indicators of well-being is presented, many of which are discussed in *Well-Being for Public Policy* (Diener et al., 2009b). For example, one concern is that people will change their answers to well-being surveys in order to alter the results and thus influence policy. However, participants taking well-being surveys do not know to what end the surveys are being used. Moreover, the surveys are structured and scored in ways that preclude participants from choosing answers that clearly further a desired policy outcome. And finally, well-being surveys have been shown to have high validity and reliability, suggesting that participants simply do not answer these surveys according to agendas.

Another concern is whether people adapt to conditions, thereby subverting the ability of the well-being measures to reveal problems. However, recent evidence shows that this claim is unsupported. One type of evidence that refutes this claim is that of well-being differences across nations. If there are marked national differences in well-being and these differences can be predicted from the objective characteristics of those nations, then this would suggest that the stable external circumstances that vary across nations have a lasting impact on happiness, and that citizens do not simply adapt to their conditions. If the reverse were true, regardless of their policies, all nations would have similar levels of well-being. However, studies by Diener, Lucas, and Scollon (2006) and Kahneman, Diener, Arora, Muller, Harter, and Tov (2009) show that nations do, in fact, show a wide variance in levels of happiness. Therefore, adaptation to such an extreme extent simply does not occur, and the well-being measures will not be subverted by this phenomenon.

In this chapter, we discuss three specific questions regarding the use of subjective well-being measures in discussions of public policy. First, why measure well-being? Do we really want or need the results of national subjective well-being measures? Should people be happy, or is happiness shallow? The second question pertains to whether well-being is an individual or public matter. Isn't it the responsibility of individuals to achieve happiness through their own personal choices, and the responsibility of the government only to provide the conditions of peace and security that allow individuals the freedom to make choices? Is the entry of governments into well-being a paternalistic affair that implies unnecessary intrusion and control in people's lives? And finally, what are the societal causes of well-being? If we do want societal well-being and we can justify the involvement of government policy to this end, then what do we know about societies that are doing well in this regard?

WHY MEASURE WELL-BEING?

As indicated above, one of the primary issues regarding the use of subjective well-being measures is why the use of such measures is helpful. For one thing, national indicators of well-being are democratic. Because the measures are representative of the thoughts and feelings of citizens rather than elite policy-makers, they indicate areas in which the general populace is flourishing or languishing.

More importantly, subjective well-being has increased in importance during the post-industrial era. While emphasizing economic development made sense during the first centuries of the industrial revolution when governments were striving to provide people with basic food, shelter, and clothing, most of the economically developed nations of the world are now in a post-industrial period. This economic change has caused a shift in what Inglehart (1981) and others called materialist to post-materialist values. Beyond money, people now desire engagement, fulfillment, and most importantly happiness. This new set of needs begs the question of why the subjective well-being of citizenry is not measured directly instead of using income, GDP, and other economic indicators as a proxy.

Perhaps the most important point that is not realized by lay people is that high levels of well-being are beneficial to the effective functioning of societies. Alternately, societies in which high levels of negative feelings, such as anger, depression, sadness, and envy, exist are inherently more unstable and are more likely to have political conflicts or revolutions. Throughout history, several have questioned the ability of "happy" people to thrive. For example, do happy people work hard and fix problems that clearly need attention, or does their giddy state make them unmotivated? Some, such as Gustave Flaubert, clearly believe that happiness is not a desired goal because it interferes with effective functioning, as evident by his statement: "To be stupid, selfish, and have good health are three requirements for happiness, though if stupidity is lacking, all is lost." However, contrary to Flaubert's assumption, there is much evidence that happy people do better in a number of areas of life, such as social relationships, work and income, health and longevity, and overall societal benefits. More importantly, it is not just that success in these areas causes well-being. Rather, there is some evidence that well-being actually causes success in these areas.

BENEFITS OF SUBJECTIVE WELL-BEING

Social Relationships

While it may seem intuitive that healthy social contact is essential to happiness, a growing body of evidence suggests that happy people also tend to have better families, friends, and supportive relationships than people with low life satisfaction. Correlational studies affirm time and time again the strong relation between happiness and sociality. However, as with all correlational studies, it is important to ascertain which factor is causal. One could ask whether happy people find it easier to create and maintain strong social relationships or, alternately, whether having these relationships leads to higher levels of happiness.

There is much evidence that having supportive social relationships raises levels of well-being (see Diener & Biswas-Diener, 2008). In general, people are happier when they are around other people, as evidenced by numerous Experience Sample Method (ESM) studies, which require participants to rate their happiness levels at random intervals throughout the day. In these studies, the highest levels of happiness occur when the participants are spending time with others. Social bonds, such as marriage, also increase subjective well-being. Married people are, on average, happier than non-married people, and happiness levels spike around the time of the wedding. Alternately, the death of a spouse causes a sharp decline in life satisfaction, and it can require as much as five to seven years for widows to achieve the satisfaction levels they felt before the death. By examining people's daily interactions and social bonds, it is clear that supportive relationships cause a certain degree of well-being.

However, we have also found that happy people tend to have higher levels of self-confidence, warmth, leadership ability, sociability, and more friends to begin with. This finding suggests that the causal arrow also moves in the opposite direction, and that happy people generate their social support systems. For example, people who have high life satisfaction prior to marriage are more likely than others to get married, stay married, and be happy in their marriages.

Work and Income

Another benefit of subjective well-being lies in the domain of work and income. While it is generally thought that those who make a high income are happier than those living in dire poverty, new studies suggest that happy people are actually more likely than others to earn more money, regardless of occupation. In one study, we obtained data on cheerfulness for students entering college in 1976 and then checked their incomes in the 1990s. Surprisingly, the least cheerful people were earning on average $50,000 a year, and the most cheerful were earning about $65,000 a year – a 30% higher salary! These results persisted even when occupation and parental income were controlled, revealing that the cheerfulness levels of these 18-year-olds had vast effects on their future income levels (Diener, Nickerson, Lucas, & Sandvik, 2002). Evidence that happiness causes economic and career success has been found again and again using populations in several countries around the world (Graham & Pettinato, 2002; Marks & Fleming, 1999). Moreover, research also suggests that happy workers are more likely to have higher supervisor ratings and be judged as more creative on the job. Happy workers also tend to have higher levels of organizational leadership, which means they are more likely to help co-workers by volunteering to take an extra shift and are less likely to take sick days or steal office supplies.

Health and Longevity

There have also been a number of studies detailing the link between well-being and health, or longevity. One classic study is the famous "nun study," conducted by Danner, Snowdon, and Friesen (2001). This study utilized the autobiographies of nuns entering the convent to compare levels of happiness to survival rates. Importantly, all the nuns lived under the same conditions and their happiness levels were derived from autobiographies completed long before health problems could set in and confound the findings. The results of the study showed that of the most cheerful quartile of nuns, 79% lived to the age of 85, and 52% lived to the age of 93! In contrast, for the least cheerful nuns, only 54% lived to the age of 85, and only

18% made it to age 93. Moreover, a study in which the autobiographies of famous psychologists were computer-scored for positive and negative feelings revealed that happy psychologists lived five years longer on average. Importantly, those psychologists who mentioned their social lives also lived longer (Pressman & Cohen, 2007).

The effects of happiness on life expectancy have also been tested at the national level. When we predicted the average longevity of nations, we found that income per capita did predict longevity, and this is widely known. People in wealthier nations tend to live longer due to the availability of better nutrition and healthcare. However, using data from the Gallup World Poll, we also found that people's feelings of their lives were strong positive predictors of longevity, and correlated with the mean life expectancy in nations even more strongly than national wealth. Furthermore, even when wealth was statistically controlled, longevity was strongly predicted by people's well-being.

Given the results of these studies, one might ask why happy people are healthier. Initial evidence is now available that shows many causal pathways involved, going from well-being to health, and not just from health to well-being. Some important findings presented by Diener and Biswas-Diener (2008) show that happy people tend to have stronger immune systems and better cardiovascular health (i.e., fewer heart attacks and less artery blockage). Moreover, happy people tend to engage in healthier behaviors, such as wearing seatbelts and sunscreen, and they tend to have fewer lifestyle diseases, such as addictions to alcohol or drugs.

Societal Benefits of Happiness

One final, but crucially important, benefit of happiness is that it is good not only for the individual but also at the societal level. People who seek happiness are shown not to be selfish people who engage in activities for their own gain and ignore societal problems but, conversely, to engage more frequently than unhappy people in altruistic, prosocial activities such as volunteering (Tov & Diener, 2008). Moreover, happy people on average tend to have more trusting, cooperative, and pro-peace attitudes, more confidence in the government and armed forces, a greater willingness to fight for their country, stronger support for democracy, and lower levels of intolerance for immigrants and racial groups (Tov & Diener, 2008; Diener & Tov, 2007). The area of societal benefits is another where the causal arrow of subjective well-being probably moves in both directions. While the happiness of citizenry may result from a more structurally sound society, high levels of subjective well-being can actually create a more stable society as well.

IS WELL-BEING AN INDIVIDUAL MATTER?

The famous phrase in the Declaration of Independence states that "all men have the right to life, liberty and the *pursuit* of happiness." One argument is that we have no right to happiness per se, only to its pursuit, and the government's responsibility is simply not to impede citizens in this endeavor. This sentiment is often used to discourage the use of well-being measures to inform public policy. Many believe that government intrusion in personal affairs such as happiness would create dangerous levels of paternalism capable of threatening individual liberties.

However, data from the Gallup World Poll show that societies around the globe differ strongly in happiness levels. These results beg the question: If happiness is only a matter of individual difference, then why do whole societies differ from each other regarding levels of well-being? Participants in the Gallup World Poll were shown Cantril's Ladder and evaluated their life using a scale of 10–0, where 10 indicates that you are living your ideal life and 0 indicates that you are living the worst possible life imaginable for you. As one can see in Figure 2.1, vast differences in nation scores emerged, with countries like Denmark scoring extremely high (8.0) and countries like Togo scoring astoundingly low (3.2).

Whether we like it or not, society has a huge influence on our happiness; we are not just lone individuals cast adrift from our nations. Moreover, many of the much feared incursions into individual life have already occurred; we have income taxes as well as a plethora of laws and regulations to govern our everyday lives. The legal drinking age is a primary example of a law that governs our behavior in ways to protect our well-being. While drinking age could be a private matter, the government has determined that there should be legal sanctions against drinking before the age of 21 because drinking before this age might be damaging to ourselves and to others. There are also laws that tell you where you can drink and that you must wear seatbelts in your own personal vehicle, laws that many believe are justifiable and even necessary to our welfare. In addition, we have organizations that reward us for acting in certain ways, such as life insurance and liability insurance, where our behavior influences the rates. In this day and age, we are no longer lone individuals, and probably never really were. There is no reason why well-being

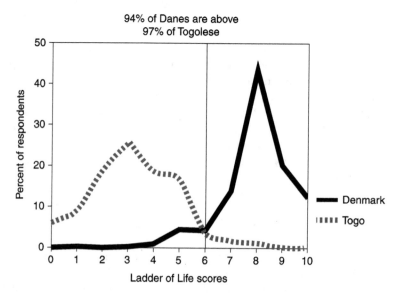

FIGURE 2.1   Ladder of Life scores for the Danes vs. Togolese.

measures should be intrusive to liberty; indeed, they can be used to protect it. And the measures are not used by themselves, but in combination with the other values of a society. Thus, not only should the well-being measures reflect the fruits of liberty, but measures of freedom can be considered along with them.

WHAT ARE THE SOCIETAL CAUSES OF WELL-BEING?

When one asks what constitutes the societal causes of well-being and, even more importantly, how the world is doing with regard to well-being, answers can be found in the Gallup World Poll. The Gallup World Poll polls 140 nations to create a representative sample of the globe with 140,000 respondents. Wave 1 of this survey represented a total of 98% of the world's population, and is therefore a tool of primary importance when examining well-being across the globe. By studying the results of the Gallup World Poll, we have found that the income of nations is a strong predictor of Ladder scores, although factors such as longevity also add to the prediction. More importantly, there are many factors that predict emotional well-being to a better degree than income. High levels of positive feelings result when participants feel that they can count on others, that they are autonomous, that they learned something new yesterday, and that they did what they did best yesterday. These four factors create psychological capital, or what Csikszentmihalyi (1990) labeled "paratelics." While people engage in telic activities in order to accomplish a further goal, for example working in order to make money, paratelic activities are engaged in because of the value they provide in and of themselves, for example playing golf simply for the enjoyment of playing golf. Other elements that make individuals happy are positive spirituality, temperament, relationships, and a sense of meaning and purpose.

When breaking down why differences in well-being occur between nations (e.g., Denmark and Sierra Leone), one can see three types of capital that influence results. The first is monetary capital, or the material wealth of the nation – how much money does the country earn on average, and thus to what degree does it satisfy the material needs of its citizenry? The second factor is social capital – can citizens in this nation count on others, how frequently have they experienced assaults, and what is the level of government corruption and interpersonal trust? The third factor is psychological capital and consists of "paratelics" – do people feel free, did they learn something yesterday, and are they free to use their talents? Because we are just able to scratch the surface of societal well-being, measures instituted on a national level would greatly help to increase our knowledge of how subjective well-being functions in societies and where it originates.

We maintain that economic measures do not entirely capture the full range of well-being in societies. Yet, Diener et al. (2009b), Inglehart (2009), and others have found extremely high correlations between the average levels of life satisfaction in nations and their GDP per capita. Importantly, factors such as longevity and educational quality tend to correlate strongly with the income of nations. Thus, an important question is whether the well-being measures provide additional useful information. In Table 2.1 we show the rankings of a number of major nations

TABLE 2.1   World nation scores and rankings for several types of well-being

Nation	Ladder	Ladder rank	Positive engagement[a]	Pos. eng. rank	Social prosperity[b]	Soc. prosp. rank	Negative affect[c]	Neg. aff. rank
USA	7.1	15	75	25	87	16	22.79	50
Ireland	7.1	13	82	5	88	13	17.16	17
Norway	7.4	6	74	31	92	1	16.72	14
Switzerland	7.5	3	73	33	90	4	16.99	16
Denmark	8.0	1	77	17	91	2	12.30	1
Austria	7.1	14	74	30	89	9	14.00	3
Netherlands	7.5	4	75	23	89	6	18.70	26
Canada	7.4	5	76	20	89	10	18.64	24
UK	7.0	18	75	21	85	24	22.22	48
Australia	7.4	8	75	24	85	22	20.00	33
Finland	7.7	2	71	42	90	3	15.77	9
Sweden	7.4	7	75	22	89	8	12.40	2
Japan	6.5	23	71	43	73	66	14.50	6
France	7.1	16	73	36	88	11	18.65	25
Singapore	6.5	24	72	41	84	25	26.65	68
Germany	6.6	21	68	54	88	14	16.35	11
Italy	6.9	19	66	62	85	23	25.72	63
Spain	7.2	12	76	19	89	7	20.91	39
Israel	7.2	11	64	66	87	17	26.10	64
Greece	6.0	31	64	70	80	36	23.17	52
New Zealand	7.3	9	78	13	86	18	18.42	23
South Korea	5.7	37	64	67	69	78	28.68	77
Portugal	5.4	41	72	38	85	21	30.18	80
Argentina	6.4	26	75	26	77	47	27.64	73
Poland	5.6	40	65	64	85	20	23.17	53
Chile	6.1	28	74	28	72	69	29.68	79
South Africa	5.1	50	73	32	72	72	21.41	43
Russia	5.0	53	57	84	68	81	21.42	44
Malaysia	6.0	31	71	44	74	61	22.48	49
Botswana	4.7	58	66	59	70	76	20.57	35

Mexico	6.6	22	79	11	79	39	19.92	32
Costa Rica	7.1	17	82	4	80	37	20.97	40
Brazil	6.6	20	78	12	74	60	25.10	60
Colombia	6.0	29	80	8	81	34	28.38	75
Ukraine	4.8	57	58	82	67	82	23.18	54
Venezuela	7.2	11	81	6	76	53	21.26	41
Peru	4.8	56	70	50	74	59	37.40	86
Armenia	4.3	71	57	83	76	52	42.96	88
Philippines	4.7	62	77	14	82	29	31.92	83
Indonesia	5.0	54	72	39	85	19	21.35	42
India	5.4	44	61	76	72	68	18.29	20
Georgia	3.7	81	40	88	74	65	23.89	57
Vietnam	5.3	45	70	46	87	15	18.86	27
Cambodia	3.6	84	59	81	69	77	31.44	82
Angola	4.2	72	66	60	67	83	27.24	72
Ghana	4.5	67	70	49	79	41	18.30	21
Bangladesh	4.3	70	49	87	75	58	30.58	81
Nepal	4.6	66	60	79	59	88	16.31	10
Nigeria	4.7	61	77	16	74	64	16.39	12
Kenya	4.0	74	68	53	71	75	16.85	15
Sierra Leone	3.6	83	61	75	63	85	34.91	85
Tanzania	3.7	82	69	52	73	67	19.81	28

[a] Positive engagement was composed of the average of six variables, where 0 was "no" and 1 was "yes" yesterday: enjoyment; smiling and laughing; doing what one does best; learning new things; choosing how to spend time; wanting more days like yesterday.

[b] Social prosperity was composed of: feeling respected; having others to count on in an emergency; feel safe when walking alone.

[c] Negative affect was composed of: worry; sadness; anger; depression.

of the world on several types of subjective well-being. The scores clearly indicate that income does not give a complete picture of the quality of life of nations.

There were 88 nations in our sample with complete data, and the nations shown are rank-ordered from highest to lowest in GDP per capita. The USA was the richest nation in our sample for 2005 income, and Tanzania was the poorest. In the first column of the table are Cantril's Ladder mean scores for the nations, with a possible range of 0–10. The Ladder score asked respondents to evaluate their lives from "worst possible" to "ideal," and the mean Ladder score of nations correlated with a GDP per capita of .84. The next three well-being variables, however, do not so strongly mirror income. The second variable is positive engagement, and it is the average response to six questions about positive engagement "yesterday," averaged for the nation. In other words, it assesses what percentage of the nation experienced positive feelings yesterday, and specifically variables such as enjoying life. It can be seen that some nations vary on positive engagement compared to their Ladder score. For example, Finland scores high on the life evaluation measure but much lower on positive engagement.

The next well-being variable shown in the table is social prosperity, and the last variable is negative affect. The table reveals that some nations consistently score well. But even for the clear "winner," Denmark, we see that its rank is somewhat lower for positive engagement. Nations such as Cambodia and Sierra Leone consistently score at a relatively low level across well-being variables, but even for them there is variation across the scores.

Some nations show striking disparities between their rankings across types of well-being. The USA is first in income, and yet only 25th for positive engagement and 50th for negative affect. Thus, the richest nation scores in the lower half of nations in terms of negative feelings, with 23% of respondents reporting "lots" of negative feelings such as anger and depression yesterday. In contrast, in Sweden half as many, 12%, report such feelings. Although respondents in Japan tend to report low negative affect, they rank low on social prosperity as well – on variables such as feeling respected and being able to count on others. A number of poor African nations score much more favorably on negative affect than they do on other well-being variables, and the Latin American cultures tend to score very high on positive engagement, but also tend to report high levels of negative feelings. Russia is a nation where income far surpasses positive engagement and social prosperity. South Korea, Japan, and Chile score much higher on income than on social prosperity, and one might speculate that the rapid economic growth of these nations somehow interfered with strong social relationships. In contrast, Costa Rica, Indonesia, and Vietnam score higher on social prosperity than on income. Thus, the well-being scores yield a much more intricate view of the quality of life of nations than is afforded by income alone.

CONCLUSIONS

Ultimately, while data support the claim that high levels of subjective well-being benefit citizens on a personal level, there is also a large body of evidence suggesting that well-being is good for societies in such areas of health and longevity, pro-peace attitudes, social capital, and income. And in many ways well-being is at least as important as money for social and psychological health. Because societies attend to and emphasize the improvement of what is measured, it is imperative that measures of subjective well-being are created and/or instituted. The creation of national accounts of well-being will not only stimulate public interest in well-being, but will also aid societies by promoting social and psychological capital. Because well-being is good for individuals and for societies, it will enormously aid the positive behavioral sciences and will continue to improve the human condition. Therefore, the importance of well-being for societies should be recognized, and raising levels of well-being should be a policy imperative.

REFERENCES

Bird, W. (2007). *Natural thinking: A report by Dr. William Bird, for the Royal Society for the Protection of Birds (RSPB), investigating the links between the natural environment, biodiversity and mental health* (2nd ed.). United Kingdom: RSPB.

Cantril, H. (1965). *The pattern of human concerns*. New Brunswick, NJ: Rutgers University Press.

Collier, C., & Christiansen, T. (1992). The state of commute in southern California. *Transportation Board Research, 1338*, 73–81.

Csikszentmihalyi, M. (1990). *Flow: The psychology of optimal experience*. New York: Harper & Row.

Danner, D. D., Snowdon, D. A., & Friesen, W. V. (2001). Positive emotions in early life and longevity: Findings from the nun study. *Journal of Personality and Social Psychology, 80*, 804–813.

Diener, E., & Biswas-Diener, R. (2008). *Happiness: Unlocking the mysteries of psychological wealth*. Malden, MA: Blackwell Publishing.

Diener, E., Kahneman, D., Tov, W., & Arora, R. (2009a). Income's association with judgments of life versus feelings. In E. Diener, D. Kahneman, & J. F. Helliwell (Eds.), *International differences in well-being* (pp. 3–15). Oxford, UK: Oxford University Press.

Diener, E., Lucas, R., Schimmack, U., & Helliwell, J. (2009b). *Well-being for public policy*. Oxford, UK: Oxford University Press.

Diener, E., Lucas, R., & Scollon, C. N. (2006). Beyond the hedonic treadmill: Revising the adaptation theory of well-being. *American Psychologist, 61*, 305–314.

Diener, E., Nickerson, C., Lucas, R. E., & Sandvik, E. (2002). Dispositional affect and job outcomes. *Social Indicators Research, 59*, 229–259.

Diener, E., & Oishi, S. (2004). Are Scandinavians happier than Asians? Issues in comparing nations on subjective well-being. In F. Columbus (Ed.), *Asian economic and political issues* (Vol. 10, pp. 1–25). Hauppauge, NY: Nova Science.

Diener, E., & Seligman, M. E. P. (2004). Beyond money: Toward an economy of well-being. *Psychological Science in the Public Interest, 5*, 1–31.

Diener, E., & Tov, W. (2007). Subjective well-being and peace. *Journal of Social Issues, 63*, 421–440.

Evans, G. W., & Wener, R. E. (2006). Rail commuting duration and passenger stress. *Health Psychology, 25*, 408–412.

Graham, C., & Pettinato, S. (2002). Frustrated achievers: Winners, losers and subjective well-being in new market economies. *Journal of Development Studies, 38,* 100–140.

Hartig, T., Evans, G. W., Jamner, L. D., Davis, D. S., & Garling, T. (2003). Tracking restoration in natural and urban field setting. *Journal of Environmental Psychology, 23,* 109–123.

Hartig, T., Mang, M., & Evans, G. W. (1991). Restorative effects of natural environment experience. *Environment and Behaviour, 23,* 3–26.

Heerwagen, J. H. (1990). The psychological aspects of windows and widow design. In R. I. Selby, K. H. Anthony, J. Choi, & B. Orland (Eds.), *Proceedings of the 21st Annual Conference of the Environmental Design Research Association* (pp. 269–280). Oklahoma City, OK: EDRA.

Inglehart, R. (1981). Post-materialism in an environment of insecurity. *American Political Science Review, 75,* 880–900.

Inglehart, R. (2009). Faith and freedom: Traditional and modern ways to happiness. In E. Diener, D. Kahneman, & J. F. Helliwell (Eds.), *International differences in well-being* (pp. 351–397). Oxford, UK: Oxford University Press.

Jacobs, S. V., Evans, G. W., Catalano, R., & Dooley, D. (1984). Air pollution and depressive symptomatology: Exploratory analyses of intervening psychosocial factors. *Population and Environment, 7,* 260–272.

Kahneman, D., Diener, E., Arora, R., Muller, G., Harter, J., & Tov, W. (2009). Prosperity and well-being on planet earth. Unpublished paper, Princeton University, *Proceedings of the National Academy of Sciences* (PNAS).

Kahneman, D., & Krueger, A. B. (2006). Developments in the measurement of subjective well-being. *Journal of Economic Perspectives, 20,* 3–24.

Kaplan, R., & Kaplan, S. (1989). *The experience of nature: A psychological perspective.* New York: Cambridge University Press.

Koslowsky, M., Kluger, A. N., & Reich, M. (1995). *Commuting stress: Causes, effects, and methods of coping.* New York: Springer.

Kuo, F. E., & Sullivan, W. C. (2001a). Aggression and violence in the inner city: Impacts of environment and mental fatigue. *Environment and Behavior, 33,* 543–571.

Kuo, F. E., & Sullivan, W. C. (2001b). Environment and crime in the inner city: Does vegetation reduce crime? *Environment and Behavior, 33,* 343–367.

Lavin, T., Higgins, C., Metcalfe, O., & Jordan, A. (2006). *Health impacts of the built environment: A review.* Dublin, Ireland: Institute of Public Health in Ireland.

Leather, P., Pygras, M., Beale, D., & Lawrence, C. (1998). Windows in the workplace: Sunlight, view, and occupational stress. *Environment and Behavior, 30,* 739–762.

Liss, S. (1991). *Nationwide personal transportation study: Early results.* Washington, DC: Office of Highway Information Management, Federal Highway Administration.

Luechinger, S. (2007). *Valuing air quality using the life satisfaction approach.* Unpublished manuscript, University of Zurich, Swiss Federal Institute of Technology.

Lyubomirsky, S., King, L., & Diener, E. (2005). The benefits of frequent positive affect: Does happiness lead to success? *Psychological Bulletin, 131,* 803–855.

Maller, C., Townsend, M., Pryor, A., Brown, P., & St. Leger, L. (2006). Healthy nature healthy people: "Contact with nature" as an upstream health promotion intervention for populations. *Health Promotion International, 21,* 45–55.

Marks, G. N., & Fleming, N. (1999). Influences and consequences of well-being among Australian young people: 1980–1995. *Social Indicators Research, 46,* 301–323.

Moore, E. O. (1981). A prison environment's effect on health care service demands. *Journal of Environmental Systems, 11,* 17–34.

Novaco, R. W. (1992). Automobile driving and aggressive behavior. In M. Wachs & M. Crawford (Eds.), *The car and the city: The automobile, the built environment, and daily urban life* (pp. 234–247). Ann Arbor: University of Michigan Press.

Novaco, R. W., & Collier, C. (1994). Commuting stress, ridesharing, and gender: Analyses from the 1993 state of the commute study in Southern California. *Transportation Board Research, 1433*, 170–176.

Novaco, R. W., Kliewer, W., & Broquet, A. (1991). Home environmental consequences of commute travel impedance. *American Journal of Community Psychology, 19,* 881–909.

Novaco, R. W., Stokols, D., & Milanesi, L. (1990). Objective and subjective dimensions of travel impedance as determinants of commuting stress. *American Journal of Community Psychology, 18,* 231–257.

Parsons, R., Tassinary, L. G., Ulrich, R. S., Hebl, M. R., & Grossman-Alexander, M. (1998). The view from the road: Implications for stress recovery and immunization. *Journal of Environmental Psychology, 18,* 113–140.

Pressman, S. D., & Cohen, S. (2007). Use of social words in autobiographies and longevity. *Psychosomatic Medicine, 69,* 262–269.

Robinson, A. (1991). Lung cancer, the motor vehicle, and its subtle influence on bodily functions. *Medical Hypotheses, 28,* 39–43.

Rohde, C. L. E., & Kendle, A. D. (1994). *Report to English Nature – human wellbeing, natural landscapes and wildlife in urban areas. A review.* University of Reading, Department of Horticulture and Landscape and the Research Institute for the Care of the Elderly, Bath.

Ryan, R. M., & Deci, E. L. (2000). Self-determination theory and the facilitation of intrinsic motivation, social development, and well-being. *American Psychologist, 55,* 68–78.

Ryff, C. D. (1989). Happiness is everything, or is it? Explorations on the meaning of psychological well-being. *Journal of Personality and Social Psychology, 57,* 1069–1081.

Schwarz, N., Kahneman, D., & Xu, J. (2009). Global and episodic reports of hedonic experience. In R. Belli, F. P. Stafford, & D. F. Alwin (Eds.), *Calendar and time diary methods in life course research* (pp. 157–174). Thousand Oaks, CA: Sage Publications.

Singer, J., Lundberg, U., & Frankenhaeuser, M. (1978). Stress on the train: A study of urban commuting. *Advances in Environmental Psychology, 1,* 41–56.

Stutzer, A., & Frey, B. S. (2008). Stress that doesn't pay: The commuting paradox. *Scandinavian Journal of Economics, 110,* 339–366.

Talbot, J. F., & Kaplan, R. (1991). The benefits of nearby nature for elderly apartment residents. *International Journal of Aging and Human Development, 33,* 119–130.

Tennessen, C. M., & Cimprich, B. E. (1995). Views to nature: Effects on attention. *Journal of Environmental Psychology, 15,* 77–85.

Tov, W., & Diener, E. (2008). The well-being of nations: Linking together trust, cooperation, and democracy. In B. A. Sullivan, M. Snyder, & J. L. Sullivan (Eds.), *Cooperation: The political psychology of effective human interaction* (pp. 323–342). Malden, MA: Blackwell Publishing.

Ulrich, R. S. (1979). Visual landscapes and psychological well-being. *Landscape Research, 4,* 17–19.

Ulrich, R. S. (1984). View through a window may influence recovery from surgery. *Science, 224,* 420–421.

Ulrich, R., Simons, R. F., Losito, E., Fiorito, E., Miles, M. A., & Zelson, M. (1991). Stress recovery during exposure to natural and urban environments. *Journal of Environmental Psychology, 11,* 201–230.

Wells, N. M., & Evans, G. W. (2003). Nearby nature; a buffer of life stress among rural children. *Environment and Behaviour, 35*, 311–330.

Welsch, H. (2006). Environment and happiness: Valuation of air pollution using life satisfaction data. *Ecological Economics, 58*, 801–813.

Wener, R. E., Evans, G. W., Phillips, D., & Nadler, N. (2003). Running for the 7:45: The effects of public transit improvements on commuter stress. *Transportation, 30*, 203–220.

White, R., & Heerwagen, J. (1998). Nature and mental health: Biophilia and biophobia. In A. Lundberg (Ed.), *Environment and mental health* (pp. 175–192). Hove, UK: Lawrence Erlbaum Associates Ltd.

White, S. M., & Rotton, J. (1998). Type of commute, behavioral aftereffects, and cardiovascular activity: A field experiment. *Environment and Behavior, 30*, 763–780.

3

Cultivating Positive Emotions to Enhance Human Flourishing

BARBARA L. FREDRICKSON and LAURA E. KURTZ

*P*ositive emotions, by definition, feel good. People enjoy feeling the pleasant emotional states of joy, inspiration, gratitude, serenity, and the like. So much so, that they often seek out opportunities to feel good in these ways. Yet do most people do this enough? And is feeling good the only reward? We answer a decisive "no" to both questions. In this chapter, we present an overview of research stemming from the broaden-and-build theory of positive emotions to justify our stance. Science now confirms that positive emotions do far more than simply feel good. Indeed, they have wide-reaching implications for psychological, social, and physical well-being in ways that fuel human flourishing.

Only in the last decade or so have we come to understand the vital downstream effects of pleasant emotional states. Historically, research on emotions centered on the negative, detailing, for instance, how people react to adversity such as the death of a loved one or the devastating conditions of war, or how emotions such as anger, fear, and contempt contribute to disease, disorders, and social unrest. Thanks in part to the advent of positive psychology, this imbalance has shifted, with positive emotions increasingly becoming the target of scientific investigation. Even though the science of positive emotions remains young, a number of findings are now ripe for application, pointing to plausible paths to improve individual and societal well-being.

THE BROADEN-AND-BUILD THEORY

The broaden-and-build theory of positive emotions (Fredrickson, 1998, 2009) holds that positive emotions momentarily broaden people's attention and thinking, enabling individuals to draw flexibly on higher level connections and wider-than-usual ranges of percepts or ideas. In turn, these broadened and flexible outlooks help people to discover and build survival-promoting personal resources. These resources can be: *cognitive*, such as the ability to mindfully attend to the present moment or come up with multiple pathways toward a goal; *psychological*, such as the ability to maintain a sense of mastery over environmental challenges or be resilient to adversity; *social*, such as the ability to give and receive love and social support; or *physical*, such as the ability to sleep well or ward off the common cold. People with ample resources such as these are more effective in flexibly meeting life's challenges and taking advantage of its many opportunities, including those associated with creating healthy lifestyles and positive trajectories of personal growth that seed human flourishing. Put simply, Fredrickson's broaden-and-build theory states that positive emotions widen people's outlooks in ways that, little by little, beneficially reshape who they are.

Over time, frequent experiences of positive emotions can trigger upward spirals between positive affect and expansive, creative thinking, which lead to personal growth and flourishing. This dynamic contrasts sharply with the downward spirals between negative affect and narrow, pessimistic thinking, which can lead to depression and have long been the focus of cognitive-behavioral therapy. And because people can control which emotions they feel and when – perhaps far more than they recognize – they can, in effect, steer themselves away from downward spirals and toward flourishing. We describe, in this chapter, new tools for doing so. Before taking up these tools, however, it is helpful to understand the strength of the empirical support upon which they rest. Key hypotheses of the broaden-and-build theory have received empirical support from multiple laboratories. We review that support in the sections that follow.

POSITIVE EMOTIONS EXPAND AWARENESS

Research affirms that positive emotions momentarily expand the scope of people's attention and thinking. Such cognitive expansion allows one to see the proverbial "big picture," become more creative, and create and execute action plans outside of one's typical routine. This ability of positive emotions to expand our awareness is termed the broaden effect. Our laboratory initiated tests of the broaden effect some years ago with a number of controlled laboratory experiments.

In one early experiment we evoked different emotional states in participants using short film clips. We randomly assigned participants to one of five experimental groups. Participants in two of the groups watched clips that evoked positive emotions, either contentment or joy, two other groups saw films intended to evoke negative emotions, either anger or fear, and the clip for the final group served as the control condition and evoked neutrality. Immediately following each film clip, we measured the breadth of participants' thought–action repertoires by asking them to list all of the things they would like to do at the moment, given how they were feeling. On tallying the listed actions, the data revealed significant between-group differences. Participants in either of the two positive emotion conditions of joy and contentment listed more things they would like to do right then relative to those in the neutral control condition. Additionally, those in the two negative emotion conditions named significantly fewer things than those in the neutral control condition, demonstrating a narrowing effect (Fredrickson & Branigan, 2005). This expanded behavioral repertoire provides clear support for the broaden effect. The experience of positive emotions opened up new possibilities – new ideas about action.

Although subtle, the broaden effect of positive emotions is reliable and has since been tested and supported in research laboratories beyond our own, using a wide range of methods. Studies of memory, attention, and verbal fluency show that, under the influence of positive emotions, people have access to a wider array of information than is typically accessible to them (Johnson, Waugh, & Fredrickson, 2010; Rowe, Hirsh, & Anderson, 2007; Talarico, Berntsen, & Rubin, 2009). Eye-tracking studies show that positive emotions literally expand one's peripheral vision, allowing people to see more of their surroundings (Wadlinger & Isaacowitz, 2006). Brain imaging studies concur. Stroke patients with visual neglect, for instance, show expanded visual awareness when listening to pleasant music, relative to unpleasant or no music, an effect apparently mediated by functional coupling of emotional and attentional brain regions (Soto, Funes, Guzman-Garcia, Warbrick, Rotshtein, & Humphreys, 2009). Likewise, brain-based measures of breadth of visual encoding indicate that induced emotions bias early visual inputs, with positive emotions increasing and negative emotions decreasing the field of view (Schmitz, De Rosa, & Anderson, 2009). Positive emotions also affect the manner in which individuals relate with one another by cultivating a unified understanding and deeper appreciation for common humanity, while bridging the divides of racial and cultural differences (Dovidio, Isen, Guerra, Gaertner, & Rust, 1998; Johnson & Fredrickson, 2005). Positivity opens people, both mentally and socially.

POSITIVE EMOTIONS UNDO LINGERING NEGATIVE EMOTIONS AND FUEL RESILIENCE

In addition to broadening one's awareness and action repertoires, positive emotions have the ability to erase the lingering traces of negative emotions. This erasing quality of positive emotions, termed the undo effect, was demonstrated in one of our earliest studies on cardiovascular reactivity and recovery in response to experimentally induced speech anxiety. To first generate a potent negative emotion in all participants, they were instructed that they would prepare a speech under considerable time pressure. Participants were told that there was a 50% chance that they would have to deliver their prepared speech, which would in turn be evaluated by their peers. However, if instead of a countdown to record their speech they saw a film clip appear on the screen, this would indicate that they would not have to give their speech after all. In actuality, all participants were shown a film clip signaling their release from the speech task. Depending on their assigned condition, participants then watched one of four possible films: a positive film evoking contentment or joy, a neutral film, or a negative film evoking sadness. Cardiovascular reactivity was tracked throughout the study to operationally test the ability of the different emotional states to undo the lingering negative emotional arousal brought about by the earlier prospect of public speaking. As predicted, the data supported the undo effect of positive emotions. All participants showed a significant spike in cardiovascular reactivity in response to speech preparation (i.e., increased heart rate, blood pressure, etc.), yet participants in each of the two positive emotion conditions showed faster cardiovascular recovery rates relative to those in the neutral and negative emotion conditions. Specifically, those who turned their attention to positive images recovered from the negative cardiovascular arousal about 20 seconds faster than those who considered neutral or sad images (Fredrickson, Mancuso, Branigan, & Tugade, 2000; see also Fredrickson & Levenson, 1998). Knowing that prolonged cardiovascular reactivity to stress may increase the likelihood for heart disease, the undo effect shows a promising way in which positive emotions may promote greater overall health (see Cohen & Pressman, 2006, for a review).

A related buffering effect of positive emotions was evident in the wake of the September 11, 2001 terrorist attack. Our laboratory closely examined the links between positive emotions and resilience, the personal resource that helps one to bounce back from adversity. Participants from an earlier study were invited to complete additional questionnaires in the days following 9/11. In the previous study, experimenters had measured participants' resilience levels using the Ego-Resiliency Scale (Block & Kremen, 1996). Experimenters were then able to determine the personality style of each participant in terms of their purported resilience levels. These differing personality styles served as the major classifying variable for the participants in the post-9/11 study, which aimed to evaluate the difference in emotional recovery outcomes between those ranking high in resilience and those ranking low. While both personality styles demonstrated clear emotional disturbance in response to 9/11, the data revealed that those with resilient personalities showed fewer signs of clinical depression and actually became psychologically stronger than they were pre-9/11 with regard to increases in optimism, tranquility, and reported life satisfaction (Fredrickson, Tugade, Waugh, & Larkin, 2003). Most importantly, however, is the underlying mechanism behind these differences – positive emotions. These were the active force driving the "bounce back" effect of the resilient personalities. Although participants both low and high on resilience reported comparable anger, fear, and sadness following the 9/11 attacks, those with highly resilient personalities concurrently reported experiencing positive emotions such as joy, love, and gratitude. These positive emotions fueled the resilience that promoted more rapid emotional growth and recovery.

Yet it does not require an international catastrophe for resiliency to take effect. In another study modeled after the anxiety-producing speech preparation protocol explained at the beginning of this section, the differences between high and low resilience personalities were again assessed. Using this same anxiety-building task along with the same surprise release from actual speech presentation, experimenters once again measured participants' physiological responses throughout the anxiety-release process. This time, however, the focus was observing the differences between people with more or less resilient personality styles. We observed that although the physiological measures of heart rate, blood pressure, and blood vessel constriction peaked equally high for all participants in response to the speech preparation task, the highly resilient participants experienced significantly more rapid recovery. That is, the hearts of the low resilience personality type participants continued to race long after those of the high resilience personalities had returned to their normal, relaxed rhythm. As anticipated, the faster rebounds of the highly resilient participants were catalyzed by their higher than average positive emotions. While other participants reported mostly only negative emotions in response to the speech preparation task, the swiftly rebounding high resilience personalities reported a mix of positive and negative emotions and attitudes (Tugade & Fredrickson, 2004). They viewed the task as an appealing challenge that they were eager to tackle. Where others felt apprehension, the resilient participants saw opportunity. It is precisely these resilient individuals who best utilize the undo effect of positive emotions to their benefit, at even the most basic physiological level, by self-generating positive emotions even in the midst of adverse circumstances.

POSITIVE EMOTIONS PROMOTE PERSONAL GROWTH

The open, expansive awareness that positive emotions bring can in turn prompt growth in personal and social resources that increase well-being. Such growth in resources fueled by the broaden effect of positive emotions is termed the build effect, which offers a new perspective on the ever-popular pursuit of happiness. Positive emotions are often taken as a sign of life satisfaction, a momentary marker of a more global state of well-being or happiness (Diener & Diener, 1996). However, when examined beyond this mere surface-level association, an alternate connection is revealed between positive emotions and life satisfaction (Cohn, Fredickson, Brown, Mikels, & Conway, 2009). This alternate connection incorporates an evolutionary perspective in which positive emotions build the personal resources, which then equip individuals to better meet life's opportunities and challenges. The increased preparedness produced through the additional resources accounts for a greater sense of satisfaction with life or, more commonly termed, happiness.

We tested this idea by revisiting the topic of resilience in a recent longitudinal study. The data revealed that individuals who report experiencing the most positive emotions in daily life show the greatest increases in resilience over the span of a month, showing yet another connection between resilience and positive emotions. In turn, people who showed the greatest increases in resilience also showed the greatest increases in their life satisfaction. Importantly, the data enabled the statistical isolation of growth in resources as the active ingredient mediating the link between positive emotions and life satisfaction. In other words, we unpacked the complex amalgam known as "happiness" into its constituent parts. In doing so, we move beyond seeing happiness as a mere collection of positive outlooks and experiences toward the view of happiness as an orderly system in which momentary good feelings have the capacity to set people on trajectories of learning and growth that equip them with the resources needed to maintain a satisfying life (Cohn et al., 2009).

POSITIVE EMOTIONS PRODUCE RELATIONAL INTIMACY

Another recent experiment examined the effects of laughter-induced positive emotions on interpersonal relationships. Pairs of friends visited our laboratory and were randomly assigned to one of three conditions: shared laughter, solo laughter, or shared serenity. All participants listened to a brief audio clip prior to engaging in a self-disclosure conversation with their friend. Participants in the shared laughter condition listened to a sampler of laughter with their friend in clear view and within reaching distance. Participants in the solo laughter condition listened to the same audio clip but in private, separated from their friend by a partition and isolated via headphones. Participants in the shared serenity condition listened to a brief clip of calming beach sounds with their friend in view, as in the shared laughter condition. Following these audio clips, all participants engaged in a self-disclosing conversation in which each member of the friendship pair had a chance to share something that had been troubling or concerning to them lately. The self-disclosure task was intended to test the security of each friendship and the ease and openness that each member felt while sharing.

Self-report data gathered after the interaction revealed that participants who engaged in shared laughter prior to self-disclosure reported greater perceived responsiveness from their friend during the interaction compared to those in the solo laughter condition (Algoe, Kurtz, & Fredrickson, 2009; Study 3). This increased perception of partner responsiveness may in turn promote increased openness and ease of disclosure by eliminating feelings of doubt or rejection. Because self-disclosure builds relational intimacy, which in turn builds relationship satisfaction (Reis, 1990), this experiment demonstrates another way in which positive emotions build consequential social resources.

POSITIVE EMOTIONS TRANSFORM PEOPLE

While the shared laughter study demonstrated the potential for the build effect from laughter-induced positive emotions, a more solid test of the build effect requires a longitudinal examination of people's lives as they unfold over time. This requires that people increase their daily diet of positive emotions over the span of weeks or months, not just in a one-hour laboratory session. In terms of the previous study, one would likely need to generate shared laughter at multiple instances across an extended period of time before experiencing durable changes in relationship satisfaction. The build effect is not instantaneous, rather it represents incremental changes forged through repeated exposure to positive emotions.

We recently conducted a randomized controlled trial of the effects of a particular form of meditation training, known as loving-kindness meditation (Salzberg, 2005), which we speculated would augment people's daily experiences of positive emotions, thus enabling a strong test of the build effect (Fredrickson, Cohn, Coffey, Pek, & Finkel, 2008). The study was performed in the context of a workplace wellness program, in which the participants, who were employed at a large computer firm in Detroit, Michigan, were offered a seven-week meditation workshop, billed to "reduce stress" free of charge. Interested participants were randomly assigned to either partake in the meditation workshop during the study or to serve as a waitlist control group that received the meditation training a few months later. Those assigned to the experimental condition attended a weekly workshop session over their lunch hour, and began a practice of daily meditations using guided meditations that we supplied them via CD. All participants in the study completed daily emotional reports, assessing the positive and negative emotions experienced throughout the day. Participants also completed pre- and post-workshop surveys evaluating their cognitive, social, psychological, and physical resources (Fredrickson et al., 2008).

The data revealed clear support for the build hypothesis, showing that positive emotions do indeed build individuals' personal resources. The practice of loving-kindness meditation increased participants' reports of positive emotions, which in turn increased a variety of personal resources, including mindfulness, social support received, self-acceptance, and a sense of purpose in life. Participants who practiced the meditation also reported having fewer illness symptoms than those participants in the control condition. These increased personal resources in turn increased participants' overall ratings of life satisfaction and reduced their depressive symptoms. Moreover, statistically we were able to isolate the increase in positive emotions as the active ingredient through which loving-kindness meditation produced these salubrious outcomes. These data provided clear support for the hypothesis, drawn from the broaden-and-build theory, that positive emotions build consequential personal resources that increase overall well-being. In the span of just three months, the positive emotions generated through loving-kindness meditation significantly transformed the study participants' lives for the better (Fredrickson et al., 2008).

REPRISE ON THE BROADEN-AND-BUILD THEORY

The broaden-and-build theory (Fredrickson, 1998, 2009) holds that positive emotions evolved as part of universal human nature because these pleasant states broadened our human ancestors' awareness in ways that, over time, built their resources for combating later threats to life and limb. Several recent longitudinal studies indicate that people who experience and express the most positive emotions actually live longer than their less positive peers, perhaps as much as 10 years longer (Danner, Snowdon, & Friesen, 2001; Moskowitz, 2003). Although the links between positive emotions and longevity are eye-catching, they are merely associations, correlations in need of an explanation. The broaden-and-build theory provides an evidence-backed explanatory framework that can account for those findings. Positive emotions broaden people's mindsets and build their resources in ways that promote human flourishing and longevity.

THE POSITIVITY RATIO

How much positive emotion is enough to promote human flourishing? Recent research from our laboratory provides an evidence-based guideline to address this important question, expressed in terms of the ratio of a person's positive to negative emotions, or what we've called the positivity ratio (Fredrickson, 2009; Fredrickson & Losada, 2005). For every negative emotion that weighs us down, we should aim to cultivate at least three positive emotions to lift us up. Three-to-one is the ratio that we've found to be the tipping point beyond which the full impact of positive emotions becomes unleashed. The 3 : 1 tipping point also honors the underlying asymmetries between positive and negative emotions. One asymmetry, termed negativity bias, or "bad is stronger than good" (Baumeister, Bratslavsky, Finkenauer, & Vohs, 2001; Cacioppo, Gardner, & Berntson, 1999), promises that, measure for measure, negative experiences captivate people's attention and energy to a much larger degree than positive experiences, which can seem weak and pale by comparison. This asymmetry in intensity is offset by a complementary asymmetry in frequency: Most experiences in life, for most people, are at least mildly positive, an imbalance termed the positivity offset (Cacioppo et al., 1999; Diener & Diener, 1996).

The positivity ratio was discovered in the context of a corporate boardroom. Losada (1999) observed the interactions of 60 teams as they conducted annual strategic planning, coding for statements that were positive or negative, self-focused or other-focused, and based on inquiry or advocacy. After classifying the teams according to their performance levels, interesting distinctions emerged. Those teams classified as high-performing, who scored high on profitability, customer satisfaction ratings, and superior, peer, and subordinate evaluations, demonstrated positivity ratios of around 6 : 1; low-performance teams had ratios below 1 : 1; and mixed-performance teams hovered around 2 : 1 (Losada, 1999). Carefully observing the intertwined relationships in these data plotted over time, Losada (1999) wrote a set of mathematical equations to capture the different dynamics he observed across the three types of business teams, resulting in a non-linear dynamic system (Losada, 1999). Because the properties of this non-linear dynamic system – the Lorenz system – have been thoroughly studied, Losada could use his mathematical model to predict the tipping point ratio at which flourishing, high performance would first emerge. That is how the 3 : 1 tipping point ratio was discovered (see Fredrickson, 2009; Fredrickson & Losada, 2005).

On the heels of that discovery, Fredrickson and Losada (2005) tested the 3 : 1 positivity ratio within the everyday lives of individuals known to be either flourishing or languishing across two, independent samples. These individuals had reported their emotional experiences each day for four weeks. We tallied their total positive emotions experienced over the course of the month, as well as their total negative emotions, and then computed each person's positivity ratio. The data were consistent with the hypothesis that a 3 : 1 positivity ratio was a psychologically meaningful tipping point. In one sample, flourishing individuals had an average ratio of 3.2 : 1, and in the second sample the ratio for flourishers was 3.4 : 1. In contrast, people classified as languishing had average ratios below 3 : 1, with averages of 2.3 : 1 and 2.1 : 1 in the two samples (Fredrickson & Losada, 2005).

The positivity ratio is also consistent with research on married couples and individuals diagnosed with depression. Marital relationships that might be classified as flourishing – those that last, with both members reporting high relationship satisfaction – had average positivity ratios of about 5 : 1. Conversely, languishing and failed marriages averaged lower than 1 : 1 ratios (Gottman, 1994). Data from patients undergoing treatment for depression echoed the previous findings. Prior to any treatment, the average positivity ratio across all patients was around 0.5 : 1. Following treatment, however, patients who were classified as having obtained optimal remission from their depression increased their positivity ratios to around 4.3 : 1. In contrast, those who showed only average remission had ratios of around 2.3 : 1, and those demonstrating no improvement remained around 0.7 : 1 (Schwartz, Reynolds, Thase, Frank, Fasiczka, & Haaga, 2002).

Across business teams, marriages, and individuals, the positivity ratio of 3 : 1 has thus been found to mark the line between languishing and flourishing. But this begs the question, why not strive for an even greater positivity ratio of 20 : 1 or 100 : 1? Is negativity even necessary?

As with many other things in life, too much positivity may actually be destructive. While still in need of empirical test, there appears to be a cap on the positivity ratio. The same mathematical model upon which the discovery of the 3 : 1 positivity ratio rests also suggests that the ratio of 11 : 1 may be the upper limit for the benefits of positive emotions (Fredrickson & Losada, 2005). This suggests that rather than strive for a top-heavy ratio packed with positivity, a moderate amount of negativity in one's life may serve as emotional grounding. Research with married couples demonstrates that some negativity, if appropriately communicated, is indeed healthy for relationship well-being. Specifically, anger and conflict engagement are normal and productive forms of negativity while exhibitions of contempt and disgust can be extremely maladaptive (Gottman, 1994). The difference between adaptive and maladaptive negativity may lie in the personal meanings or appraisals that undergird specific negative emotions, as well as their ease of remediation. For instance, when people feel guilty, they make a moral judgment about some inappropriate action they've taken in the past. Their misstep can perhaps be rectified with a change in future action choices. By contrast, when people feel ashamed about that same misstep, they are making a more wide-sweeping moral judgment about themselves as unacceptable people, an appraisal that is far more difficult to overcome. Appropriate negativity, therefore, is specific and easier to resolve. Inappropriate negativity, on the other hand, can overwhelm people both in magnitude and duration, often being exaggerated relative to the actual circumstances at hand. Appropriate negativity may well be necessary from time to time, as it enables one to maintain grounded in reality.

REDUCING NEEDLESS NEGATIVITY

One benefit of having the positivity ratio as a guideline to achieve human flourishing is that there are always three ways to increase a ratio: decrease the denominator, increase the numerator, or both. The vast legacy of clinical psychology, especially cognitive-behavioral therapy, provides ample tools for decreasing negativity.

Although appropriate negativity is healthy in moderation, inappropriate negativity is often pointless and can be reduced. In her 2009 book, *Positivity*, Fredrickson outlines several tools for doing so. For instance, examining one's habitual cognitive appraisals of specific situations is extremely helpful in this regard as it draws attention to unnecessary negative thinking, rumination, and mindlessness. Focusing one's efforts on avoiding the downward pull of these cognitive traps improves awareness for recognizing future needless negativity and provides one with the tools necessary to combat its debilitating effects at the roots. Assessing one's immediate environment is also useful for decreasing daily diets of negativity. An excessive intake of media violence has been shown to decrease empathy and kindness in its viewers (Huesmann & Taylor, 2006). Immersing oneself in a culture of gossip and sarcasm or surrounding oneself with negative people can also drastically impact your positivity ratio. Becoming more mindful of recurring sources of negativity in one's daily life can be an important step toward reaching the tipping point to emotional flourishing. The next step is cultivating positivity.

CULTIVATING POSITIVITY

Increasing the numerator of heartfelt positivity is arguably the most important step to improve people's odds of flourishing. We underscore, however, that the positivity that generates true change needs to be heartfelt and sincere, not blatantly fabricated. Indeed, insincere positivity can be corrosive, both physically and interpersonally. As just one potent example, an imaging study of men with coronary heart disease found that insincere positivity, as evidenced in facial expression, predicted heart wall collapse just as did facial expressions of anger (Rosenberg et al., 2001). So while it may be easier to force a smile than to genuinely produce one, the consequences of such a positive façade can be harmful.

Although the task of fostering sincere positivity may at first appear daunting, the burgeoning field of positive psychology reveals a number of techniques to help boost daily diets of positive emotions, which Fredrickson also reviews in her 2009 book, *Positivity*. Rather than force oneself to "be positive" in a heavy-handed way, the advice that emerges from positive psychology is to lightly create the mindset of positivity. Better mottos than "be positive" are "be open, be appreciative, be curious, and be kind." First, allowing oneself to be open and truly accepting of one's current circumstances creates multiple opportunities to seed positivity. Being open to one's environment, inviting change, and letting go of expectations for how something should or should not be produces an increased feeling of acceptance for present conditions while enabling one to take notice of the beauty, kindness, and comforts that life often brings. Second, appreciating these newly found gifts by savoring the experience and gently reliving the positive emotions they create also helps one to extract additional positivity from everyday life (Bryant & Veroff, 2007). Coinciding with the suggestion of being open is the importance of being curious. Following one's interests and expanding one's skill repertoire by pursuing new things can also facilitate in the growth of positivity (Kashdan, 2009). Finally, creating high-quality connections with others has been shown to be an extremely valuable tool for improving one's positivity (Diener & Seligman, 2002; Franklin, 2001). Making regular efforts to generate tenderness and compassion for another individual leads to greater increases in positivity than merely living life as usual (Fredrickson et al., 2008).

POSITIVITY: RECAPPED AND APPLIED

The science of positive emotions is still a fresh topic within the field of psychology. Even so, a tremendous amount of valuable insight has already been gained – insight upon which ongoing research continues to build. Researchers have identified a number of scientifically supported benefits of positive emotions. Positive emotions broaden people's awareness, allowing them to step beyond the narrow confines of negativity to explore new situations and ideas. Through this increased openness, positive emotions set people on positive trajectories of growth that build their personal resources, creating increasing social integration and emotional stability. Positive emotions also fuel resilience, serving as the means through which people can resist downward spirals in the face of adversity, and instead be buoyed by positivity's upward spirals.

The science of emotions also reveals that people have far more control over what emotions they experience, and when, than they typically give themselves credit for. Everyone is capable of keeping their inappropriate negative emotions in check and of increasing their daily intake of positive emotions. Indeed, opportunities to experience positive emotions abound, waiting to be noticed, explored, and amplified. With 3 : 1 positioned as the emotional guideline – the tipping point positivity ratio that separates languishing from flourishing – pathways to improving society come into view.

REFERENCES

Algoe, S. B., Kurtz, L. E., & Fredrickson, B. L. (2009). *Shared laughter and interpersonal closeness.* Unpublished data, University of North Carolina at Chapel Hill.

Baumeister, R. F., Bratslavsky, E., Finkenauer, C., & Vohs, K. D. (2001). Bad is stronger than good. *Review of General Psychology, 5,* 323–370.

Block, J., & Kremen, A. M. (1996). IQ and ego-resiliency: Conceptual and empirical connections and separateness. *Journal of Personality and Social Psychology, 70,* 346–361.

Bryant, F., & Veroff, J. (2007). *Savoring: A new model of positive experience.* Mahwah, NJ: Lawrence Erlbaum Associates, Inc.

Cacioppo, J. T., Gardner, W. L., & Berntson, G. G. (1999). The affect system has parallel and integrative processing components: Form follows function. *Journal of Personality and Social Psychology, 76,* 839–855.

Cohen, S., & Pressman, S. D. (2006) Positive affect and health. *Current Directions in Psychological Science, 15,* 122–125.

Cohn, M. A., Fredrickson, B. L., Brown, S. L., Mikels, J. A., & Conway, A. M. (2009). Happiness unpacked: Positive emotions increase life satisfaction by building resilience. *Emotion, 9,* 361–368.

Danner, D. D., Snowdon, D. A., & Friesen, W. V. (2001). Positive emotions in early life and longevity: Findings from the nun study. *Journal of Personality and Social Psychology, 80,* 804–813.

Diener, E., & Diener, C. (1996). Most people are happy. *Psychological Science, 7,* 181–185.

Diener, E., & Seligman, M. E. P. (2002). Very happy people. *Psychological Science, 13,* 81–84.

Dovidio, J. F., Isen, A. M., Guerra, P., Gaertner, S. L., & Rust, M. (1998). Positive affect, cognition, and the reduction of intergroup bias. In C. Sedikides (Ed.), *Intergroup cognition and intergroup behavior* (pp. 337–366). Mahwah, NJ: Lawrence Erlbaum Associates, Inc.

Franklin, H. (2001). Beyond toxicity: Human health and the natural environment. *American Journal of Preventive Medicine, 20*, 234–239.

Fredrickson, B. L. (1998). What good are positive emotions? *Review of General Psychology, 2*, 300–319.

Fredrickson, B. L. (2009). *Positivity: Groundbreaking research reveals how to embrace the hidden strength of positive emotions, overcome negativity, and thrive.* New York: Crown.

Fredrickson, B. L., & Branigan, C. (2005). Positive emotions broaden the scope of attention and thought–action repertoires. *Cognition and Emotion, 19*, 313–332.

Fredrickson, B. L., Cohn, M. A., Coffey, K. A., Pek, J., & Finkel, S. M. (2008). Open hearts build lives: Positive emotions, induced through loving-kindness meditation, build consequential personal resources. *Journal of Personality and Social Psychology, 95*, 1045–1062.

Fredrickson, B. L., & Levenson, R. W. (1998). Positive emotions speed recovery from the cardiovascular sequelae of negative emotions. *Cognition and Emotion, 12*, 191–220.

Fredrickson B. L., & Losada M. F. (2005). Positive affect and the complex dynamics of human flourishing. *American Psychologist, 60*, 678–686.

Fredrickson, B. L., Mancuso, R. A., Branigan, C., & Tugade, M. M. (2000). The undoing effect of positive emotions. *Motivation and Emotion, 24*, 237–258.

Fredrickson, B. L., Tugade, M. M., Waugh, C. E., & Larkin, G. (2003). What good are positive emotions in crises?: A prospective study of resilience and emotions following the terrorist attacks on the United States on September 11th, 2001. *Journal of Personality and Social Psychology, 84*, 365–376.

Gottman, J. M. (1994). *What predicts divorce: The relationship between marital processes and marital outcomes.* Hillsdale, NJ: Lawrence Erlbaum Associates, Inc.

Huesmann, R. L., & Taylor, L. D. (2006). The role of media violence in violent behavior. *Annual Review of Public Health, 27*, 393–415.

Johnson, K. J., & Fredrickson, B. L. (2005). Positive emotions eliminate the own-race bias in face perception. *Psychological Science 16*, 875–881.

Johnson, K. J., Waugh, C. E., & Fredrickson, B. L. (2010). Smile to see the forest: Expressed positive emotion broadens attentional scope and increase attentional flexibility. *Cognition and Emotion, 24*, 299–321.

Kashdan, T. B. (2009). *Curious?* New York: HarperCollins.

Losada, M. F. (1999). The complex dynamics of high performance teams. *Mathematical and Computer Modelling, 30*, 179–192.

Moskowitz, J. T. (2003). Positive affect predicts lower risk of AIDS mortality. *Psychosomatic Medicine, 65*, 620–626.

Reis, H. T. (1990). The role of intimacy in interpersonal relationships. *Journal of Social and Clinical Psychology, 9*, 15–30.

Rosenberg, E. L., Ekman, P., Jiang, W., Babyak, M., Coleman, R. E., Hanson, M., et al. (2001). Linkages between facial expressions of anger and transient myocardial ischemia in men with coronary artery disease. *Emotion, 1*, 107–115.

Rowe, G., Hirsh, J. B., & Anderson, A. K. (2007). Positive affect increases the breadth of attentional selection. *Proceedings of the National Academy of Sciences of the USA, 104*, 383–388.

Salzberg, S. (2005). *The force of kindness: Change your life with love and compassion.* Boulder, CO: Sounds True.

Schmitz, T. W., De Rosa, E., & Anderson, A. K. (2009). Opposing influences on affective state valence on visual cortical encoding. *Journal of Neuroscience, 29,* 7199–7207.

Schwartz, R. M., Reynolds, C. F., III, Thase, M. E., Frank, E., Fasiczka, A. L., & Haaga, D. A. F. (2002). Optimal and normal affect balance in psychotherapy of major depression: Evaluation of the balanced states of mind model. *Behavioural and Cognitive Psychotherapy, 30,* 439–450.

Soto, D., Funes, M. J., Guzman-Garcia, A., Warbrick, T., Rotshtein, P., & Humphreys, G. W. (2009). Pleasant music overcomes the loss of awareness in patients with visual neglect. *Proceedings of the National Academy of Sciences of the USA.* doi 10.1073/pnas.0811681106.

Talarico, J. M., Berntsen, D., & Rubin, D. C. (2009). Positive emotions enhance recall of peripheral details. *Cognition and Emotion, 23,* 380–398.

Tugade, M. M., & Fredrickson, B. L. (2004). Resilient individuals use positive emotions to bounce back from negative emotional experiences. *Journal of Personality and Social Psychology, 86,* 320–333.

Wadlinger, H. A., & Isaacowitz, D. M. (2006). Positive mood broadens visual attention to positive stimuli. *Motivation and Emotion, 30,* 89–101.

4

Character Strengths and Virtues: Their Role in Well-Being

CHRISTOPHER PETERSON and NANSOOK PARK

W hat is the good of a person? Answers to this question lie at the heart of traditional moral philosophy as well as contemporary positive psychology (Peterson, 2006). Despite the importance of good character, scholars largely neglected this topic throughout much of the 20th century. Positive psychology has refocused scientific attention on character, identifying it as one of the pillars of this new field and central to the understanding of the psychological good life (Seligman & Csikszentmihalyi, 2000). In their introduction to positive psychology, Seligman and Csikszentmihalyi (2000) described the study of positive traits as a central pillar of this new field, and Park and Peterson (2003) proposed that positive traits link together the other central topics of positive psychology: positive experiences, positive social relationships, and positive institutions. Positive traits enable positive experiences and close relationships with others, which in turn have important consequences in the contexts of families, schools, workplaces, and communities. Positive psychology specifically emphasizes building individual and societal well-being by identifying and fostering strengths of character (Peterson, 2006; Peterson & Park, 2003).

Good character is what we look for in our leaders, what we look for in our teachers and students in classrooms, what we look for in our colleagues at work, what parents look for in their children, and what friends look for in each other. Good character is not simply the absence of deficits and problems but rather a well-developed family of positive traits.

Character strengths not only prevent undesirable life outcomes (Botvin, Baker, Dusenbury, Botvin, & Diaz, 1995) but are important in their own right as indicators and indeed causes of healthy life-long development (Colby & Damon, 1992; Weissberg & Greenberg, 1997). Growing evidence shows that certain strengths of character – for example, hope, kindness, social intelligence, self-control, and perspective – can buffer against the negative effects of stress and trauma, preventing or mitigating disorders in their wake. In addition, character strengths help people to thrive. Good character is associated with desired outcomes such as school success, leadership, tolerance and the valuing of diversity, ability to delay gratification, kindness, and altruism (see Park, 2004, for a review).

For the past several years, we have been involved in a project describing important strengths of character and devising ways to measure them. Our research program is sometimes called the Values in Action (VIA) Project, after the non-profit organization – the VIA Institute – that sponsored the initial work. Classification includes two dozen strengths of character on which our research has focused (Peterson & Seligman, 2004). Various VIA measures comprise a family of assessment devices that measure individual differences in the strengths in the classification and allow comparative studies of character strengths. The most general use of the term VIA is to describe a vocabulary for psychologically informed discourse on the qualities of a person that are worthy of moral praise.

HISTORY OF THE VIA PROJECT

Positive psychology's foray into character began in 1999 when a core group of scholars assembled to create a tentative list of human strengths. Christopher Peterson and Martin Seligman continued this work, elaborating the initial list, presenting it at numerous workshops and conferences, and refining it after discussions with participants. Between meetings, Peterson and Seligman devised a framework for defining and conceptualizing strengths. Also critical were surveys of literatures that addressed good character, from psychiatry, youth development, philosophy, and psychology (e.g., Peterson, 2003).

Especially helpful were virtue catalogs – list of character strengths from historical luminaries such as Charlemagne and Benjamin Franklin, contemporary figures such as William Bennett and John Templeton, and imaginary sources such as the Klingon Empire and Harry Potter books. Also consulted were virtue-relevant messages in Hallmark greeting cards, bumper stickers, *Saturday Evening Post* covers by Norman Rockwell, personal ads, popular song lyrics, graffiti, and Tarot cards.

Another part of the project was the development of ways to assess character strengths. Peterson began to devise character measures for adults, and Nansook Park took the lead in devising measures for children and youth and for directing subsequent cross-cultural and applied investigations.

When the VIA Project began, the initial question was how best to approach good character. Is character but one thing, either present or absent? Is character culturally bound or socially constructed, making generalization futile? Can character, however it is defined, be explained by a single theory drawn from psychology, education, philosophy, or theology?

We chose to approach good character as a family of characteristics, each of which existed in degrees, a decision that has been amply supported by subsequent research showing that character indeed is plural. We decided not to wed our approach to a given theory. After all, an impetus for the VIA Project was the need to know more about good character, and no consensual theory had emerged within psychology or elsewhere. We took to calling our project an *aspirational* classification, meaning that it attempted to specify mutually exclusive and exhaustive categories of moral traits without claiming finality or assuming a deep theory (Bailey, 1994).

The field of virtue ethics helped us think through the meaning of good character. Consider the following representative definition of a virtue (Yearley, 1990, p. 13):

> a disposition to act, desire, and feel that involves the exercise of judgment and leads to a recognizable human excellence or instance of human flourishing. Moreover, virtuous activity involves choosing virtue for itself and in light of some justifiable life plan.

This definition of a virtue sounds very much like the meaning of a trait as used in personality psychology, although virtue is a more specific construct than personality. Character is personality morally evaluated (Baumrind, 1998). That is, character strengths are the subset of personality traits on which we place moral value.

THE VIA CLASSIFICATION

As candidate strengths accumulated through our research and discussion, a way to reduce and systematize the ever-growing list was needed. Highly useful here was a literature review by Katherine Dahlsgaard, who read the texts of the world's influential religious and philosophical traditions (e.g., the books of *Exodus* and *Proverbs* in the case of Judaism, the *Analects* in the case of Confucianism), exhaustively listed the virtues discussed in each, and then abstracted a core set of virtues acknowledged as important in all (Dahlsgaard, Peterson, & Seligman, 2005):

- Wisdom and knowledge – cognitive strengths entailing the acquisition and use of knowledge.
- Courage – emotional strengths involving the exercise of will to accomplish goals in the face of opposition, external or internal.
- Humanity – interpersonal strengths that involve "tending and befriending" others.
- Justice – civic strengths underlying healthy community life.
- Temperance – strengths protecting against excess.
- Transcendence – strengths that forge connections to the larger world or universe and provide meaning.

This list is limited to literate traditions, but fieldwork by Biswas-Diener (2006) found that these sorts of virtues were also acknowledged and cultivated among the non-literate Maasai and Inughuit. Accordingly, the six core virtues identified by Dahlsgaard provided an overall scheme for classifying more specific character strengths.

The second step in simplifying the list was specifying criteria for saying that a candidate's character strength belonged in the classification:

- Ubiquity – widely recognized and celebrated across cultures.
- Fulfilling – contributes to individual fulfillment, satisfaction, and happiness broadly construed.
- Morally valued – valued in its own right and not as a means to an end.
- Does not diminish others – elevates others who witness it, producing admiration, not jealousy.
- Non-felicitous opposite – has one or more obvious antonyms that are "negative."
- Trait-like – an individual difference with demonstrable generality and stability.
- Measurable – has been successfully measured by researchers as an individual difference.
- Distinctiveness – not redundant (conceptually or empirically) with other character strengths.
- Paragons – strikingly embodied in some individuals.
- Prodigies – precociously shown by some children or youth.
- Selective absence – missing altogether in some individuals.
- Institutions – the deliberate target of societal practices and rituals that try to cultivate it.

These criteria were abstracted from the best examples of character strengths that had been gathered and then used to winnow the list. Not all of the VIA character strengths meet all 12 criteria, but in each case the majority of the criteria are satisfied (Park & Peterson, 2006b). The current VIA Classification includes 24 positive traits organized in terms of the six core virtues (Table 4.1).

Caveats are in order. First, the hierarchical organization – strengths under virtues – is a conceptual scheme and not a hypothesis to be tested with data. Indeed, our empirical investigations of the structuring of character strengths yield a coherent picture but not exactly the one implied in Table 4.1.

Second, there are culture-bound strengths – positive traits valued in some places but not others. Consider ambition, achievement, and autonomy in the contemporary United States. Their absence from the VIA Classification means that they failed the ubiquity criterion, not that they are unimportant. Indeed, depending on the interests and purposes of a researcher or practitioner, attention to these culture-bound strengths in particular may be important.

Third, some of the 24 strengths are probably cut from a different moral cloth than the others. Strengths such as humor and zest are not morally valued in their own right but become morally valued when coupled with other strengths in the classification. So, a humorous person is simply funny, but a humorous person who is kind is very special and morally praiseworthy. We call these value-added strengths and intend to study them further. More generally, we intend to study strength configurations, under the assumption that the whole may be different from the sum of the parts – the specific character strengths that a person may or may not possess.

Fourth, changes in the classification are expected. Some currently included strengths may be dropped, and others may be combined. Still other strengths may

TABLE 4.1   The VIA Classification of Strengths

1   Wisdom and knowledge
- Creativity: thinking of novel and productive ways to do things
- Curiosity: taking an interest in all of ongoing experience
- Open-mindedness: thinking things through and examining them from all sides
- Love of learning: mastering new skills, topics, and bodies of knowledge
- Perspective: being able to provide wise counsel to others

2   Courage
- Honesty: speaking the truth and presenting oneself in a genuine way
- Bravery: *not* shrinking from threat, challenge, difficulty, or pain
- Persistence: finishing what one starts
- Zest: approaching life with excitement and energy

3   Humanity
- Kindness: doing favors and good deeds for others
- Love: valuing close relations with others
- Social intelligence: being aware of the motives and feelings of self and others

4   Justice
- Fairness: treating all people the same according to notions of fairness and justice
- Leadership: organizing group activities and seeing that they happen
- Teamwork: working well as member of a group or team

5   Temperance
- Forgiveness: forgiving those who have done wrong
- Modesty: letting one's accomplishments speak for themselves
- Prudence: being careful about one's choices; *not* saying or doing things that might later be regretted
- Self-regulation: regulating what one feels and does

6   Transcendence
- Appreciation of beauty and excellence: noticing and appreciating beauty, excellence, and/or skilled performance in all domains of life
- Gratitude: being aware of and thankful for the good things that happen
- Hope: expecting the best and working to achieve it
- Humor: liking to laugh and joke; bringing smiles to other people
- Religiousness: having coherent beliefs about the higher purpose and meaning of life

be added, and among those suggested to us in recent years are compassion, patience, and tranquility. Our criteria provide explicit guidelines for changing the VIA Classification.

The VIA Classification was presented in a monograph describing what was known and what was not known about each of the included strengths: paradigm cases, consensual definition, historical background, measurement, correlations and consequences of having or lacking the strength, development, enabling and disabling conditions, gender and cultural differences, and interventions thought to build the strength (Peterson & Seligman, 2004). The monograph was intended as a framework for conducting future research and creating new interventions.

MEASURES

Just as important for the VIA Project as specifying widely valued strengths of character was assessing them. In the absence of our assessment efforts, the VIA Project would be just one more virtue catalog (Park & Peterson, 2006b). To date, we have devised and evaluated: (1) focus groups to flesh out the everyday meanings of character strengths among different groups, such as school children; (2) self-report questionnaires suitable for adults and young people; (3) structured interviews to identify what we call signature strengths; (4) informant reports of how target individuals rise to the occasion (or not) with appropriate strengths of character (e.g., hope when encountering setbacks); (5) a content analysis procedure for assessing character strengths from unstructured descriptions of self and others; (6) strategies for scoring positive traits from archived material such as obituaries; and (7) case studies of nominated paragons of specific strengths.

We also emphasize our ongoing interest in devising interventions to change specific character strengths. To the degree that our interventions successfully target specific character strengths as we measure them, we have additional evidence that they are discrete individual differences.

Space does not permit a detailed description of what we have learned about the reliability and validity of these different methods. Suffice it to say that we have successfully established the internal consistency of our questionnaire measures and their test–retest stability over several months. We have investigated their validity with the known-groups procedure and more generally by mapping out their correlates (Park & Peterson, 2006c). Although we anticipate that these different methods will converge in the strengths they identify for given individuals, we note that each assessment strategy should also provide unique information about good character (see Hedge, Borman, & Birkeland, 2001). Available data suggest convergence but not redundancy.

To develop and validate measures for adults, we did not rely on college student samples. Although young adults have strengths of character, we were persuaded by previous thinkers from Aristotle (350 BCE/2000) to Erik Erikson (1963) that good character is most apt to be found among those who are mature, who have done more than rehearse work and love.

In addition to traditional methods of collecting data, we also used the Internet to reach a wide range of adults. We placed our tentative questionnaires on-line (see http://www.authentichappiness.org). Critical to the appeal of this method is that, upon completion of the measures, respondents are given instant feedback about their top five strengths. In addition to expediting our research, this strategy has taught us something about character: Being able to put a name to what one does well is intriguing to people and even empowering (Resnick & Rosenheck, 2006). At the time of this writing, more than 1,000,000 people from all 50 US states and more than 200 different nations, from Azerbaijan to Zimbabwe, have completed our questionnaires.

These Internet respondents are not a representative sample of the US or world population, but we emphasize the diversity of our respondents across virtually all demographic contrasts (other than computer literacy). Researchers have recently shown that Internet studies typically enroll more diverse samples than conventional studies using psychology-subject pool samples at colleges or universities and that they are as valid as traditional research methods (Gosling, Vazire, Srivastava, & John, 2004).

Our measures of the VIA strengths allow a systematic study of character in multidimensional terms. Past research on good character has focused on one component of character at a time, leaving unanswered questions about the underlying structure of character within an individual. Some individuals may be creative and honest but are neither brave nor kind, or vice versa (Park, 2004). Furthermore, measuring a range of positive traits may reduce concerns about socially desirable responding by allowing most research participants to say something good about themselves. Although we are open to the possibility that some people may altogether lack the strengths in the VIA Classification, the data show that virtually everyone has some notable strengths of character. We have taken to calling these signature strengths, and they are akin to what Gordon Allport (1961) once identified as someone's personal traits. Signature strengths are morally evaluated traits that a person owns, celebrates, and frequently exercises. In interviews with adults, we find that everyone can readily identify a handful of strengths as very much their own, typically between three and seven (just as Allport proposed). We hypothesize that the exercise of signature strengths is particularly fulfilling.

EMPIRICAL FINDINGS

Measures make empirical research possible, and here is some of what we have learned to date.

Distribution and Demographics

Our Internet procedure makes it possible to compare people around the world. In one study, we compared scores from 111,676 adult respondents from 54 nations and all 50 US states and found striking convergence in the relative prevalence of the 24 different VIA strengths (Park, Peterson, & Seligman, 2006). In almost all nations, from the most commonly endorsed strengths were kindness, fairness, authenticity, gratitude, and open-mindedness, and the lesser strengths included prudence, modesty, and self-regulation. Except for religiousness, comparisons within the US sample showed no differences as a function of state or geographical region. We speculate that our results revealed something about universal human nature and/or the character requirements minimally needed for a viable society.

We also looked at demographic correlates of the VIA strengths within the US sample. There are some modest and sensible differences. Females score higher than males for the interpersonal strengths of gratitude, kindness, and love. Older adults score higher than younger adults on strengths of temperance. Respondents with more education love learning more than those with less education. Those who are married are more forgiving than those who are unmarried. African-Americans and Asian-Americans are more religious than European-Americans.

In contrast to adults, the most common strengths among youth were gratitude, humor, and love, and the lesser strengths included prudence, forgiveness, religiousness, and self-regulation (Park & Peterson, 2006c). Hope, teamwork, and zest were relatively more common among youth than adults, whereas appreciation of beauty, authenticity, leadership, and open-mindedness were relatively more common among adults than youth.

What about the strengths of very young children? Coding of open-ended parental descriptions of young children revealed sensible patterns (Park & Peterson, 2006a). The modal child, as seen by his or her parents, is one who is loving, kind, creative, humorous, and curious. These results also confirm theoretical speculation that some strengths of character – e.g., honesty, gratitude, modesty, forgiveness, and open-mindedness – are not common among young children. We would not expect these strengths to be common because they depend on cognitive sophistication that only occurs with development.

Correlates and Consequences

Evidence concerning the correlates of the VIA strengths is accumulating. So, among adults, several strengths in particular show a robust relation with life satisfaction, happiness, and psychological well-being measured in different ways: love, gratitude, hope, curiosity, and zest (Park, Peterson, & Seligman, 2004). Among youth, the robust predictors of life satisfaction are love, gratitude, hope, and zest (Park & Peterson, 2006c). And among very young children, those described by their parents as showing love, zest, and hope are also described as happy (Park & Peterson, 2006a).

In addition to life satisfaction, the following outcomes are related to character strengths in the VIA Classification:

- Academic achievement among school children is predicted by perseverance, which is hardly surprising, but also by love and gratitude, interesting findings that remind us that learning is not something that happens just within people but also something that happens between them.
- Leadership ability among West Point cadets is predicted by the strength of love.
- Teaching effectiveness among new teachers is predicted by zest, humor, and social intelligence.
- The tendency to regard one's work as a calling (as opposed to a way to pay the bills) is predicted by zest.
- More generally, work satisfaction across dozens of different occupations is predicted by the character strengths of zest and hope.

In our current studies, we are using longitudinal designs and focusing on "hard" outcome measures such as workplace productivity and health (Peterson & Park, 2006).

Origins and Development

We know less about the origins of character strengths than their consequences. Character strengths are of course influenced by nurture *and* nature. Not surprisingly, the character strengths of parents and children converge, especially between fathers and sons and between mothers and daughters. A twin study that compared similarities in the VIA strengths in identical versus fraternal twins showed that strengths are moderately heritable, as are many individual differences (Steger, Hicks, Kashdan, Krueger, & Bouchard, 2007). The study also showed that shared family environment influenced some of the strengths (e.g., love of learning), an unusual finding in this type of research, which rarely finds any influence of growing up in a given family once common genetics are controlled (Dunn & Plomin, 1992). Perhaps family influence is more relevant for positive characteristics than for the negative characteristics usually on focus in twin studies. And for virtually all of the VIA strengths, non-shared family environment (e.g., peers and teachers) proved the most important influence.

We have learned that dramatic events can increase character strengths. For example, in the six months after the 9/11 attacks, the character strengths of faith (religiousness), hope, and love were elevated among US respondents but not among Europeans (Peterson & Seligman, 2003). These strengths, the so-called theological virtues of St. Paul, are core Western virtues and may reflect the operation of processes specified in terror management theory, which proposes that the possibility of death leads people to reaffirm central cultural beliefs and values (Pyszczynski, Solomon, & Greenberg, 2002).

We have learned that successful recovery from physical illness is associated with modest increases in the strengths of bravery, kindness, and humor, whereas successful recovery from psychological disorder is associated with modest increases in the strengths of appreciation of beauty and love of learning (Peterson, Park, & Seligman, 2006). Furthermore, we have learned that exposure to trauma results in increases in the character strengths of religiousness, gratitude, kindness, hope, and bravery – precisely the components of post-traumatic growth (Peterson, Park, Pole, D'Andrea, & Seligman, 2008).

These findings do not mean that people need trauma, illness, or disorder to increase their character strengths. In fact, our data showed that, in general, people with these unfortunate life histories reported lower life satisfaction than people who did not. However, these results suggest that in the wake of negative life events certain character strengths may work as a buffer and help to maintain or even increase well-being despite challenges.

These results have a larger significance for positive psychology. When the field was first articulated by Seligman and Csikszentmihalyi (2000), it was carefully distanced from business-as-usual psychology and its concern with problems. But as critics of positive psychology have observed, it is not always possible to segregate the positive in life from the negative (Lazarus, 2003), and our data suggest that crisis may be the crucible of good character. In any event, these sorts of findings would not have been discovered without the premise of positive psychology that attention to strength is worthwhile even following challenge.

None of these studies done to date was fine-grained, and we do not know the exact process by which strengths of character develop. However, we have some ideas about how character strengths are created, increased, and sustained.

We regard character strengths as habits, evident in thoughts, feelings, and actions (see Aristotle, 350 BCE/2000). They are not latent entities. When we say that character strengths are trait-like, we mean simply that the habits to which they refer are relatively stable across time and relatively general across situations. No further meaning is intended, and the fact that character strengths are moderately heritable does not mean that they are immutable or that they are singular things (Peterson, 2006).

As habits, character strengths are established like any habit: by practice, by prevailing rewards and punishments, and by social modeling. The efficient acquisition and maintenance of character strengths is cognitively mediated – enabled by thoughts and beliefs. Finally, the situation matters not only in the acquisition of character strengths but also in their use. It is easier to display certain character strengths in some settings than in others.

Deliberate Cultivation

Some researchers have looked also at how character strengths included in the VIA Classification can be cultivated. This work is just beginning and only a handful of strengths have been seriously considered, such as hope (optimism), gratitude, kindness, social intelligence, leadership, creativity, and fairness (Park & Peterson, 2009). The problem with these endeavors, as seen from the vantage of the VIA Project, is that they focus on one strength of character at a time. Unanswered is whether other strengths, not on focus and not measured, are changed as well.

Structure and Tradeoffs

As noted, the classification of character strengths under core virtues is a conceptual scheme and not an empirical claim. The question remains of how the strengths in the VIA Classification are related to one another. One answer comes from an exploratory factor analysis of data from an adult sample, in which we first standardized subscale scores within individual respondents, thereby removing response sets such as extremity (Peterson, 2006). Oblique factor analysis (which allows factors to be correlated) revealed a clear two-factor solution, shown in Figure 4.1 along with our interpretation of the two factors: heart versus head and self-oriented versus other-oriented. This is a circumplex model, meaning that strengths close together are more likely to co-occur, whereas those more distant are less likely.

Can someone have all of the character strengths, or are tradeoffs among them inevitable as people conduct their everyday lives? Figure 4.1 implies that tradeoffs

FIGURE 4.1   The structure of character (see text).

do occur and that people make them in characteristic ways. All things being equal, some of us will tend to be kind, whereas others of us will tend to be honest. The structure of these tradeoffs might reveal something about how the real world allows good character to present itself.

Note in Figure 4.1 how many of the character strengths associated with happiness and life satisfaction tend to reside north of the equator (in the heart quadrants), whereas those associated with achievement are located south (in the head quadrants). Perhaps the very small associations found between life satisfaction and education, income, and status – despite all the apparent benefits that these bring – reflects the operation of these tradeoffs. Additional analyses suggest that respondents with a high school degree tend to score higher than those with college degrees on many of the "focus on others" strengths, and those with a college degree tend to score higher than those with a high school degree on many of the "focus on self" strengths (see Snibbe & Markus, 2005).

We are in the process of looking at the location in the circumplex of people in different occupations as well as people who live in different US cities. Sensible patterns are emerging, and the heart-versus-head dimension appears to be a powerful one. For example, although our previous work comparing character strengths found few differences across US states, perhaps this was the wrong level of analysis. In contrast, there are striking differences across US cities in the prevalence of head strengths versus heart strengths. Cities such as San Francisco and Seattle have residents relatively high on strengths such as creativity, curiosity, love of learning, and appreciation of beauty and excellence, but relatively low on most emotional and interpersonal strengths such as kindness, love, and modesty. Other cities, such as El Paso and Omaha, show the exact opposite pattern. We conclude that all cities are "good" but in different ways.

THE FUTURE

We will continue to refine our measures and to use empirical findings to generate theory. As noted, our attention is turning to hard outcome measures, to cultural differences and similarities, to development, to interventions, and to the processes by which strengths of character give rise to actual behavior. Our project supports the premise of positive psychology that attention to good character sheds light on what makes life worth living and how to build a thriving society.

Two centuries ago, Thomas Jefferson wrote that "happiness is the aim of life, [but] virtue is the foundation of happiness." In his 2009 inaugural address, Barack Obama reminded everyone that virtue remains the foundation of a flourishing nation. In his 18-minute speech, he mentioned virtually every one of the character strengths that we have been studying, and he provided everyday but compelling examples for each. Character matters, then and now.

REFERENCES

Allport, G. W. (1961). *Pattern and growth in personality*. New York: Holt, Rinehart, & Winston.
Aristotle. (2000). *Nicomachean ethics* (R. Crisp, Trans.). Cambridge, UK: Cambridge University Press. (Originally written ~350 BCE)
Bailey, K. D. (1994). *Typologies and taxonomies: An introduction to classification techniques*. Thousand Oaks, CA: Sage Publications.
Baumrind, D. (1998). Reflections on character and competence. In A. Colby, J. James, & D. Hart (Eds.), *Competence and character through life* (pp. 1–28). Chicago: University of Chicago Press.
Biswas-Diener, R. (2006). From the equator to the north pole: A study of character strengths. *Journal of Happiness Studies, 7*, 293–310.
Botvin, G. J., Baker, E., Dusenbury, L., Botvin, E. M., & Diaz, T. (1995). Long-term follow-up results of a randomized drug abuse prevention trial in a white middle-class population. *Journal of the American Medical Association, 273*, 1106–1112.
Colby, A., & Damon, W. (1992). *Some do care: Contemporary lives of moral commitment*. New York: Free Press.
Dahlsgaard, K., Peterson, C., & Seligman, M. E. P. (2005). Shared virtue: The convergence of valued human strengths across culture and history. *Review of General Psychology, 9*, 209–213.
Dunn, J., & Plomin, R. (1992). *Separate lives: Why siblings are so different*. New York: Basic Books.

Erikson, E. (1963). *Childhood and society* (2nd ed.). New York: Norton.

Gosling, S. D., Vazire, S., Srivastava, S., & John, O. P. (2004). Should we trust Web-based studies? A comparative analysis of six preconceptions about Internet question-naires. *American Psychologist, 59*, 93–104.

Hedge, J. W., Borman, W. C., & Birkeland, S. A. (2001). History and development of multi-source feedback as a methodology. In D. W. Bracken, C. W. Timmreck, & A. H. Church (Eds.), *The handbook of multisource feedback* (pp. 15–32). San Francisco: Jossey-Bass.

Lazarus, R. S. (2003). Does the positive psychology movement have legs? *Psychological Inquiry, 14*, 93–109.

Park, N. (2004). Character strengths and positive youth development. *Annals of the American Academy of Political and Social Science, 591*, 40–54.

Park, N., & Peterson, C. (2003). Virtues and organizations. In K. S. Cameron, J. E. Dutton, & R. E. Quinn (Eds.), *Positive organizational scholarship: Foundations of a new discipline* (pp. 33–47). San Francisco: Berrett-Koehler.

Park, N., & Peterson, C. (2006a). Character strengths and happiness among young children: Content analysis of parental descriptions. *Journal of Happiness Studies, 7*, 323–341.

Park, N., & Peterson, C. (2006b). Methodological issues in positive psychology and the assessment of character strengths. In A. D. Ong & M. van Dulmen (Eds.), *Handbook of methods in positive psychology* (pp. 292–305). New York: Oxford University Press.

Park, N., & Peterson, C. (2006c). Moral competence and character strengths among adolescents: The development and validation of the Values in Action Inventory of Strengths for Youth. *Journal of Adolescence, 29*, 891–905.

Park, N., & Peterson, C. (2009). The cultivation of character strengths. In M. Ferrari & G. Potworowski (Eds.), *Teaching for wisdom* (pp. 57–75). Mahwah, NJ: Lawrence Erlbaum Associates, Inc.

Park, N., Peterson, C., & Seligman, M. E. P. (2004). Strengths of character and well-being. *Journal of Social and Clinical Psychology, 23*, 603–619.

Park, N., Peterson, C., & Seligman, M. E. P. (2006). Character strengths in fifty-four nations and the fifty US states. *Journal of Positive Psychology, 1*, 118–129.

Peterson, C. (2003). Classification of positive traits in youth. In R. M. Lerner, F. Jacobs, & D. Wertlieb (Eds.), *Promoting positive child, adolescent, and family development: A handbook of program and policy innovations* (Vol. 4, pp. 227–255). Thousand Oaks, CA: Sage Publications.

Peterson, C. (2006). *A primer in positive psychology.* New York: Oxford University Press.

Peterson, C., & Park, N. (2003). Positive psychology as the evenhanded positive psycholo-gist views it. *Psychological Inquiry, 14*, 141–146.

Peterson, C., & Park, N. (2006). Character strengths in organizations. *Journal of Organizational Behavior, 27*, 1–6.

Peterson, C., Park, N., Pole, N., D'Andrea, W., & Seligman, M. E. P. (2008). Strengths of character and posttraumatic growth. *Journal of Traumatic Stress, 21*, 214–217.

Peterson, C., Park, N., & Seligman, M. E. P. (2006). Greater strengths of character and recovery from illness. *Journal of Positive Psychology, 1*, 17–26.

Peterson, C., & Seligman, M. E. P. (2003). Character strengths before and after September 11. *Psychological Science, 14*, 381–384.

Peterson, C., & Seligman, M. E. P. (2004). *Character strengths and virtues: A handbook and classification.* New York: Oxford University Press/Washington, DC: American Psychological Association.

Pyszczynski, T., Solomon, S., & Greenberg, J. (2002). *In the wake of 9/11: The psychology of terror.* Washington, DC: American Psychological Association.

Resnick, S. G., & Rosenheck, R. A. (2006). Recovery and positive psychology: Parallel themes and potential synergies. *Psychiatric Services, 57,* 120–122.

Seligman, M. E. P., & Csikszentmihalyi, M. (2000). Positive psychology: An introduction. *American Psychologist, 55,* 5–14.

Snibbe, A. C., & Markus, H. R. (2005). You can't always get what you want: Educational attainment, agency, and choice. *Journal of Personality and Social Psychology, 88,* 703–720.

Steger, M. F., Hicks, B. M., Kashdan, T. B., Krueger, R. F., & Bouchard, T. J. (2007). Genetic and environmental influences on the positive traits of the Values in Action classification, and biometric covariance with normal personality. *Journal of Research in Personality, 41,* 524–539.

Weissberg, R. P., & Greenberg, M. T. (1997). School and community competence-enhancement and prevention programs. In W. Damon (Ed.), *Handbook of child psychology* (pp. 877–954). New York: John Wiley & Sons.

Yearley, L. H. (1990). *Mencius and Aquinas: Theories of virtue and conceptions of courage.* Albany, NY: State University of New York Press.

Part III

Applications for Improving Health, Education, and Positive Human Development

5

How Psychosocial Resources Enhance Health and Well-Being

SHELLEY E. TAYLOR

*P*sychosocial resources are the skills, beliefs, talents, and individual personality factors that influence how people manage stressful events. They include self-esteem, optimism, a sense of mastery, active coping skills, and social support. Without them, stress can take a great toll on psychological well-being, on biological responses to stress, and ultimately on health, but with these resources come at least three kinds of benefits. First, psychosocial resources help people to appraise potential stressors in more benign ways. Threatening events seem less so when people are armed with psychosocial resources. Second, they help people cope with the inevitable taxing events that they encounter. Psychosocial resources are reliably related to active coping strategies that involve enlisting social support, managing emotional responses to stress, and gathering information and taking direct action. People with psychosocial resources are less likely to cope through maladaptive avoidant behaviors, such as substance abuse or withdrawal. Finally, psychosocial resources foster resilience in the face of major stressors, such as natural disasters and health threats (Taylor, 1983).

For the past 30 years, we have examined how psychosocial resources affect mental and physical health. We have examined these processes in laboratory studies that manipulate stress and also among people who are going through intensely stressful events, such as coping with HIV or cancer. Figure 5.1 illustrates the approach that has guided our thinking. We regard the early environment and genetic predispositions as origins of psychosocial resources; we look at neural responses to threat and low chronic negative affect as correlates of psychosocial resources; we examine downstream consequences of psychosocial resources on biological stress regulatory systems; and we explore how the cumulative adverse effects of stress responses provoke accumulating damage that, in turn, predisposes to mental and physical health risks.

PSYCHOSOCIAL RESOURCES: BACKGROUND

What Are Psychosocial Resources?

Psychosocial resources are critical for regulating responses to threat and have been demonstrated to beneficially affect both mental and physical health. Although different investigators have focused on different resources, four that have been consistently tied to beneficial mental and physical health outcomes are optimism, mastery, self-esteem, and social support (e.g., Folkman & Moskowitz, 2004; Scheier & Carver, 2003; Taylor & Stanton, 2007).

Optimism refers to outcome expectancies that good things rather than bad things will happen to the self (Scheier, Weintraub, & Carver, 1986). It has been tied to a broad array of mental and physical health benefits, including greater psychological well-being (Kubzansky, Wright, Cohen, Weiss, Rosner, & Sparrow, 2002; Park, Moore, Turner, & Adler, 1992; Scheier & Carver, 1992; Segerstrom, Taylor, Kemeny, Reed, & Visscher, 1996), lower vulnerability to infection (Cohen, Doyle, Turner, Alper, & Skoner, 2003; Segerstrom, Taylor, Kemeny, & Fahey, 1998), faster recovery from illness (Scheier et al., 1989), and a slower course of advancing disease (Antoni & Goodkin, 1988; Reed, Kemeny, Taylor, & Visscher, 1999; Reed, Kemeny, Taylor, Wang, & Visscher, 1994) (see Carver & Scheier, 2002; Scheier & Carver, 2003, for reviews).

Personal control or mastery refers to whether a person feels able to control or influence his/her outcomes (Thompson, 1981). Studies have shown a relationship between a sense of control and better psychological health (Rodin, Timko, & Harris, 1985; Taylor, Helgeson, Reed, & Skokan, 1991), as well as better physical health outcomes, including lower incidence of coronary heart disease (CHD; Karasek, Theorell, Schwartz, Pieper, & Alfredsson, 1982), better self-rated health, better functional status, and lower mortality (Seeman & Lewis, 1995). A belief in personal control is related to reduced mental and physical health risks conferred by low socioeconomic status (SES); among people of low SES with strong beliefs in personal mastery, mental and physical health outcomes are equivalent to those seen in high-SES groups (Lachman & Weaver, 1998).

A positive sense of self or high self-esteem is also protective against adverse mental and adverse health outcomes. For example, research consistently ties a positive sense of self to lower autonomic and cortisol responses to stress (e.g., Cresswell, Welch, Taylor, Sherman, Gruenewald, & Mann, 2005; Seeman & Lewis, 1995). Ties to health outcomes are modest but consistently positive as well (Adler, Marmot, McEwen, & Stewart, 1999; Taylor & Seeman, 1999).

Social support is the perception or reality of having people in your life who care for you and will help you in stressful times, if you need it (Wills, 1991). Research consistently shows that social support reduces negative affect during times of stress and promotes psychological adjustment to a broad array of chronically stressful conditions (see Taylor, 2010, for a review). Social support also contributes to physical health and survival. Indeed, it is the most significant and reliable psychosocial predictor of health outcomes, with effects on health on par with smoking and lipid levels (House, Landis, & Umberson, 1988).

Psychosocial Resources and Biological Stress Responses

Laboratory studies have demonstrated that people with strong psychosocial resources have lower biological responses to stress. What are these biological responses? There are two major stress systems in the body: the sympathetic nervous system and the hypothalamic-pituitary-adrenal (HPA) system. In response to stress, these systems are activated and mobilize the organism for fight or flight. These responses are protective in the short term, but in the long term they carry costs. These systems may lose their resilience, laying the groundwork for chronic illness. In laboratory studies, researchers assess heart rate and blood pressure as indicators of sympathetic functioning and cortisol as a hormone indicative of the functioning of the HPA axis. As is true of heart rate and blood pressure, one expects to see cortisol levels increase in response to stress, and so cortisol profiles that are flat and elevated are among the signs that researchers consider to be diagnostic of compromised functioning of the HPA axis (McEwen, 1998).

Our research has shown lower heart rate, lower blood pressure, and lower cortisol responses to stress among those with strong psychosocial resources. For example, in one study we employed a composite measure of the resources noted above and found lower heart rate responses to stress tasks in the laboratory, lower blood pressure responses, faster sympathetic recovery, and a lower baseline level of cortisol (Taylor, Lerner, Sherman, Sage, & McDowell, 2003).

Psychosocial Resources and Health

As noted, there is clear evidence that psychosocial resources affect health. Our own research indicates that survival rates among men with AIDS is longer and progression of the HIV virus in asymptomatic seropositive men is less rapid among men who have strong psychosocial resources (Reed et al., 1994, 1999). Other researchers have found that psychosocial resources can affect the course of cardiovascular disease and recovery from surgical procedures, such as coronary artery bypass graft surgery (Helgeson, 1999, 2003; Scheier et al., 1989).

Armed with this evidence, pivotal questions become: What are the origins of psychosocial resources? What are the pathways by which psychosocial resources and their origins ultimately translate into good health?

ORIGINS OF PSYCHOSOCIAL RESOURCES

Psychosocial resources have origins both in genes and in the early environment. Early environment affects health not only in childhood, but throughout adulthood into old age, controlling for other risk factors. Essentially, a harsh early environment predicts early onset chronic disease, controlling for other variables. The two lines of research that have demonstrated this relationship most clearly is work showing that childhood social class predicts health outcomes (Chen, Matthews, & Boyce, 2002) and research showing that a harsh early family environment predicts health risks (Repetti, Taylor, & Seeman, 2002). Research on physical and emotional abuse and on early isolation reveals adverse effects (e.g., Fries, Shirtcliff, & Pollak, 2008; Tottenham et al., 2010), but even families that are not abusive but merely conflict-ridden, neglectful, chaotic, or cold and non-nurturant show these adverse health effects (Repetti et al., 2002). Thus, the damage done by a harsh early environment is not limited to circumstances of extreme abuse. Research by Vincent Felitti and colleagues using enrollees in the Kaiser program in Southern California reported strong dose–response relationships between adversity in the early family environment and diagnosis of a broad array of health conditions (from the Kaiser archives) ranging from depression to ischemic heart disease (Felitti et al., 1998). This dose–response relationship – the greater the adversity, the greater the health risk – is important evidence for the role of the early environment in health outcomes.

As Figure 5.1 shows, we regard the early environment as an important input to the development of psychosocial resources. Substantial research links economic adversity (low childhood SES) to problems in the enlistment or use of psychosocial resources, including social support, optimism, mastery, and self-esteem (Adler et al., 1999). A harsh early family environment has also been tied reliably to psychosocial deficits, including difficulty managing emotions in challenging circumstances and the development of chronic negative emotional states with high levels of hostility, anxiety, and depression (Repetti et al., 2002).

Genetic factors are also clearly implicated in psychosocial resources. For example, twin studies indicate that approximately 25% of the variance in optimism

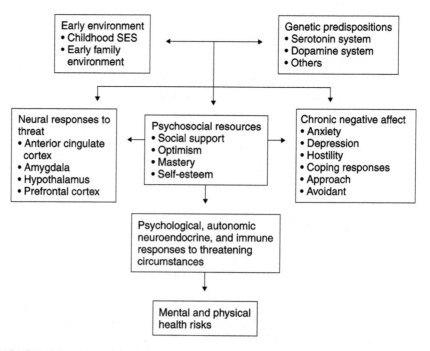

FIGURE 5.1 A model of the impact of psychosocial resources on health and well-being.

appears to be genetically based (Plomin, Scheier, Bergeman, Pedersen, Nesselroade, & McClearn, 1992). Kessler, Kendler, Heath, Neale, and Eaves (1992) reported a genetic basis for social support, which may reflect the ability to perceive social support as available, the availability to enlist it, or both. Empirical studies suggest that genes in conjunction with the early environment can affect how people cope with stress, for example with depression (Taylor, Way, Welch, Hilmert, Lehman, & Eisenberger, 2006b) or with aggression (Caspi et al., 2002; Eisenberger, Way, Taylor, Welch, & Lieberman, 2007).

PATHWAYS TO GOOD HEALTH

The robust effect of early environment on health across the lifespan is often greeted with surprise. It is not immediately clear why socioeconomic or family environmental conditions in early life would affect the early onset of chronic disorders in adulthood, such as Type 2 diabetes, heart disease, or cancer. To make these pathways more transparent, our laboratory has focused on several possible mechanisms: first, the brain's responses to stress, and, second, alterations in biological stress regulatory systems.

The research on harsh early environments suggests several reliable effects on the coping skills of offspring. Children from risky families evidence higher levels of avoidant coping, such as trying to tune out stressors as much as possible (Johnson & Pandina, 1991; O'Brien, Margolin, John, & Krueger, 1991; Valentiner, Holahan, & Moos, 1994). But if they are confronted with stressors they cannot avoid, they may show overly aggressive responses to stressors that are perceived by others to be only moderately challenging (Reid & Crisafulli, 1990). And finally, offspring from these harsh family environments show ineffective coping, that is, coping that does not seem to reduce the stress they are experiencing (Brody & Flor, 1998; Dishion, 1990).

In a recent investigation (Taylor, Eisenberger, Saxbe, Lehman, & Lieberman, 2006a), we examined the neural bases of these coping resources in the context of the family environment. The focal question of this study was: Does the early environment compromise how the brain deals with stress? We focused on two brain regions that have been implicated in previous research as being involved in the regulation of stress responses. These are the amygdala, portions of which have been tied to threat detection and fear responses, and a region of the prefrontal cortex, specifically, the right ventrolateral prefrontal cortex (RVLPFC), which may regulate amygdala responses to threat.

We conducted an investigation to see if the reactivity of these regions to threat cues is affected by the type of early environment a person grew up in (Taylor et al., 2006a). Thirty young adults participated. They completed validated questionnaire and interview assessments of the early environment and then responded to three tasks in the functional magnetic resonance imaging (fMRI) scanner. In one condition, they observed faces that conveyed negative emotions, specifically fear and anger. This observation task typically evokes amygdala activity because fearful or angry faces are threat cues. In other trials, they were asked to label the emotions, that is, to indicate whether the faces were expressing fear, anger, or some other emotion. This task has been found to evoke RVLPFC activity, as people are processing what the emotions mean. In a control task, participants simply indicated the gender of the face, namely, whether the person pictured was more likely to be named Sam or Helen. What one would typically see in a study such as this is: (1) amygdala activity in response to the observation of negative faces, (2) RVLPFC activity in response to labeling the faces, and (3) a negative correlation between activity in the RVLPFC and amygdala during the labeling task. This is exactly what you see among children who have grown up in nurturant families.

However, among children who have grown up in non-nurturant families, the findings are quite different. In the observation-of-faces task, offspring from harsh family environments showed lower amygdala activity. This pattern suggests that in the observation task, participants from non-nurturant families may have been tuning out the stimuli, consistent with what the behavioral literature on coping among offspring of risky families has found. In the task that involves labeling emotions, however, a very different pattern of responding was found. This is a task that people are not able to avoid, and so offspring from harsh families have higher amygdala responses to the labeling task than those from nurturant families. And of particular interest is a positive, rather than negative, relationship between activity in the RVLPFC and in the amygdala. That is, offspring from risky families appear to be trying to recruit the prefrontal cortex to manage emotional responses to stress, but it is not reducing their amygdala activity, as appears to be the case for offspring from nurturant families.

What do these results mean? They suggest that offspring from risky families may shut out threatening cues with which they do not need to engage, but when they are forced by task demands to engage, their amygdala responses are stronger and they do not recruit prefrontal brain regions effectively for regulating amygdala responses to threatening stimuli. We conclude, then, that growing up in a risky family environment marked by harsh parenting has effects on the brain's detection of threat and the regulation of responses to threat by the prefrontal cortex. Offspring from risky families do not appear to develop effective coping skills for managing circumstances, and such deficits can actually be seen in the brain's responses to threat.

HOW CAN PSYCHOSOCIAL RESOURCES AFFECT THESE PATHWAYS?

Psychosocial resources play a vital role in the links between early environment and adult health outcomes. We begin this section by discussing the role of social support in these processes. As noted, social support, whether perceived or utilized, has a strong and beneficial effect on health. It is not immediately clear why and how social support has such beneficial effects on health outcomes, although a strong possibility is that social support keeps stress reactivity low by helping people to appraise potential stressors more positively, by helping them to regulate their responses to threat, or both.

To address this question, Eisenberger, Taylor, Gable, Hilmert, and Lieberman (2007) examined how social support may influence the neural regulation of stress responses. The goal of the study was to see if people who have a lot of social support are less likely to experience social threats as threatening and if they also experience lesser stress reactivity. The procedures for this three-part study were as follows. First, the 20 participants completed a daily experience sampling procedure. They carried a pager for nine days and were beeped several times a day and asked to rate how supportive their most recent interaction partner had been. At the end of the nine-day period, the support that they reported receiving was summed.

Participants then came into the laboratory and completed a virtual social exclusion task (Eisenberger, Lieberman, & Williams, 2003). In this task, the participant plays a virtual ball-tossing task in the scanner with two other people he believes to be participants. Although all three participants throw the ball to each other at the beginning of the game, over time the participant is gradually excluded, as the other two people play with each other and ignore the participant. In fact, the game is pre-programmed, and there are no other participants. People who play this game are surprisingly devastated by being excluded in this virtual ball-tossing task and express considerable social distress. Moreover, this distress is correlated with activity in a particular region of the brain, namely the dorsal anterior cingulate cortex (dACC). We predicted that people who had a lot of social support over the previous nine-day period would be less likely to experience social distress and would show less activity in the dACC in response to social exclusion.

In the third part of the study, participants took part in the Trier Social Stress Task (TSST; Kirschbaum, Pirke, & Hellhammer, 1993). The TSST is a standardized laboratory procedure involving two specific tasks. Participants count backwards as rapidly as possible, say by 13s from 2095, while an experimenter urges them to go faster or interrupts them to start over when they have made a mistake. In the second task, participants are asked to spend five minutes preparing a speech, which they then deliver to an audience that has been pre-trained to be unresponsive and to communicate signs of boredom and a poor impression of the speech. Typically these tasks evoke strong increases in heart rate and blood pressure and a rise in cortisol levels. We expected to see that people with strong levels of social support would show lesser increases in heart rate, blood pressure, and cortisol during the stress tasks.

As predicted, we found that people who had strong experiences of social support had lower dACC activity in response to the scanner social exclusion task than those with lower levels of social support. If there are many people that you can count on who are supportive and care for you, being excluded from a virtual social task may not matter as much as it would to people who do not have as much social support. With respect to the neuroendocrine evidence, we found that people who had many experiences of social support on a daily basis also showed lower cortisol activity during the laboratory portion of the TSST. We conducted mediational analyses and found that individual differences in activity in the dACC mediated the relationship between social support and cortisol reactivity during the TSST. These findings tell us that social support is influencing the brain's response to threat tasks, which in turn keeps biological responses to stress at lower levels.

In a related investigation, we examined whether individual differences in psychosocial resources might affect stress responses in similar ways (Taylor, Burklund, Eisenberger, Lehman, Hilmert, & Lieberman, 2008). Specifically, we created a composite measure of optimism, self-esteem, mastery, and related resources and asked whether they, too, influence how the brain processes threat. In this study, participants completed questionnaire assessments of psychosocial resources and participated in the TSST described earlier. Participants also completed the fMRI fearful faces task described earlier. We expected to see that psychosocial resources would be protective against stress by leading to lesser amygdala activity during the observation of fearful or angry faces, greater RVLPFC activity while they were being labeled, and lower cortisol responses to stress during the TSST.

This is essentially what we found. Psychosocial resources were tied to greater RVLPFC activity during the labeling of fearful and angry faces and to lower amygdala activity as expected. Psychosocial resources were also tied to lower cortisol and systolic blood pressure responses during the TSST. Most important, lower amygdala activity mediated the relation of psychosocial resources to lower cortisol reactivity. This evidence, then, tells us that individual differences in psychosocial resources influence the brain's response to threat, which in turn reduces neuroendocrine responses to stress.

PSYCHOSOCIAL RESOURCES AND HEALTH OUTCOMES

Does the model pictured in Figure 5.1 predict health outcomes? In other words, by knowing a person's psychosocial resources, can we make educated guesses about what their health will be like across the lifespan? In one effort to address this important and complex question, we developed a collaborative relationship with the CARDIA study (Coronary Artery Risk Development In Young Adults). CARDIA is a large prospective study of risk factors for coronary artery disease in African-Americans and Whites. It has so far followed participants over a 15-year period, enabling an examination of our model (Figure 5.1) with regard to specific health outcomes.

We have thus far addressed three such outcomes. The first is metabolic functioning. Metabolic functioning is a composite risk factor for diabetes, coronary artery disease, hypertension, and other chronic health conditions. It is composed of such indicators as cholesterol, insulin, glucose, triglycerides, and waist circumference. We also examined the relation of the model to C-reactive protein, an indicator of inflammatory processes that has been implicated as a risk factor for both mental disorders (e.g., depression) and physical health disorders (e.g., heart disease). And third, we examined whether the model can predict the development of hypertension.

We had 3225 participants complete our assessments of childhood SES and early family environment and also complete a physical exam to assess metabolic functioning, C-reactive protein, and blood pressure. We used structural equation modeling to examine the viability of a model similar to that pictured in Figure 5.1. Unfortunately though, from a psychosocial standpoint, we were able to look at only depression, hostility, and social support as the psychosocial measures. Nonetheless, the model proved to be a good fit for explaining variability in all three of the health outcomes, including not only blood pressure but change in blood pressure over time. These findings provide direct evidence that psychosocial factors are implicated in health risks tied to low SES in childhood and to a harsh early family environment.

CONCLUSIONS AND IMPLICATIONS

Are there applications of this work? The realization that psychosocial resources arise in the early family environment and from genes may imply that these patterns are established very early in life and that there may not be much room for improvement. Accordingly, this would seemingly limit possibilities for intervention. This is clearly not the case, however. For example, some of our genetics work has shown that when people are in a supportive environment, even genes that would normally predispose to adverse stress responses such as depression and anxiety are expressed differently and may even become protective against the adverse effects of stress (Taylor et al., 2006b). How might we engineer a positive social environment?

A first point of intervention concerns the early environment. Because the damage of low socioeconomic conditions and a harsh family environment occurs so early in life, it is important to intervene at the earliest possible time. Children who may be at risk need to be identified very early, as babies or toddlers or even prenatally, so that the psychosocial environment can be improved. Interventions with families to improve parenting practices, for example, are essential and for the most part appear to be successful (McLoyd, 1998). However, an important predictor of decline in the psychosocial environment of the family is economic downturns: When people are under stress, fear losing their jobs, or are having difficulty meeting their financial obligations, family relations deteriorate. As such, economic downturns represent a high-risk circumstance for the kinds of risky family dynamics documented here. Interventions, then, need to start early with such things as parenting classes, training manuals, and skill training in emotion regulation and empathy, for parents and children alike.

Our research also clearly points to a mechanism that links social support to health outcomes via neural regulation of stress reactivity. Accordingly, attempting to personally engineer one's environment so that it is relatively low in stress and high in social support is another way to guard against the adverse effects of stress, even those that may be related to genes. The lesson to be learned is that everyone should be encouraged to build supportive social networks and participate actively in them. Those who are unable to do so on their own may need assistance.

Another strategy is to cultivate psychosocial resources for improving well-being. There are a number of books that can help people to do this, including Sonja Lyubomirsky's (2008) *The How of Happiness*, Seligman's (2006) *Learned Optimism*, Diener and Biswas-Diener's (2008) *Happiness*, and Fredrikson's (2009) *Positivity*.

Not everyone can engineer their personal environment in such a way as to foster psychosocial resources on their own. But, there is every reason to believe that therapeutic interventions, such as cognitive-behavioral treatments to modify coping skills, can help people think about their lives differently and deal with stress more effectively. So, for people who are unable to achieve this re-engineering, there are numerous sources of help.

In conclusion, the importance of psychosocial resources such as social support, optimism, a sense of mastery, self-esteem, and active coping skills should not be underestimated. These resources, the groundwork for which is laid early in life, help people to stave off psychological distress and ill health across the lifespan.

ACKNOWLEDGMENTS

Preparation of this chapter was supported by a grant from the National Institute of Aging (AG030309).

REFERENCES

Adler, N. E., Marmot, M., McEwen, B. S., & Stewart, J. (1999). *Socioeconomic status and health in industrial nations: Social, psychological, and biological pathways*. New York: New York Academy of Sciences.

Antoni, M. H., & Goodkin, K. (1988). Host moderator variables in the promotion of cervical neoplasia—I: Personality facets. *Journal of Psychosomatic Research, 32*, 327–338.

Brody, G. H., & Flor, D. L. (1998). Maternal resources, parenting practices, and child competence in rural, single-parent African-American families. *Child Development, 69*, 803–816.

Carver, C. S., & Scheier, M. F. (2002). Optimism. In C. R. Snyder & S. J. Lopez (Eds.), *Handbook of positive psychology* (pp. 231–243). New York: Oxford University Press.

Caspi, A., McClay, J., Moffitt, T. E., Mill, J., Martin, J., Craig, I. W., et al. (2002). Role of genotype in the cycle of violence in maltreated children. *Science, 297*, 851–854.

Chen, E., Matthews, K. A., & Boyce, W. T. (2002). Socioeconomic differences in children's health: How and why do these relationships change with age? *Psychological Bulletin, 128*, 295–329.

Cohen, S., Doyle, W. J., Turner, R. B., Alper, C. M., & Skoner, D. P. (2003). Emotional style and susceptibility to the common cold. *Psychosomatic Medicine, 65*, 652–657.

Creswell, J. D., Welch, W. T., Taylor, S. E., Sherman, D. K., Gruenewald, T., & Mann, T. (2005). Affirmation of personal values buffers neuroendocrine and psychological stress responses. *Psychological Science, 16*, 846–851.

Diener, E., & Biswas-Diener, R. (2008). *Happiness: Unlocking the mysteries of psychological wealth*. Oxford, UK: Blackwell Publishing.

Dishion, T. J. (1990). The family ecology of boys' peer relations in middle childhood. *Child Development, 61*, 874–891.

Eisenberger, N. I., Lieberman, M. D., & Williams, K. D. (2003). Does rejection hurt? An fMRI study of social exclusion. *Science, 302*, 290–292.

Eisenberger, N. I., Taylor, S. E., Gable, S. L., Hilmert, C. J., & Lieberman, M. D. (2007). Neural pathways link social support to attenuated neuroendocrine stress responses. *NeuroImage, 35*, 1601–1612.

Eisenberger, N. I., Way, B. M., Taylor, S. E., Welch, W. T., & Lieberman, M. D. (2007). Understanding genetic risk for aggression: Clues from the brain's response to social exclusion. *Biological Psychiatry, 61*, 1100–1108.

Felitti, V. J., Anda, R. F., Nordenberg, D., Williamson, D. F., Apitz, A. M., Edwards, V., et al. (1998). Relationship of childhood abuse and household dysfunction to many of the leading causes of death in adults. *American Journal of Preventative Medicine, 14*, 245–258.

Folkman, S., & Moskowitz, J. T. (2004). Coping: Pitfalls and promise. *Annual Review of Psychology, 55*, 745–774.

Fredrikson, B. L. (2009). *Positivity: Groundbreaking research reveals how to embrace the hidden strength of positive emotions, overcome negativity, and thrive.* New York: Crown.

Fries, A. B., Shirtcliff, E. A., & Pollak, S. D. (2008). Neuroendocrine dysregulation following early social deprivation in children. *Developmental Psychobiology, 50*, 588–599.

Helgeson, V. S. (1999). Applicability of cognitive adaptation theory to predicting adjustment to heart disease after coronary angioplasty. *Health Psychology, 18*, 561–569.

Helgeson, V. S. (2003). Cognitive adaptation, psychological adjustment and disease progression among angioplasty patients: 4 years later. *Health Psychology, 22*, 30–38.

House, J. S., Landis, K. R., & Umberson, D. (1988). Social relationships and health. *Science, 241*, 540–545.

Johnson, V., & Pandina, R. J. (1991). Effects of family environment on adolescent substance use, delinquency, and coping styles. *American Journal of Drug and Alcohol Abuse, 17*, 71–88.

Karasek, R. A., Theorell, T., Schwartz, J., Pieper, C., & Alfredsson, L. (1982). Job, psychological factors and coronary heart disease: Swedish prospective findings and U.S. prevalence findings using a new occupational inference method. *Advances in Cardiology, 29*, 62–67.

Kessler, R. C., Kendler, K. S., Heath, A. C., Neale, M. C., & Eaves, L. J. (1992). Social support, depressed mood, and adjustment to stress: A genetic epidemiological investigation. *Journal of Personality and Social Psychology, 62*, 257–272.

Kirschbaum, C., Pirke, K., & Hellhammer, D. H. (1993). The "Trier Social Stress Test" – a tool for investigating psychobiological stress responses in a laboratory setting. *Neuropsychobiology, 28*, 76–81.

Kubzansky, L. D., Wright, R. J., Cohen, S., Weiss, S., Rosner, B., & Sparrow, D. (2002). Breathing easy: A prospective study of optimism and pulmonary function in the normative aging study. *Annals of Behavioral Medicine, 24*, 345–353.

Lachman, M. E., & Weaver, S. L. (1998). The sense of control as a moderator of social class differences in health and well-being. *Journal of Personality and Social Psychology, 74*, 763–773.

Lyubomirsky, S. (2008). *The how of happiness: A scientific approach to getting the life you want.* New York: Penguin Press.

McEwen, B. S. (1998). Protective and damaging effects of stress mediators. *New England Journal of Medicine, 338*, 171–179.

McLoyd, V. C. (1998). Socioeconomic disadvantage and child development. *American Psychologist, 53*, 185–204.

O'Brien, M., Margolin, G., John, R. S., & Krueger, L. (1991). Mothers' and sons' cognitive and emotional reactions to simulated marital and family conflict. *Journal of Consulting and Clinical Psychology, 59*, 692–703.

Park, C. L., Moore, P. J., Turner, R. A., & Adler, N. E. (1992). The roles of constructive thinking and optimism in psychological and behavioral adjustment during pregnancy. *Journal of Personality and Social Psychology, 73*, 584–592.

Plomin, R., Scheier, M. F., Bergeman, S. C., Pedersen, N. L., Nesselroade, J. R., & McClearn, G. E. (1992). Optimism, pessimism, and mental health: A twin/adoption study. *Personality and Individual Differences, 13*, 921–930.

Reed, G. M., Kemeny, M. E., Taylor, S. E., & Visscher, B. R. (1999). Negative HIV-specific expectancies and AIDS-related bereavement as predictors of symptom onset in asymptomatic HIV-positive gay men. *Health Psychology, 18,* 354–363.

Reed, G. M., Kemeny, M. E., Taylor, S. E., Wang, H. Y. J., & Visscher, B. R. (1994). Realistic acceptance as a predictor of decreased survival time in gay men with AIDS. *Health Psychology, 13,* 299–307.

Reid, R. J., & Crisafulli, A. (1990). Marital discord and child behavior problems: A meta-analysis. *Journal of Abnormal Child Psychology, 18,* 105–117.

Repetti, R. L., Taylor, S. E., & Seeman, T. E. (2002). Risky families: Family social environments and the mental and physical health of offspring. *Psychological Bulletin, 128,* 330–366.

Rodin, J., Timko, C., & Harris, S. (1985). The construct of control: Biological and psychosocial correlates. *Annual Review of Gerontology and Geriatrics, 5,* 3–55.

Scheier, M. F., & Carver, C. S. (1992). Effects of optimism on psychological and physical well-being: Theoretical overview and empirical update. *Cognitive Therapy Research, 16,* 201–228.

Scheier, M. F., & Carver, C. S. (2003). Self-regulatory processes and responses to health threats: Effects of optimism on well-being. In J. Suls & K. A. Wallston (Eds.), *Social psychological foundations of health* (pp. 395–428). Oxford, UK: Blackwell Publishing.

Scheier, M. F., Matthews, K. A., Owens, J., Magovern Sr., G. J., Lefebvre, R. C., Abbott, R. A., et al. (1989). Dispositional optimism and recovery from coronary artery bypass surgery: The beneficial effects on physical and psychological well-being. *Journal of Personality and Social Psychology, 57,* 1024–1040.

Scheier, M. F., Weintraub, J. K., & Carver, C. S. (1986). Coping with stress: Divergent strategies of optimists and pessimists. *Journal of Personality and Social Psychology, 51,* 1257–1264.

Seeman, M., & Lewis, S. (1995). Powerlessness, health, and mortality: A longitudinal study of older men and mature women. *Social Science and Medicine, 41,* 517–525.

Segerstrom, S. C., Taylor, S. E., Kemeny, M. E., & Fahey, J. L. (1998). Optimism is associated with mood, coping, and immune change in response to stress. *Journal of Personality and Social Psychology, 74,* 1646–1655.

Segerstrom, S. C., Taylor, S. E., Kemeny, M. E., Reed, G. M., & Visscher, B. R. (1996). Causal attributions predict health behavior in HIV seropositive gay men. *Health Psychology, 15,* 485–493.

Seligman, M. (2006). *Learned optimism: How to change your mind and your life.* New York: Vintage Books.

Taylor, S. E. (1983). Adjustment to threatening events: A theory of cognitive adaptation. *American Psychologist, 41,* 1161–1173.

Taylor, S. E. (2010). Social support: A review. In H. S. Friedman (Ed.), *Oxford handbook of health psychology.* New York: Oxford University Press.

Taylor, S. E., Burklund, L. J., Eisenberger, N. I., Lehman, B. J., Hilmert, C. J., & Lieberman, M. D. (2008). Neural bases of moderation of cortisol stress responses by psychosocial resources. *Journal of Personality and Social Psychology, 95,* 197–211.

Taylor, S. E., Eisenberger, N. I., Saxbe, D., Lehman, B. J., & Lieberman, M. D. (2006a). Neural responses to emotional stimuli are associated with childhood family stress. *Biological Psychiatry, 60,* 296–301.

Taylor, S. E., Helgeson, V. S., Reed, G. M., & Skokan, L. A. (1991). Self-generated feelings of control and adjustment to physical illness. *Journal of Social Issues, 47,* 91–109.

Taylor, S. E., Lerner, J. S., Sherman, D. K., Sage, R. M., & McDowell, N. K. (2003). Are self-enhancing cognitions associated with healthy or unhealthy biological profiles? *Journal of Personality and Social Psychology, 85*, 605–615.

Taylor, S. E., & Seeman, T. E. (1999). Psychosocial resources and the SES–health relationship. In N. Adler, M. Marmot, B. McEwen, & J. Stewart (Eds.), *Socioeconomic status and health in industrial nations: Social, psychological, and biological pathways* (pp. 210–225). New York: New York Academy of Sciences.

Taylor, S. E., & Stanton, A. (2007). Coping resources, coping processes, and mental health. *Annual Review of Clinical Psychology, 3*, 129–153.

Taylor, S. E., Way, B. M., Welch, W. T., Hilmert, C. J., Lehman, B. J., & Eisenberger, N. I. (2006b). Early family environment, current adversity, the serotonin transporter polymorphism, and depressive symptomatology. *Biological Psychiatry, 60*, 671–676.

Thompson, S. C. (1981). Will it hurt less if I can control it? A complex answer to a simple question. *Psychological Bulletin, 90*, 89–101.

Tottenham, N., Hare, T., Quinn, B., McCarry, T., Nurse, M., Gilhooly, T., et al. (2010). Prolonged institutional rearing is associated with atypically larger amygdala volume and difficulties in emotion regulation. *Developmental Science, 13*, 46–61.

Valentiner, D. P., Holahan, C. J., & Moos, R. H. (1994). Social support, appraisals of event controllability, and coping: An integrative model. *Journal of Personality and Social Psychology, 66*, 1094–1102.

Wills, T. A. (1991). Social support and interpersonal relationships. In M. S. Clark (Ed.), *Prosocial behavior* (pp. 265–289). Newbury Park, CA: Sage Publications.

6

Tailoring Positive Psychology Interventions to Treat Depressed Individuals

NANCY L. SIN, MATTHEW D. DELLA PORTA,
and SONJA LYUBOMIRSKY

W hen Scott finally sought treatment, it was apparent that he had been struggling for some time. He was unshaven and wore large, crumpled clothes that overwhelmed his thin frame. At 27, Scott seemed to move with the labored, slouched shuffling of an elderly man. Slowly and dully, with frequent pauses, Scott explained that he had been feeling persistently sad and withdrawn for several years, starting in college. However, his mental health had steadily deteriorated ever since he began a new job several months earlier. Scott felt inadequate and worthless, particularly at work. His poor self-esteem was further compounded by his lack of meaningful friendships. Scott found no delight in activities he used to enjoy, such as biking, playing classical guitar, and reading philosophy books. When not dragging himself through the workday, Scott passed the time by sitting or lying motionless at home for hours on end. He doubted he would ever feel good again. What can positive psychology do for Scott?

Traditionally, psychologists have equated mental health with the absence of mental illness – that is, Scott would be considered psychologically well when his depressive symptoms are relieved. A shift in mental health practice and research began to unfold in the final years of the 20th century, when the field of positive psychology emerged to unite disparate theory and knowledge on positive functioning and to advance work on *positive* mental health (Seligman, Steen, Park, & Peterson, 2005). Increasingly, psychological well-being is now understood as both the absence of mental illness and the presence of positive psychological resources, such as positive affect and satisfaction with one's life (Diener, 1984), autonomy, competence, relatedness (Ryan & Deci, 2001), self-acceptance, purpose, and personal growth (Ryff, 1989).

A NEED FOR NOVEL TREATMENTS FOR DEPRESSION

In a given one-year period, approximately 5.4% of the US population will meet the criteria for Major Depressive Disorder, and many others suffer from depressive symptoms or chronic low-level depression (Narrow, Rae, Robins, & Regier, 2002). Depression is enormously debilitating for individuals, families, and society, costing the USA tens of billions of dollars each year in lost productivity, medical expenses, and more (e.g., Wang, Simon, & Kessler, 2003). Despite a variety of empirically supported treatments for depression, why do a startling number of people continue to suffer from this incapacitating illness?

We suggest two possible explanations. First, many people do not seek treatment for depression – only about 14.8% of individuals potentially diagnosable with Major Depressive Disorder actually receive appropriate counseling from a mental health provider during a one-year period (Young, Klap, Sherbourne, & Wells, 2001). Many individuals with depression are perhaps reluctant or unwilling to seek treatment because of the stigma associated with mental illness. Others may be unable to obtain treatment because they lack the requisite financial resources. One promising solution to this problem would be to offer treatments that people can administer themselves; for example, self-help books, DVDs, or interactive digital Web-based and mobile-based programs based on research. Computerized treatments for depression – such as *Beating the Blues*, an eight-session cognitive-behavioral program with homework exercises – are efficacious options for depressed individuals who cannot or prefer not to engage in traditional face-to-face therapy (Cavanagh & Shapiro, 2004; Proudfoot, Goldberg, Mann, Everitt, Marks, & Gray, 2003). Although these alternative options should not take the place of professional, individualized treatment, especially in cases of moderate or severe depression, they are nevertheless better than no treatment at all.

A second possible reason why many people continue to suffer from depression is that established treatments are not effective for everyone. In fact, fewer than half of patients who receive cognitive-behavioral therapy (CBT) – arguably one of the most effective and widely researched depression treatments – will completely recover from depression (e.g., Elkin et al., 1989). Perhaps the therapeutic techniques used to treat the acute phase of depression are not as helpful for preventing relapses or for eliminating residual symptoms (Fava, Rafanelli, Cazzaro, Conti, & Grandi, 1998), or perhaps particular components of CBT fail to provide a good "fit" with some clients' personalities, goals, values, resources, or lifestyles. In sum, novel treatment approaches should be accessible, customizable to the individual's needs, and promote the building of durable resources to protect against relapse.

WHY USE POSITIVE PSYCHOLOGY TO TREAT DEPRESSION?

Depression is often conceptualized as an overabundance of negatives – namely, negative moods and negative cognitions (e.g., Abramson, Seligman, & Teasdale,

1978). It is not surprising then that existing depression treatments are primarily focused on alleviating and fixing these negatives and less concerned with building positive resources. However, negative affect and positive affect are two independent constructs (Watson & Tellegen, 1985); the absence of negative feelings is not equivalent to the presence of positive ones. According to a frequently mentioned analogy, psychologists should not aim to merely raise a person's mental health from a –5 to a neutral 0; instead, the aim should be to raise that person to a +5 or higher. Treatments should thus strive to cultivate an individual's well-being, rather than only ameliorate depressive symptoms (Lyubomirsky, 2008).

Positive emotions are valuable for more than just feeling good. They can foster successful outcomes in a variety of life domains, including relatively better job performance, more creativity, greater marital satisfaction, and enhanced social relationships (Lyubomirsky, King, & Diener, 2005). The benefits of positive emotions are especially relevant to those suffering from depression: Positive emotions have been shown to speed recovery from the cardiovascular effects of negative emotions (Fredrickson & Levenson, 1998; Tugade & Fredrickson, 2004), improve broad-minded coping skills (Fredrickson & Joiner, 2002), and buffer against relapses (Fava & Ruini, 2003).

Even momentary positive feelings can produce lasting changes in one's life. According to Fredrickson's (2001) broaden-and-build theory, positive emotions broaden thinking and attention. Broadened mindsets bring about novel ideas and actions (e.g., the urge to play and explore) and lead to the building of long-term personal resources, including social, psychological, intellectual, and physical skills and reserves. Indeed, among individuals with depression, relatively higher levels of approach-oriented motivation are associated with less severe depression and a greater likelihood of recovery (Kasch, Rottenberg, Arnow, & Gotlib, 2002). In contrast to the narrowing of attention (Gasper & Clore, 2002) and behavioral inhibition (Kasch et al., 2002) characteristic of negative states, positive emotions trigger upward spirals toward greater psychological well-being (Fredrickson & Joiner, 2002).

ENHANCING WELL-BEING VIA POSITIVE PSYCHOLOGY INTERVENTIONS

Much skepticism exists regarding whether well-being can be sustainably increased. Is it possible for a person to become happier, and if so, how? Genetics (i.e., one's temperament and happiness "set point") and – to a lesser extent – life circumstances (e.g., age, marital status, income level) determine a sizable portion of one's well-being (Lyubomirsky, Sheldon, & Schkade, 2005). Nevertheless, considerable "room" remains for one to climb up or drop down in happiness, as approximately 40% of the individual differences in well-being can be accounted for by one's activities and perceptions of life circumstances (Lyubomirsky, Sheldon et al., 2005). Indeed, studies have shown that well-being can be boosted by engaging in intentional, effortful activities, such as writing letters of gratitude (Lyubomirsky, Dickerhoof, Boehm, & Sheldon, in press; Seligman et al., 2005), counting one's blessings (Emmons & McCullough, 2003; Froh, Sefick, & Emmons, 2008; Lyubomirsky, Sheldon et al., 2005), practicing optimism (Sheldon & Lyubomirsky, 2006), performing acts of kindness (Sheldon, Boehm & Lyubomirsky, in press; Lyubomirsky, Sheldon et al., 2005), and using one's signature strengths (Seligman et al., 2005). These activities – empirically tested in so-called *positive psychology interventions* – are similar in that they promote positive feelings, positive thoughts, and/or positive behaviors, rather than directly aiming to fix any negatives.

A recent meta-analysis of 51 studies revealed that positive psychology interventions are effective for enhancing well-being and ameliorating depressive symptoms (Sin & Lyubomirsky, 2009). The magnitudes of these effects are medium-sized (mean r = .29 for well-being, mean r = .31 for depression) and are quite impressive, given that many of these interventions are self-administered positive activities rather than therapy. To put the effectiveness of positive psychology interventions into perspective, consider the classic Smith and Glass (1977) meta-analysis of 375 psychotherapy studies. Smith and Glass found that psychotherapy had an average effect size r of .32 on various outcomes, such as self-esteem and adjustment. In contrast, studies of positive psychotherapies (albeit few in number) show average r effect sizes of about .30 to .57 on well-being and depression outcomes. Thus, although the development, research, and implementation of these interventions are in their infancy, positive psychology interventions show immense promise for improving the lives of many.

POSITIVE PSYCHOLOGY INTERVENTIONS FOR NON-DEPRESSED INDIVIDUALS

One of the first research investigations to test the possibility of boosting happiness via intentional positive activities was conducted by Fordyce (1977, 1983). In a series of classroom-based studies, Fordyce taught his students to modify their behaviors and attitudes to mimic those of very happy people. Students assigned to practice these techniques (e.g., strengthen close relationships, develop optimistic thinking, and become involved in meaningful work) every day for several weeks experienced greater boosts in well-being and larger declines in depressive symptoms than did students in the comparison group.

More recently, researchers have focused on testing the impact of specific positive activities, such as practicing optimism, performing kind acts, and cultivating gratitude, in randomized controlled experiments.

Optimism

A simple yet powerful way to enhance positive mood is by visualizing one's "best possible selves" in the future. In a pioneering study, once a day for four consecutive days, participants were instructed to "imagine that everything has gone as well as it possibly could" and to write about it for 20 minutes (King, 2001). These individuals experienced a greater boost to positive mood than those who engaged in a neutral activity. Furthermore, this optimism exercise had remarkable health benefits –

individuals who wrote about their best possible selves had relatively less illness five months later. Even more impressive are findings from a recent follow-up study, which found similar benefits for an analogous intervention that involved only two minutes of writing on only two consecutive days (Burton & King, 2008).

In a four-week study, participants who imagined and wrote about their best possible selves witnessed an immediate boost in positive affect compared to those in the control group (Sheldon & Lyubomirsky, 2006). This boost was sustained over the four-week period, perhaps because participants felt relatively more self-concordant motivation (or intrinsic interest) for this activity and, in turn, practiced it more frequently. Finally, the benefits of thinking optimistically were replicated in two follow-up studies (Lyubomirsky et al., in press), in which students wrote about their best possible selves for 15 minutes a week over the course of eight weeks (Study 1), and community-dwelling adults wrote for 10 minutes a week over the course of six weeks (Study 2). Notably, significant differences in well-being between the experimental and control groups remained in these studies even six months and one month, respectively, after the intervention ended.

Kindness

An association exists between kindness and happiness, such that happy people tend to engage in more prosocial behaviors (Lyubomirsky, King et al., 2005; Otake, Shimai, Tanaka-Matsumi, Otsui, & Fredrickson, 2006). To experimentally test whether performing a kind act would lead to an increase in happiness, Dunn, Aknin, and Norton (2008) gave participants either $5 or $20 and instructed them to spend the money on themselves or on others that day. Participants who spent the money on others – typical purchases included donations to the homeless, toys for siblings, and meals for friends – reported feeling greater happiness than those who spent the money on themselves. Interestingly, the amount of money spent did not matter – participants who spent $5 on others felt just as good as those who spent $20.

The positive emotional benefits of kindness extend beyond performing actual behaviors to simply recalling them. Otake and colleagues (2006) conducted a "counting kindnesses" intervention by assigning individuals to keep track of their own kind behaviors towards others for one week. Compared to the control group, those who counted kindnesses experienced a greater boost in happiness one month later. Furthermore, the largest increases in happiness and gratitude occurred for individuals who reported enacting a greater number of kind behaviors.

However, the quantity of kind acts is only one of many factors to consider when assessing their well-being benefits. Lyubomirsky, Sheldon et al. (2005) demonstrated that the timing of kind acts – particularly if the acts are small – matters. In their six-week study, individuals who performed five kind acts (e.g., cooking dinner for others, babysitting a sibling) all in a single day showed an increase in well-being, but individuals whose five kind acts were spread over a week were no happier than the control group. Because many of these kind acts were small, spreading them throughout the week may have diminished their salience. Another critical factor to consider in kindness – or any other – interventions is variety or novelty. A 10-week intervention revealed that although regularly committing acts of kindness improves well-being, this effect is observed only for individuals who vary the types of kind acts they enact, as opposed to performing the very same activities each week (Sheldon et al., in press).

These findings suggest that the pursuit of happiness need not be a self-focused or self-absorbed endeavor. By helping others, people are likely to feel more confident in their abilities to enact change, build better relationships, and trigger an upward spiral of positive emotions and positive interpersonal exchanges (Lyubomirsky, King et al., 2005; Otake et al., 2006).

Gratitude

Not surprisingly, the cultivation of gratitude – a cognitive construct closely related to the behavior of kindness – has been found to promote well-being. The intentional practice of attending to, savoring, and being thankful for one's fortunate circumstances can counteract the effects of hedonic adaptation, by which an individual gradually "takes something for granted." Grateful thinking also can be an effective coping strategy during difficult times, when the ability to derive positive meaning from negative events gains special significance.

In a series of studies, Emmons and McCullough (2003) directed participants to "count their blessings" by listing five things for which they were grateful. (Examples included "the generosity of friends," "to God for giving me determination," and "for wonderful parents.") Participants were assigned to engage in this self-guided activity weekly for 10 weeks or daily for 2–3 weeks. Relative to those in the comparison groups, individuals in the gratitude condition reported greater psychological well-being, fewer physical symptoms, and improvements in health behaviors. Moreover, the counting of blessings led to more positive moods, better sleep, and a greater sense of social connectedness in a sample of participants with neuromuscular disease.

Similarly, Lyubomirsky, Sheldon et al. (2005) showed that the cultivation of grateful thinking across a six-week period can produce a boost in well-being. However, the frequency of the activity was found to be a moderating variable, such that individuals who counted blessings once a week became happier, but not those who counted blessings three times a week. It is likely that overpracticing any one positive activity may weaken its freshness and meaning.

Although gratitude-inducing exercises appear to have a powerful impact on well-being, not everyone is likely to benefit from this activity. In their four-week experimental study, Sheldon and Lyubomirsky (2006) found that only those participants who applied high effort and were intrinsically driven to write letters of gratitude obtained the benefits of the intervention. Likewise, a more recent study revealed that writing gratitude letters weekly over an eight-week period did not produce gains in well-being for everyone (Lyubomirsky et al., in press). Only those individuals who had an intrinsic desire to become happier – as well as those who continued to practice the activity even after the intervention ended – experienced enhanced well-being. In fact, the motivation to become happier was such a powerful factor that these individuals continued to show increased well-being six months post-intervention.

POSITIVE PSYCHOLOGY INTERVENTIONS FOR INDIVIDUALS WITH DEPRESSION

A growing number of positive psychology interventions have been tested on individuals with depressive symptoms and those diagnosed with depression. In an on-line study, Seligman and colleagues (2005) randomly assigned 411 volunteers – who were mildly depressed, on average – to engage for one week in one of five purported happiness-enhancing activities or a placebo control activity. The positive activities were to write and deliver a gratitude letter, write about three good things in life, write about a time when they were at their best, identify signature strengths, and use signature strengths in a new way. For the placebo exercise, participants were instructed to write about their early memories. Participants experienced a boost in happiness and a decline in depressive symptoms immediately post-intervention, regardless of the assigned activity. However, whereas participants in the placebo condition returned to and remained at their baseline state one week later, those who completed the happiness-enhancing exercises were more likely to continue garnering the benefits. Two of the activities – writing about three good things and using signature strengths in a new way – resulted in lasting improvements in depression and happiness for six months. This study demonstrates that even simple, self-guided exercises can bring long-term benefits to mildly depressed or dysphoric individuals, especially for those who continue to engage in the exercise after the intervention period is long over.

Such evidence supports the efficacy of single happiness-promoting exercises in non-clinical dysphoric populations. However, little research has been done to test programs consisting of multiple positive psychology-based exercises to treat clinical populations. An exception is pioneering work on positive psychotherapy (PPT) and well-being therapy (WBT), which reveals that clinical depression can be alleviated by nurturing positive emotions, building inner strengths, and fostering engagement and life meaning.

In a six-week study, 40 mildly-to-moderately depressed young adults were assigned to participate in group PPT or to a no-treatment control condition (Seligman, Rashid, & Parks, 2006). Group PPT consisted of varying positive exercises each week, including using one's strengths, practicing active and constructive responding, and savoring everyday activities. During the 2-hour weekly sessions, participants engaged in group discussions, received guidance on how to carry out the positive exercises, and were assigned homework. Although the treatment was not individually tailored for each participant, group PPT was nonetheless efficacious for ameliorating depressive symptoms and raising life satisfaction. The results for the lasting relief of depression are impressive – on average, PPT participants were non-depressed a year later, whereas those in the no-treatment control group remained mildly-to-moderately depressed.

How do positive therapies compare to more traditional treatments for depression? To answer this question, Seligman and colleagues (2006) randomly assigned 20 individuals diagnosed with Major Depressive Disorder to receive either 14 sessions of PPT or treatment as usual (i.e., whatever treatment the therapists deemed suitable for their clients). Another group of individuals, receiving both treatment as usual and antidepressant medication, were matched to PPT clients based on the severity of depression. For this study, PPT was administered using a manualized protocol that focused on both positive and negative aspects of the client. Customized to address the client's immediate concerns, PPT aimed to balance the overwhelming negatives of depression by establishing congenial and empathetic rapport, identifying and using the client's strengths, coaching the client to attend to and remember the good in his or her life, and teaching positive social behaviors. The results showed a remarkable advantage for PPT: Compared to treatment as usual and treatment as usual plus medication, PPT produced greater happiness, more symptomatic improvement, and higher remission rates.

Furthermore, therapies that enhance well-being may confer an advantage over traditional treatments for relieving the *residual* symptoms of major depression. One such therapy, WBT, aims to improve six dimensions of psychological well-being: autonomy, personal growth, environmental mastery, purpose in life, positive relations, and self-acceptance (Fava & Ruini, 2003; Ryff, 1989). WBT emphasizes the self-monitoring of episodes of well-being, identifying and changing beliefs that interrupt well-being, and reinforcing beliefs that promote well-being (Fava & Ruini, 2003). Indeed, a preliminary study of 20 patients with remitted affective disorders (including depression) showed that WBT resulted in greater increases in psychological well-being compared to CBT (Fava et al., 1998). Although both treatment approaches significantly reduced residual symptoms, observer-rated methods indicated that WBT led to more improvement than did CBT (Fava et al., 1998).

Emerging research on interventions that promote specific positive perspectives (including forgiveness, hope, mindfulness, and loving-kindness) have also been shown to enhance mental health and reduce depression. A meta-analysis of several controlled forgiveness interventions suggests that the process of willfully giving up resentment and developing empathy for an offender can improve one's emotional health, as measured by scales of depression, anxiety, hope, and self-esteem (Baskin & Enright, 2004).

Snyder and colleagues (1991) conceptualize hope as a cognitive process for actively pursuing one's goals. Hope therapy is designed to help individuals set meaningful goals, identify pathways to pursue goals, as well as strengthen motivation and monitor progress towards those goals (Cheavens, Feldman, Gum, Michael, & Snyder, 2006). A randomized, wait-list controlled investigation using 32 community members – many of whom had previously undergone psychological treatment and met the criteria for a mental disorder – showed that hope-based group therapy reduced depression and enhanced life meaning and self-esteem (Cheavens et al., 2006).

Finally, burgeoning empirical research extols the benefits of training the mind through regular meditation practice. Mindfulness meditation involves intentional, non-judgmental awareness and acceptance of the present moment (Kabat-Zinn, 1990). Interventions rooted in mindfulness (such as mindfulness-based stress reduction and mindfulness-based cognitive therapy) have been shown to improve well-being and to alleviate physical and psychological distress in patients with chronic fatigue syndrome (Surawy, Roberts, & Silver, 2005), fibromyalgia

(Grossman, Tiefenthaler-Gilmer, Raysz, & Kesper, 2007), rheumatoid arthritis (Zautra et al., 2008), traumatic brain injury (Bédard et al., 2003), and other chronic ailments and stressors (see Grossman, Niemann, Schmidt, & Walach, 2004, for a quantitative review). Mindfulness meditation has also been used to benefit treatment-resistant individuals with depression (Eisendrath, Delucchi, Bitner, Fenimore, Smit, & McLane, 2008), reduce residual depressive symptoms (Kuyken et al., 2008), decrease rumination (Ramel, Goldin, Carmona, & McQuaid, 2004), and prevent relapse in recurrent depression (Kuyken et al., 2008). Similarly, loving-kindness meditation – wherein individuals cultivate feelings of love and compassion for the self and others – has been shown to lower depressive symptoms and enhance life satisfaction through increases in personal resources (Fredrickson, Cohn, Coffey, Pek, & Finkel, 2008).

Taken together, a growing number of experimental interventions support the success of focusing on building positive feelings, cognitions, and behaviors. These interventions offer a novel, yet efficacious, approach to treating symptoms of depression in psychiatric and non-psychiatric, medical and non-medical populations. Moreover, these novel treatments foster increases in essential components of mental well-being, including happiness, life satisfaction, purpose in life, and self-esteem.

FACTORS MODERATING THE EFFICACY OF POSITIVE PSYCHOLOGY INTERVENTIONS

It is unlikely that all individuals would engage in and experience a given happiness-promoting activity in the same manner or profit from it to the same degree. As we discuss below, an activity that is beneficial for one person, group, or context can be ineffective or even detrimental to another. It is therefore crucial to identify factors that might improve or limit the success of positive psychology interventions.

Therapeutic Guidance

Not surprisingly, more individual attention from a therapist is associated with a relatively greater boost in well-being and improvement in depressive symptoms (Sin & Lyubomirsky, 2009). Individual positive psychology interventions bring the greatest benefits, followed by group interventions (Baskin & Enright, 2004; Sin & Lyubomirsky, 2009). Self-administered positive activities – that is, positive activities conducted without therapeutic guidance – are not as effective as individual therapy or group therapy. Nevertheless, partaking in self-administered positive activities significantly enhances well-being, compared to engaging in neutral activities or no activity at all (Sin & Lyubomirsky, 2009).

Duration of Intervention and Continued Practice

Interventions that are longer in duration (measured in hours or weeks) tend to be more effective for both treating depression and boosting happiness than relatively shorter interventions (Sin & Lyubomirsky, 2009). Longer interventions may allow for more practice, greater opportunity to turn activities into long-lasting habits, and – in the case of therapies – more therapeutic guidance. Similarly, individuals who continue to practice positive activities after a formal intervention has ended experience relatively greater increases in happiness (Lyubomirsky et al., in press; Seligman et al., 2005; Sheldon & Lyubomirsky, 2006).

Self-Selection, Motivation, and Outcome Expectations

Interventions that people freely choose to engage in – fully aware that the intervention may make them happier – tend to be more successful for lifting depressive symptoms and enhancing well-being than interventions to which people are assigned (Lyubomirsky et al., in press; Sin & Lyubomirsky, 2009). Individuals who volunteer or self-select themselves into an intervention are presumably more motivated to become happier than those who are randomly assigned into an intervention, and may be relatively more diligent and enthusiastic about following instructions or carrying out recommendations.

Person–Activity Fit

A proper "fit" or match between a person and a particular happiness-increasing activity is likely to impact the effectiveness of an intervention. Individuals have strengths, needs, values, interests, and preferences that predispose them to benefit more from some happiness-enhancing activities than others (Lyubomirsky, 2008; Lyubomirsky, Sheldon et al., 2005). For example, a sociable person may find it more rewarding to perform acts of kindness and to deepen social bonds than to engage in a more solitary activity such as writing about her positive traits.

Social Support

Positive psychology interventions may bring more success when a person has a supportive social network. Social support is valuable in a number of ways. Close others can provide ongoing encouragement and confidence-building, particularly during trying times or when the initial motivation or excitement has waned. They can be a source of inspiration for positive psychology activities (e.g., being recipients of gratitude letters). Finally, friends and family can give feedback and substantive advice regarding one's progress towards greater well-being.

Depression Status

Depression status has been shown to moderate the efficacy of positive psychology interventions, such that depressed individuals generally experience more improvement in well-being and greater reductions in depressive symptoms relative to non-depressed ones (Sin & Lyubomirsky, 2009). However, this finding is confounded with treatment format; studies that use clinically depressed participants tend to treat them with individual or group therapies (which offer attention and guidance from a clinician) rather than self-administered interventions. To our knowledge, studies have not compared the efficacy of self-administered positive interventions in depressed versus non-depressed samples.

AN EXPERIMENTAL LONGITUDINAL INTERVENTION WITH DYSPHORIC INDIVIDUALS: PRELIMINARY EVIDENCE

Background

The majority of positive psychology interventions, such as writing letters of gratitude or writing about one's best possible selves, have been tested using non-clinical participants. Although it is plausible to extrapolate from the extant research by presuming that positive activities should also benefit individuals "deficient" in well-being, emerging evidence suggests that this is not necessarily the case. For example, a recent study revealed that the rehearsal of positive self-statements such as "I'm a lovable person" – a technique commonly advocated by therapists, self-help books, and Senator Al Franken's parody via the persona of Stuart Smalley – can backfire for those with low self-esteem (Wood, Perunovic, & Lee, 2009). Whereas individuals with high self-esteem experienced a lift in their moods after repeating positive self-statements, those with low-self esteem felt worse. The authors of this study speculated that this exercise may highlight the discrepancy between the positive statements and one's own views. Similarly, it is possible that other previously validated positive activities may have null or even detrimental effects on the well-being of some individuals.

To test whether a well-documented positive activity such as writing letters of gratitude would engender a sustained increase in happiness in a dysphoric (non-clinically depressed) sample, we conducted an eight-week randomized experimental longitudinal study. This study was motivated by the following research questions: (1) Will the regular practice of an effortful, positive activity (compared to a neutral placebo activity) boost the well-being of dysphoric participants? and (2) How much does "expected efficacy" (i.e., expecting a particular activity to make you happier or not) impact the benefits derived from it? In addition, we tested several moderators to evaluate the boundary conditions that influence the efficacy of engaging in a gratitude or placebo activity: (1) social support; (2) person–activity "fit"; and (3) beliefs about the pursuit of happiness.

Method and Procedure

Fifty-eight undergraduate psychology students were randomly assigned to perform one of two activities: a happiness-boosting activity (writing a gratitude letter) or a placebo activity (listening to and writing about classical music). Furthermore, participants' expected efficacy of these activities was manipulated by presenting them with bogus *New York Times*™ articles claiming that the activity either has or has not been found to increase well-being. Participants were also presented with fake weekly poll results, leading them to believe that the majority of participants in an ongoing study rated the activity as making them happier or not making them happier. Thus, the four experimental conditions were gratitude/high expectation ($n = 14$), gratitude/low expectation ($n = 17$), placebo/high expectation ($n = 14$), and placebo/low expectation ($n = 13$).

Students were instructed to log on to the study web site once a week for four weeks to complete a 15-minute writing exercise. In the *gratitude* conditions, students were asked to write a letter of gratitude to someone who has affected their lives but whom they never properly thanked. They were allowed to write to the same person or a new person each week; actual delivery of the gratitude letter was not encouraged. In the *placebo* conditions, students were instructed to listen to classical music (streaming on the website) and write about the shapes, colors, and other elements that the music brought to mind. We chose songs that have previously been shown to have no positive or negative effects on mood (Gerrards-Hesse, Spies, & Hesse, 1994). Although the activity was of a neutral valence, participants who expected the activity to make them happier were expected to show a "placebo effect."

Measures

The participants were considered dysphoric, as determined by scores on the Beck Depression Inventory II (with the average score being 16.67, indicating mild depression; Beck, Steer, & Brown, 1996). Before the intervention began, we assessed participants' *social support* using the Provisions of Social Relations Scale (Turner, Frankel, & Levin, 1983). On this 15-item measure, participants indicated the extent to which they felt supported by family and friends. *Person–activity "fit"* was measured by having participants rate the extent to which the two activities (expressing gratitude and listening to classical music) were natural and enjoyable. Finally, we assessed participants' beliefs about the *pursuit of happiness* – their desire and willingness to become happier – using the Pursuit of Happiness Scale (Lyubomirsky, 2000). Sample items included "How desirable is happiness for you?" and "How much do you actively pursue happiness?"

Immediately pre-intervention, immediately post-intervention, and three weeks post-intervention, participants completed the following measures of well-being: the Satisfaction With Life Scale (Diener, Emmons, Larsen, & Griffin, 1985), the Subjective Happiness Scale (Lyubomirsky & Lepper, 1999), and the positive affect items of the Positive Affect Negative Affect Schedule – Revised (Watson & Clark, 1999).

Results and Discussion

Our findings were unexpected, in that the practice of gratitude actually *diminished* the well-being of dysphoric participants from before to immediately after the intervention. Our speculation is that dysphoric individuals may have experienced the exercise of writing a gratitude letter to someone that they "have never properly thanked" as a frustrating and difficult charge. Indeed, not surprisingly, perceiving a task to be difficult can engender negative affect (Winkielman & Cacioppo, 2001; Winkielman & Schwarz, 2001). Alternately, writing the gratitude letter may have backfired if it led our dysphoric participants to think that they had little for which to be grateful. With depressive thoughts and emotions constantly in the way, dysphoric individuals may have had trouble completing the gratitude task and may have come to believe that they were "failing" at it.

Interestingly, however, by the three-week follow-up assessment, those participants who expressed gratitude *and* expected to benefit from this practice evidenced a marginal *increase* in well-being. In contrast, our participants who practiced gratitude but did *not* expect to become happier reported decreases in well-being immediately following the intervention that were sustained at the three-week follow-up. This finding suggests that this latter group experienced the negative effects of both the exasperating gratitude activity and the lack of expectation for a payoff. The challenging nature of writing gratitude letters appears to have been exacerbated by having low expectations for an eventual benefit.

In contrast, our participants who listened to classical music (but had low expectations that this would make them happier) reported an *increase* in well-being during the intervention. We conjecture that this so-called "placebo" condition may have functioned as a distraction condition. Although our participants did not expect the placebo activity to "work," prior research indicates that dysphoric individuals who are distracted in a laboratory setting report temporary decreases in depressive symptoms (Lyubomirsky & Nolen-Hoeksema, 1995; Nolen-Hoeksema, Wisco, Lyubomirsky, 2008). Also, the reported increases in well-being by those who completed the placebo activity without expecting to become happier could have occurred because these participants engaged in the music exercise without the burden of trying to increase their well-being. Therefore, contrary to our expectations, the condition that turned out to be most optimal for experiencing gains in well-being for our dysphoric participants was one that they perceived to be relatively easy and that did not burden them with the expectation to become happier.

Moderator analyses further revealed that several factors impacted the efficacy of the intervention. First, not surprisingly, participants who had a high level of social support *and* a high expectation to become happier reported an increase in well-being immediately after the intervention, relative to participants who had a low expectation to become happier. Second, person–activity "fit" was important for participants in the placebo condition, such that a good fit was associated with greater increases in well-being. A perceived match between the assigned activity and participants' motives, traits, and inclinations could have facilitated their progress towards becoming happier. However, due to the challenging nature of the gratitude activity (compared to the placebo exercise) for the dysphoric participants, fit with the placebo activity may have been more beneficial than fit with writing a letter of gratitude. Finally, strong beliefs about the pursuit and desirability of happiness were found to moderate the efficacy of the placebo activity. Again, the challenging nature of the gratitude activity may have exacerbated the negative emotions of our dysphoric participants, despite a reported willingness to pursue happiness. Individuals who believed in the importance and desirability of the pursuit of happiness and who engaged in the placebo activity (i.e., listening to classical music) did not experience the frustrations and difficulties shared by those prompted to write gratitude letters and were thus presumably in a better position to garner the well-being benefits from the exercise.

Conclusions

Contrary to prior research demonstrating the well-being benefits of writing gratitude letters (Emmons & McCullough, 2003; Lyubomirsky et al., in press; Seligman et al., 2005; Watkins, Woodward, Stone, & Kolts, 2003), our study showed that expressing gratitude may be a difficult and counterproductive exercise for dysphoric individuals. On the other hand, a relatively easier neutral activity – listening to and writing about classical music – produced a temporary boost in well-being for those who expected the activity to make them happier, perhaps because it served as a distraction from ruminative thoughts. High levels of social support, person–activity "fit," and desire to pursue happiness contributed to enhanced well-being for participants who engaged in the neutral activity. The findings suggest that some positive psychology interventions (such as writing gratitude letters) may be burdensome and ineffective for depressed or dysphoric individuals, even if they have a supportive social network, feel that they "match" with the activity, and are motivated to become happier. Although the practice of grateful thinking appears to have limitations with respect to the treatment of dysphoric individuals, future research should explore how this activity and other positive psychology interventions can be tailored to meet the needs, preferences, styles, and resources of clients with depressive symptoms.

FINAL REMARKS

By pushing for greater emphasis on well-being, the field of positive psychology has challenged the conventional notion that mental health is equivalent to the absence of disorder (Fava & Ruini, 2003; Ryff, 1989). The prevalence of Major Depressive Disorder, as well as subclinical depression, speaks to the need for novel treatments that are effective, accessible, easily administered, individually tailored, and protective against future recurrence of depression. Growing research shows that positive psychology interventions – that is, experimental studies testing treatment programs and activities that primarily aim to cultivate positive emotions and personal strengths, rather than only fixing negatives – have been successful in reducing depressive symptoms and enhancing well-being. However, these interventions are not one-size-fits-all. Our preliminary study suggests that not all previous findings from happiness interventions with healthy individuals will generalize to depressed or dysphoric samples, because the motivational, affective, and cognitive deficits characteristic of depression can limit or even reverse the beneficial effects of effortful happiness-promoting activities. We encourage researchers and clinicians to consider the role of expectations and other moderating factors (such as social support, person–activity "fit," and beliefs about the pursuit of happiness) when administering positive psychology treatments for individuals with depression.

Interventions that build on the positives in people's lives show great promise for enhancing well-being, whether it be for making euthymic individuals happier or as a complement to traditional treatments for depression.

REFERENCES

Abramson, L. Y., Seligman, M. E. P., & Teasdale, J. D. (1978). Learned helplessness in humans: Critique and reformulation. *Journal of Abnormal Psychology, 87*, 49–74.

Baskin, T. W., & Enright, R. D. (2004). Intervention studies on forgiveness: A meta-analysis. *Journal of Counseling and Development, 82*, 79–90.

Beck, A. T., Steer, R. A., & Brown, G. K. (1996). *Manual for the Beck Depression Inventory – II*. San Antonio, TX: Psychological Corporation.

Bédard, M., Felteau, M., Mazmanian, D., Fedyk, K., Klein, R., Richardson, J., et al. (2003). Pilot evaluation of a mindfulness-based intervention to improve quality of life among individuals who sustained traumatic brain injuries. *Disability and Rehabilitation, 25*, 722–731.

Burton, C. M., & King, L. A. (2008). Effects of (very) brief writing on health: The two-minute miracle. *British Journal of Health Psychology, 13*, 9–14.

Cavanagh, K., & Shapiro, D. A. (2004). Computer treatment for common mental health problems. *Journal of Clinical Psychology, 60*, 239–251.

Cheavens, J. S., Feldman, D. B., Gum, A., Michael, S. T., & Snyder, C. R. (2006). Hope therapy in a community sample: A pilot investigation. *Social Indicators Research, 77*, 61–78.

Diener, E. (1984). Subjective well-being. *Psychological Bulletin, 95*, 542–575.

Diener, E., Emmons, R. A., Larsen, R. J., & Griffin, S. (1985). The Satisfaction With Life Scale. *Journal of Personality Assessment, 49*, 71–75.

Dunn, E. W., Aknin, L. B., & Norton, M. I. (2008). Spending money on others promotes happiness. *Science, 319*, 1687–1688.

Eisendrath, S. J., Delucchi, K., Bitner, R., Fenimore, P., Smit, M., & McLane, M. (2008). Mindfulness-based cognitive therapy for treatment-resistant depression: A pilot study. *Psychotherapy and Psychosomatics, 77*, 319–320.

Elkin, I., Shea, M. T., Watkins, J. T., Imber, S. D., Sotsky, S. M., Collins, J. F., et al. (1989). National Institute of Mental Health Treatment of Depression Collaborative Research Program: General effectiveness of treatments. *Archives of General Psychiatry, 46*, 971–982.

Emmons, R. A., & McCullough, M. E. (2003). Counting blessings versus burdens: An experimental investigation of gratitude and subjective well-being in daily life. *Journal of Personality and Social Psychology, 84*, 377–389.

Fava, G. A., Rafanelli, C., Cazzaro, M., Conti, S., & Grandi, S. (1998). Well-being therapy: A novel psychotherapeutic model for residual symptoms of affective disorders. *Psychological Medicine, 28*, 475–480.

Fava, G. A., & Ruini, C. (2003). Development and characteristics of a well-being enhancing psychotherapeutic strategy: Well-being therapy. *Journal of Behavior Therapy and Experimental Psychiatry, 34*, 45–63.

Fordyce, M. W. (1977). Development of a program to increase personal happiness. *Journal of Counseling Psychology, 24*, 511–521.

Fordyce, M. W. (1983). A program to increase happiness: Further studies. *Journal of Counseling Psychology, 30*, 483–498.

Fredrickson, B. L. (2001). The role of positive emotions in positive psychology: The broaden-and-build theory of positive emotions. *American Psychologist*, 56, 218–226.

Fredrickson, B. L., Cohn, M. A., Coffey, K. A., Pek, J., & Finkel, S. M. (2008). Open hearts build lives: Positive emotions, induced through loving-kindness meditation, build consequential personal resources. *Journal of Personality and Social Psychology*, 95, 1045–1062.

Fredrickson, B. L., & Joiner, T. (2002). Positive emotions trigger upward spirals toward emotional well-being. *Psychological Science*, 13, 172–175.

Fredrickson, B. L., & Levenson, R. W. (1998). Positive emotions speed recovery from the cardiovascular sequelae of negative emotions. *Cognition and Emotion*, 12, 191–220.

Froh, J. J., Sefick, W. J., & Emmons, R. A. (2008). Counting blessings in early adolescents: An experimental study of gratitude and subjective well-being. *Journal of School Psychology*, 46, 213–233.

Gasper, K., & Clore, G. L. (2002). Attending to the big picture: Mood and global versus local processing of visual information. *Psychological Science*, 13, 34–40.

Gerrards-Hesse, A., Spies, K., & Hesse, F. W. (1994). Experimental inductions of emotional states and their effectiveness: A review. *British Journal of Psychology*, 85, 55–78.

Grossman, P., Niemann, L., Schmidt, S., & Walach, H. (2004). Mindfulness-based stress reduction and health benefits: A meta-analysis. *Journal of Psychosomatic Research*, 57, 35–43.

Grossman, P., Tiefenthaler-Gilmer, U., Raysz, A., & Kesper, U. (2007). Mindfulness training as an intervention for fibromyalgia: Evidence of postintervention and 3-year follow-up benefits in well-being. *Psychotherapy and Psychosomatics*, 76, 226–233.

Kabat-Zinn, J. (1990). *Full catastrophe living: Using the wisdom of your body and mind to face stress, pain and illness*. New York: Delacourt.

Kasch, K. L., Rottenberg, J., Arnow, B. A., & Gotlib, I. H. (2002). Behavioral activation and inhibition systems and the severity and course of depression. *Journal of Abnormal Psychology*, 111, 589–597.

King, L. A. (2001). The health benefits of writing about life goals. *Personality and Social Psychology Bulletin*, 27, 798–807.

Kuyken, W., Byford, S., Taylor, R. S., Watkins, E., Holden, E., White, K., et al. (2008). Mindfulness-based cognitive therapy to prevent relapse in recurrent depression. *Journal of Counseling and Clinical Psychology*, 76, 966–978.

Lyubomirsky, S. (2000, October). *In the pursuit of happiness: Comparing the United States and Russia*. Paper presented at the Annual Meeting of the Society for Experimental Psychology, Atlanta, GA.

Lyubomirsky, S. (2008). *The how of happiness: A scientific approach to getting the life you want*. New York: Penguin Press.

Lyubomirsky, S., Dickerhoof, R., Boehm, J. K., & Sheldon, K. M. (in press). Becoming happier takes both a will and a proper way: An experimental longitudinal intervention to boost well-being. *Emotion*.

Lyubomirsky, S., King, L. A., & Diener, E. (2005). The benefits of frequent positive affect: Does happiness lead to success? *Psychological Bulletin*, 131, 803–855.

Lyubomirsky, S., & Lepper, H. S. (1999). A measure of subjective happiness: Preliminary reliability and construct validation. *Social Indicators Research*, 46, 137–155.

Lyubomirsky, S., & Nolen-Hoeksema, S. (1995). Effects of self-focused rumination on negative thinking and interpersonal problem-solving. *Journal of Personality and Social Psychology*, 69, 176–190.

Lyubomirsky, S., Sheldon, K. M., & Schkade, D. (2005). Pursuing happiness: The architecture of sustainable change. *Review of General Psychology*, 9, 111–131.

Narrow, W. E., Rae, D. S., Robins, L. N., & Regier, D. A. (2002). Revised prevalence estimates of mental disorders in the United States: Using a clinical significance criterion to reconcile 2 surveys' estimates. *Archives of General Psychiatry, 59*, 115–123.

Nolen-Hoeksema, S., Wisco, B. E., & Lyubomirsky, S. (2008). Rethinking rumination. *Perspectives on Psychological Science, 3*, 400–424.

Otake, K., Shimai, S., Tanaka-Matsumi, J. Otsui, K., & Fredrickson, B. L. (2006). Happy people become happier through kindness: A counting kindness intervention. *Journal of Happiness Studies, 7*, 361–375.

Proudfoot, J., Goldberg, D., Mann, A., Everitt, B., Marks, I., & Gray, J. A. (2003). Computerized, interactive, multimedia cognitive-behavioural program for anxiety and depression in general practice. *Psychological Medicine, 33*, 217–227.

Ramel, W., Goldin, P. R., Carmona, P. E., & McQuaid, J. R. (2004). The effects of mindfulness meditation on cognitive processes and affect in patients with past depression. *Cognitive Therapy and Research, 28*, 433–455.

Ryan, R. M., & Deci, E. L. (2001). On happiness and human potentials: A review of research on hedonic and eudaimonic well-being. *Annual Review of Psychology, 52*, 141–166.

Ryff, C. D. (1989). Happiness is everything, or is it? Explorations on the meaning of psychological well-being. *Journal of Personality and Social Psychology, 57*, 1069–1081.

Seligman, M. E. P., Rashid, T., & Parks, A. C. (2006). Positive psychotherapy. *American Psychologist, 61*, 774–788.

Seligman, M. E. P., Steen, T. A., Park, N., & Peterson, C. (2005). Positive psychology progress: Empirical validation of interventions. *American Psychologist, 60*, 410–421.

Sheldon, K. M., Boehm, J. K., & Lyubomirsky, S. (in press). Variety is the spice of happiness: The hedonic adaptation prevention (HAP) model. In I. Boniwell & S. David (Eds.), *Oxford Handbook of Happiness*. Oxford: Oxford University Press.

Sheldon, K. M., & Lyubomirsky, S. (2006). How to increase and sustain positive emotion: The effects of expressing gratitude and visualizing best possible selves. *Journal of Positive Psychology, 1*, 73–82.

Sin, N. L., & Lyubomirsky, S. (2009). Enhancing well-being and alleviating depressive symptoms with positive psychology interventions: A practice-friendly meta-analysis. *Journal of Clinical Psychology: In Session, 65*, 467–487.

Smith, M. L., &. Glass, G. V. (1977). Meta-analysis of psychotherapy outcome studies. *American Psychologist, 32*, 752–760.

Snyder, C. R., Harris, C., Anderson, J. R., Holleran, S. A., Irving, L. M., Sigmon, S. T., et al. (1991). The will and the ways: Development and validation of an individual-differences measure of hope. *Journal of Personality and Social Psychology, 60*, 570–585.

Surawy, C., Roberts, J., & Silver, A. (2005). The effect of mindfulness training on mood and measures of fatigue, activity, and quality of life in patients with chronic fatigue syndrome on a hospital waiting list: A series of exploratory studies. *Behavioural and Cognitive Psychotherapy, 33*, 103–109.

Tugade, M. M., & Fredrickson, B. L. (2004). Resilient individuals use positive emotions to bounce back from negative emotional experiences. *Journal of Personality and Social Psychology, 86*, 320–333.

Turner, R. J., Frankel, B. G., & Levin, D. M. (1983). Social support: Conceptualization, measurement, and implications for mental health. *Research in Community and Mental Health, 3*, 67–111.

Wang, P. S., Simon, G., & Kessler, R. C. (2003). The economic burden of depression and the cost-effectiveness of treatment. *International Journal of Methods in Psychiatric Research, 12*, 22–33.

Watkins, P. C., Woodward, K., Stone, T., & Kolts, R. L. (2003). Gratitude and happiness: Development of a measure of gratitude and relationships with subjective well-being. *Social Behavior and Personality*, *31*, 431–452.

Watson, D., & Clark, L. A. (1999). *The PANAS-X: Manual for the Positive and Negative Affect Schedule – Expanded Form*. Retrieved February 21, 2008, from http://www.psychology.uiowa.edu/faculty/Clark/PANAS-X.pdf

Watson, D., & Tellegen, A. (1985). Toward a consensual structure of mood. *Psychological Bulletin*, *98*, 219–235.

Winkielman, P., & Cacioppo, J. T. (2001). Mind at ease puts a smile on the face: Psychophysiological evidence that processing facilitation elicits positive affect. *Journal of Personality and Social Psychology*, *81*, 989–1000.

Winkielman, P., & Schwarz, N. (2001). How pleasant was your childhood? Beliefs about memory shape inferences from experienced difficulty of recall. *Psychological Science*, *12*, 176–179.

Wood, J. V., Perunovic, W. Q. E., & Lee, J. W. (2009). Positive self-statements: Power for some, peril for others. *Psychological Science*, *20*, 860–866.

Young, A. S., Klap, R., Sherbourne, C. D., & Wells, K. B. (2001). The quality of care for depressive and anxiety disorders in the United States. *Archives of General Psychiatry*, *58*, 55–61.

Zautra, A. J., Davis, M. C., Reich, J. W., Nicassario, P., Tennen, H., Finan, P., et al. (2008). Comparison of cognitive behavioral and mindfulness meditation interventions on adaptation to rheumatoid arthritis for patients with and without history of recurrent depression. *Journal of Consulting and Clinical Psychology*, *76*, 408–421.

7

Education in 2025: How Positive Psychology can Revitalize Education

HANS HENRIK KNOOP

> In my opinion, any prediction of the future beyond a 5-year horizon has to be extremely qualified – to be taken more as a stimulus to one's imagination than as a statement of actual expected outcomes. That being said, there can be little doubt that education will have to change very soon – or all of us are going to be in deep trouble.
>
> (Csikszentmihalyi, 2009)

A RAPIDLY APPROACHING FUTURE

*B*eing invited to write about basic concepts regarding the application of positive psychology in education it is hardly appropriate to do so without a perspective on the deeper future, in which any educational effort is ultimately tested. The children beginning school this year are being prepared for a future that may well extend into the 22nd century. We have few qualified ideas about what will happen then, apart from those provided by informed imagination. Technological evolution is happening faster and faster, at a rate that leaves out any hope of a complete overview for individuals – indeed, even the rate itself is accelerating (Kurzweil, 2006). If it ever were, cultural evolution is clearly no longer entirely in the hands of humans, let alone in the hands of educators. For all we know, evolution, be it driven by biology, culture, or autonomous technology, contains its own inclination towards propagation.

From this perspective, formal education in the future may not play quite the role in people's lives as originally conceived of by those who designed it – including us, now, as we speak of the future. For even though the business of education is obviously also about propagating ideas, carefully selected by decision-makers ranging from politicians to teachers, the current level of adaptability in formal education in many places of the world is simply too slow to predict its viability in future contexts. Already today, any Internet-savvy learner (and who isn't potentially?) is able to self-educate by watching and reading thousands of world-class lectures on the Internet, or by watching easy-to-understand representations of even the most difficult academic subjects in excellent multimedia popularized formats. Moreover, there are rich possibilities to do so jointly with others using advanced social software – ranging from the more formal such as Google Scholar, Wikipedia, and TED Conferences, to more informal applications such as Facebook, Flickr, and Youtube. And, to be sure, there are already lots of hybrid forms, springing from the human inclination for social learning. Any fairly normal child intuitively seems to grasp the logic of these new forms of digitalized media, and though we should certainly not be blind to their potential shortcomings, as educators we need to recognize how much a child is able to learn in a very short timespan when the learning environment fully employs new technology. Clearly, quite soon something quite drastic has to happen in mainstream formal education around the world – not in disrespect, but with respect for education, which continues to be our most important lever for realizing the ideal of having free and enlightened citizens on Planet Earth. Certainly, education should continue to honor the best academic and cultural traditions, but there is little hope for that without radical improvements of standard educational practice.

THE NECESSITY OF QUALIFIED PREDICTION

Boldly spoken, however, regardless of the difficulty in predicting the future, educa-tion will not make much sense without convincing ideas of what will be needed when the next generation takes over. Moreover, and more generally, without predictions guiding our awareness and choices, we are assured of a future emerging more or less randomly. With the weaponry in our hands today, that future is not likely to be a long one, at least not for humans (e.g., Joy, 2000; Rees, 2003).

A more humble reason to attempt educational prediction of the future is to avoid repeating some of the mistakes that mainstream education has suffered up until now, maybe most notably the pedagogically catastrophic twin assumptions that children are born more or less the same (as blank slates) and that children have to be forced to learn (by an outer authority) in order to learn effectively. These assumptions sat well with the 19th century industrial model of mass schooling, but there is now overwhelming scientific evidence that they run completely contrary to human nature and that the mere prevalence of these assumptions is enough to predict long-term failure of any educational system – or, more precisely, guarantee non-optimal functioning, performance, learning, and well-being. Today, geneticists, neuroscientists, and psychologists are united in recognizing individuals as just *that*, autonomous entities with capacities and preferences for learning specific content in specific ways. Furthermore, it is now clear that, like all other living organisms, humans evolved through and for *self-organization, deep interaction with the environment*, and are thus optimized for *active learning and creativity*. In the words of Ryan and Deci (2000, p. 68):

> . . . three innate psychological needs have crystallized through scientific studies of motivation: competence, autonomy, and relatedness – all of which, when

satisfied yield enhanced self-motivation and mental health and when thwarted
lead to diminished motivation and well-being.

The individuals responsible for designing the industry-model school system that
persists around the globe cannot have understood much of what indeed they created
– for had they known, they would not have done so: Everyone loses by inefficient
education (except the competitors of course), and institutions that pacify, standardize,
and alienate people are squarely counterproductive to any viable democracy.

As is usually the case with evolution, the problem may solve itself one way or
the other. Obviously, no society can survive based on an educational system that is
not competitive, that is, an educational system that does not promote the well-
being of learners and teachers, and thus learning, creativity, and social responsibility. In what follows we shall therefore take a closer look at education, with
particular focus on schools, which in many societies are the only institutions left
where, at least potentially, all citizens meet and share experiences for a few years.

WHAT IS A COMPETITIVE SCHOOL?

The fitness of any society depends on the quality of its institutions. This may sound
somewhat tautological, as society is often defined by its institutions. But because
we face a global lack of trust in institutions, the issue is acutely important (Gallup,
2002; GFK, 2003; GlobeScan, 2005; World Economic Forum, 2007). Bad schools
will promote dysfunctional societies, both in the short and the long term.
Competitive schools further competitive societies. What then, specifically, defines
a competitive school? Is it a school that can compete with the neighboring school?
Is it a school that tops the ranking charts, when half of all schools, by definition, will
rank below average at any time? Is it a school aimed at beating neighboring countries? Or is it just the best place in the local community for learners to learn what
is really important to learn? In the view of this author, we are far best served by the
last alternative. And it will be quite easy to evaluate whether a school is actually
such a place: by simply asking teachers and learners, listening to their words, and
taking them seriously at all levels of educational government.

Up until now psychology does not appear to have played much of a role in the
design of societies or institutions – apart from what may have been privately intended
by those in power. For a variety of reasons "mass sciences" such as economics, political science, law, and sociology (where individual differences are blotted out conceptually and statistically) have been the primary sources of reference for decision-makers
– sometimes with quite serious consequences, such as the factory-like classrooms
or the dull office landscapes for knowledge workers where many find it difficult to
concentrate, not the least when working with more complex content.

With these broader contextual observations in mind, the following is a
condensed version of some of the strongest evidence-based issues for schools and
education that have emerged from positive psychology and related fields of inquiry.
For the sake of overview and perspective, the text is stipulating two learning
scenarios – in 2010 and 2025, respectively – and is consequently organized in two

parts: how a good school in the future will be, in many ways, the same as a good school today; and how, in many ways, it will be a radically different school.

FIFTEEN HYPOTHESES ABOUT HOW LEARNING WILL BE MUCH THE SAME IN 2025 AS IT IS NOW

In 15 years – in 2025 – we probably have not yet changed significantly as a biological species, despite the prevalence of genetic therapies, cloning, implanted artificial intelligence, and other advanced medical technology on the market. Thus, at least biologically, we may expect to function in pretty much the same way as we do today. This gives educators a set of processual reference points quite congruent to what they are today if educational success is to be obtained. Based on this assumption, one might thus predict the hypotheses below, all derived from positive psychology and related disciplines. Although for obvious reasons these hypotheses cannot be tested before 2025, the evidence we have now suggests that they are likely to be confirmed.

The model presented in Figure 7.1 indicates the simple mechanism underlying these predictions. In each hypothesis, we expect that *if some specific beneficial event is present in the learning environment of the school, learners are likely to learn more, they will tend to be inclined to learn more, and they will tend to be more inclined to contribute to the greater good.* This extension is justified by three well-known psychological insights: (1) If something feels good (i.e., if a person experiences positive emotions, engagement, and meaning), people are likely to learn better (e.g., Fredrickson, 2009); (2) if something feels good (in this case, the content of each hypothesis), people are likely to want more of it because they will expect greater utility thereby (e.g., Bransford, Brown, & Cocking, 1999; Kahneman, 2008); (3) if a person thrives in a given setting, the setting will be interpreted as benign by

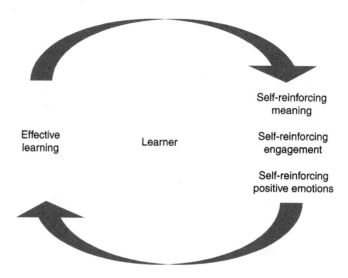

Effective learning

Learner

Self-reinforcing meaning

Self-reinforcing engagement

Self-reinforcing positive emotions

FIGURE 7.1   How good comes from good in education (Knoop, 2008).

the person, who will in turn be likely to exert prosocial reciprocity, that is, care more for the structure and functioning of the particular setting, as well as for the social structure and the environment that supports it (e.g., Hauser, 2006; Pinker, 2002).

Bearing in mind these introductory remarks, the hypotheses are as follows:[1]

(1) The more *physically and mentally healthy* learners are, the more they will learn, the more inclined they will be to learn further, and the more inclined they will be to contribute to the greater good (e.g., Baumeister, 2005; Bloom & Nelson, 2001; Fredrickson, 2009; Institute of Medicine (U.S.), 2001).

(2) The more *autonomy and control over their own situation* that learners experience while learning, the more they will learn, the more inclined they will be to learn further, and the more inclined they will be to contribute to the greater good (e.g., Camazine, Deneubourg, Franks, Sneyd, Theraulaz, & Bonabeau, 2001; Csikszentmihalyi, 1993, 1996; Deci & Ryan, 2000; Kauffman, 2000; Pinker, 1997, 2002; Ryan & Deci, 2000).

(3) The better *role models for learning and creativity* that teachers are (i.e., the more curious, innovative, socially caring, and technically skilled teachers are), the more learners will learn, the more inclined they will be to learn further, and the more inclined they will be to contribute to the greater good (e.g., Allen, Witt, & Wheeless, 2006; Bandura, 1989; Lyhne & Knoop, 2008).

(4) The more *intrinsically motivated* learners are (i.e., the more they *enjoy learning*), the more they will learn, the more inclined they will be to learn further, and the more inclined they will be to contribute to the greater good (e.g., Anderson, Manoogian & Reznick, 1976; Csikszentmihalyi, Abuhamdeh, & Nakamura, 2005; Csikszentmihalyi & Rathunde, 1993; Deci & Ryan, 1991; Fredrickson, 2009; Harter, 1978; Knoop & Lyhne, 2005; Ryan, 1995; Sheldon, Ryan, Rawsthorne, & Ilardi, 1997; Shernoff & Hoogstra, 2001).

(5) The more *positivity* – specifically joy, gratitude, serenity, interest, hope, pride, amusement, inspiration, awe, and love – learners experience in their lives, the more they will learn, the more inclined they will be to learn further, and the more inclined they will be to contribute to the greater good (e.g., Csikszentmihalyi, 1990; Damasio, 2000; Fredrickson, 1998, 2001, 2009; Fredrickson & Losada, 2005; Myers, 1993; Seligman, 2002).

(6) The more of an *attractive future* learners see for themselves, the more they will learn, the more inclined they will be to learn further, and the more inclined they will be to contribute to the greater good (e.g., Frankl, 1985; Massimini & Delle Fave, 1991; Schmuck & Sheldon, 2001; Senge, 1990; Senge, Kleiner, Roberts, Ross, & Smith, 1994; Wilson, 2002; Wong & Fry, 1998).

(7) The better the teaching matches the *intellectual strengths* (talents/ intelligences) of learners, the more they will learn, the more inclined they will be to learn further, and the more inclined they will be to contribute to the greater good (e.g., Gardner, 1999, 2000; Linley, 2008; Nakamura, 1988; Rathunde, 1992, 1996).

(8) The better the teaching matches the *character strengths* of learners, the more they will learn, the more inclined they will be for further learning,

and the more inclined they will be to contribute to the greater good. (e.g., Linley, 2008; Peterson, 2006; Peterson & Seligman, 2004).

(9) The better the teaching matches the *preferred styles* of learners, the more they will learn, the more inclined they will be for further learning, and the more inclined they will be to contribute to the greater good (e.g., Dunn & Dunn, 2005, 2008; Grigorenko, Jarvin, & Sternberg, 2002; Kolb, 1984).

(10) The more *aesthetically rich and sense stimulating* the learning environment is, the more learners will learn, the more inclined they will be for further learning, and the more inclined they will be to contribute to the greater good (e.g., Kahneman, 2008; Knoop, 2002; Pinker, 2009; Wright, 2001).

(11) The more teaching and learning resemble a *journey of discovery* in which the individual learner plays the main character, the more learners will learn, the more inclined they will be for further learning, and the more inclined they will be to contribute to the greater good (e.g., Chaisson, 2001; Gopnik, Meltzoff, & Kuhl, 2001; Kashdan, 2009; Wright, Pinker, & Seligman, 2002).

(12) The more *creative* learners are allowed to be, the more they will learn, the more inclined they will be for further learning, and the more inclined they will be to contribute to the greater good (e.g., Amabile, 1996; Csikszentmihalyi & Knoop, 2008; Dingfelder, 2003; Robinson, 2001, 2009; Runco, 2004).

(13) The more *authentically, socially connected* learners are, the more they will learn, the more inclined they will be for further learning, and the more inclined they will be to contribute to the greater good (e.g., Bandura, 1986, 1989, 1997; Bowlby, 1979; Seligman, 2002; Zimbardo, 2007).

(14) The more learners experience a *combination of being socially differentiated, unique individuals (who are thus potentially interesting to others) and socially integrated/authentically connected members of a community (which thereby can function)*, the more they will learn, the more inclined they will be for further learning, and the more inclined they will be to contribute to the greater good (e.g., Brown, 1991; Csikszentmihalyi, 1993; Csikszentmihalyi & Knoop, 2008; Knoop, 2005, 2007a, 2007b; Wilson, 1998; Wright, 2001).

(15) The more learners experience a *combination of positive support and positive challenge*, the more they will learn, the more inclined they will be to learn further, and the more inclined they will be to contribute to the greater good (e.g., Bowlby, 1979; Damon, 2003; Elliot & Dweck, 2005).

A developmentally organized connection between these processual ideals is indirectly illustrated in the model presented in Figure 7.2, where the lower principles regarding universal tendencies are general occurrences in nature, and thus relevant beyond human life, while the upper principles regarding democracy are almost exclusively relevant for humans only. The principles between these extremes are ordered according to increasing degree of "cultivation," that is, increasing degree of *intentional* human involvement. Thus, the model attempts to sum up the main processual principles for a good school, and for activity more broadly, now and in the future.

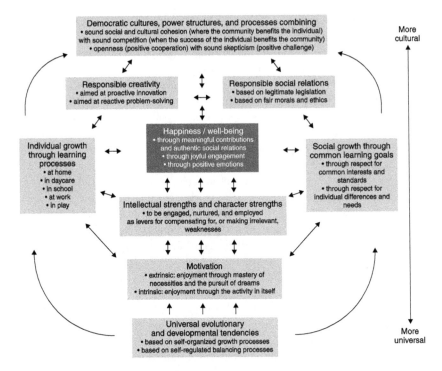

FIGURE 7.2   General, processual ideals that predict academic and social success across political spectra, disciplines, and personal aspirations (Knoop, 2008).

From this conceptual platform and status, anno 2010, it becomes possible to look forward to the new possibilities and new risks that are likely to confront education in the year 2025, and that would be highly unwise to ignore.

THIRTEEN SCENARIOS ABOUT WHAT WILL BE VERY DIFFERENT IN 2025

(1) In 2025, there will be a great many new ways to improve *physical and mental health*. It will be possible to acquire quite exact individualized information about what one's specific body needs are in order to be in optimal balance and form, and it will be possible to get specific treatment for a number of mental illnesses that we do not yet understand in 2010 and that hinder learning and well-being for many – ranging from attentional difficulties and depression to schizophrenia. These new opportunities may in principle benefit all, but there is a risk that they will primarily unfold in the hands of the most affluent, in which case social inequality and tension will increase. Moreover, we can expect considerable ethical challenges in relation to new life-prolonging, intelligence-improving and

happiness-inducing technologies and *smart drugs*, all of which probably will not be equally accessible either.

(2) Based on a far better understanding of individual learners' strengths, in 2025 it will be much easier than in 2010 to teach precisely enough to accommodate learners' need for *autonomy and control* over their situation in school. However, this potential increase in personal control has to be viewed in the light of globalization of technology, transport, and information, which in 2025 will imply that learners are even more directly exposed to a potentially overwhelming technological world in which they may also feel themselves more powerless than earlier generations. More specifically, there will be huge ethical challenges connected to being first-hand witness to so many of the world's biggest problems and, to some extent, being forced to distance/desensitize themselves to avoid being overwhelmed by feelings of grief, guilt, and the like.

(3) As in 2010, teachers in 2025 will be curious, innovative, socially caring, and technically skilled – and thus be good *role models* for learning and creativity. However, the general access to virtual content of very high quality forces the teacher, far more than in 2010, to act as a *leader of a social organization* rather than just as a traditional conveyer of knowledge through standard methods. This represents a considerable educational challenge when, increasingly, educational content is downloaded from international data-bases that are not under political and administrative control.

(4) Schools in 2025 will be organized to accommodate a very high degree of learner *enjoyment through learning*, not least because it will be necessary in order to remain attractive to learners and parents, who will otherwise be likely to choose other schools that are better at honoring this basic human, and scientifically rational, educational ideal. However, for the individual learner the process of learning will look far more like an individual journey into new realms of knowledge, into natural history, cultural history, and arts. Advanced digital technologies will open up even better opportunities for establishing virtual spaces of experience for both individual learners and groups, and it will be possible to create many more sensory-rich experiences/representations of abstract concepts than was possible in 2010. One ethical challenge of a particularly profound kind may arise from the possibility that very basic philosophical concepts regarding the fabric of reality (ontology) and our chances of grasping it (epistemology) will become so well represented through advanced multimedia technology that learners will be able to, so to speak, look *very* directly "down" into the dizzying existential depth (endless regress) and probably also experience profound weirdness when exposed to virtual quantum physics directly. Such break-throughs may not only challenge our ordinary perception of the world but may also induce significant levels of existential doubt and unease if not interpreted effectively in a way that is socially integrating.

(5) Following the best estimates of trends identified in 2010 into the future, the digital technological evolution and development in 2025 will presumably happen at least a thousand times as fast as in 2010 – and since digital

technology boosts the production of knowledge, already in 2025 the amount of information produced per time unit will be so vast that there is a significant risk that humans will not be able to see very far into the future. Given so, this implies that learners will also find it harder to imagine an *attractive future* than is the case in 2010 – at least in a very concrete way. The extreme version of this has been called *the singularity* – a condition that arises when the knowledge production is so rapid that it will no longer be possible to look into the future because the entire cognitive capacity of a person will be needed to process the information transmitted in the immediate now – a condition that thus contains its own "event horizon."

(6) In 2025, it will be possible to tailor learning quite precisely in accord with the learners' *intellectual strengths* because ultrahigh-definition brain scans and advanced psychological testing, to a far greater extent than in 2010, will make it possible to map these strengths. However, by 2025 it will be common knowledge that *character strengths* are a more direct way to higher levels of happiness and well-being than intellectual strengths. A character strength such as "love" thus brings immediate happiness when unfolded, while an intellectual strength such as linguistic intelligence only does so indirectly by paving the way for good communicative experiences. Thus, it will be of special importance for teachers to ensure that the character strengths of individual learners are brought productively into play. Moreover, character strengths appear to be an important precondition for much engagement, a main predictor of effective learning for learners and teachers alike.

(7) In 2025, all learners will have a solid understanding of their own preferred *styles* across a variety of relevant setting types – and consequently be able to make effective use of this understanding, which will be especially important in relation to content that is difficult to grasp and/or difficult to concentrate on. This obviously poses new demands on the physical as well as the virtual frames of learning environments, and even more so as parents and learners will compare the school settings with the ever more advanced learning alternatives in well-equipped homes.

(8) In 2025, both the physical and virtual learning environments will be *aesthetically rich and sense stimulating*, adjusted to accommodate the educational aims. It will be firmly acknowledged that sensory richness strengthens learning and memory, by enabling more intense experiences for the learners. However, it should be noted that, even more than in 2010, it will be a significant challenge to teachers in 2025 that the learners already *have* sensed and experienced so much that they may be habituated to a very high level of sensing, as habituation (in technical terms, *hedonistic adaptation*) more or less by definition tends to decrease the impression of subsequent sensory inputs. In this perspective there may be a massive temptation for learners to indulge in continuous superficial, flat, and fleeting experiences, in which case it poses a continuous challenge for teachers to help learners dwell long enough on content, moments, and situations to get a chance to savor and appreciate the deeper qualities of it all.

(9) In 2025, it will be possible to take advantage of digital media to simulate almost everything during teaching. This not only enables pupils to gain sensory-rich experiences of academic concepts and theories that in 2010 are mostly still communicated in very abstract ways, but it also opens up simulated *journeys of discovery* in time and space into much deeper academic and technical realms. Furthermore, by utilizing the many possibilities in *virtual reality*, learners are no longer just passive receivers of information in these simulated journeys (that in 2010 are still mostly known from seated experiences in planetaria and cinemas) but can much more actively control the direction and pace of their journey themselves (see Appendix 7.1 for examples). A certain feature of these simulators that deserves special mention is that they incorporate, to a much higher degree than in 2010, learners' bodily competences involving physical balance and coordination, thereby engaging areas in the brain that in 2010 are, by and large, detached from the standard industrial model of teaching – based on sitting still and awaiting the teacher's orders. This may be a big breakthrough because for millions of years humans have learned almost everything through some kind of physical movement *also*, and because we still tend to remember things better when we get them in our hands and experience the physical utility of what is learned. Indeed, like many a scholar has argued, any learning worth its name must imply some kind of transfer to new situations, that is, it must be physically advantageous *also*.

(10) Compared to 2010, in 2025 there will be fantastic possibilities for creativity in school. Meanwhile, learners will also be exposed to massive global creativity through the media, which they may often rate themselves against and which, of course, will be difficult if not impossible to match on almost any occasion. Furthermore, an unpleasant truth may be that machines also become increasingly "creative," causing a very real risk that human creativity will be increasingly inferior to that of machines in many areas. Historically it has often been alienating when humans were rendered expendable because of machines, as the Luddite movement reminds us.

(11) Via both mobile and stationary media it will be possible to be on-line everywhere, and thus be in contact with anyone, anywhere, anytime in 2025. Seen overall, this will be potentially strengthening for the combined *social connectedness*. This virtual freedom to organize socially is a potential advantage that obviously comes with high demands regarding the *quality* of the social relations that are ultimately established – not least the ability of individuals to formulate meaningful projects in concert with others. Also, it will be ethically taxing to deal with the fact that often a de-regulated global network will be of bigger advantage for the stronger than the weaker players, thus implying another risk for bipolar social demographic development. On the other hand, global regulation may imply an enormous bureaucracy that will be vulnerable both due to its inertia and due to its extraordinarily large capacity for corruption.

(12) In 2025, it will be clear to everyone that the viability of a social system, such as a society or a school, stands and falls with its ability to *combine strong social differentiation (that develops individuality and mutual interest between people) with strong social integration (that makes it possible to live and function together)*. In 2025, it will be generally acknowledged that the overall aim of any school worth its name is to enable both the flourishing of the individual learner, with all the implied unpredictability and developmental uniqueness, and the individual learner's predictable, non-unique developmental path (such as the acquisition of reading and writing skills). The process towards this acknowledgment will be demanding and throughout the process there lurks the danger of unbalance between the differentiating and the integrating forces.

(13) There are strong indications that the complementary values of science, "openness" and "skepticism," should also be valid in many other domains of life, for, in social life, openness towards new things means positive support, while, in social life, sound skepticism is synonymous with positive challenge. Since both values are obvious necessities for a safe and dynamic human community, in 2025 the *combination of positive support and positive challenge* will be common values. In part, this should prove effective in preventing conflicts based on religious differences. By mutual commitment to listen appreciatively and criticize respectfully it has become possible for very different religious belief systems to co-exist *as belief systems*. For instance, it has become possible for Christians and Muslims to agree that the gods in which they *believe* are, by definition, beyond what can be *known* with certainty by humans, wherefore people can no longer argue authoritatively about politics on the basis of religious beliefs. Consequently, religions will no longer be the basis for the application of power, and for that reason will no longer be criticized as untruthful either. Religions will finally be recognized for what they are: belief systems to which citizens are free to connect or not – in mutual agreement that one does not *become* a better person by believing, even though it may make one *feel* better.

CONCLUSIONS

If the opportunities presented in these scenarios are resolved in a positive direction, life will be better, safer, and more comfortable than ever, and schools will have a major role in making sure that the opportunities will not be squandered. The education of the future will be concerned not only with optimizing the experience of the individual learners because it is subjectively the best, but also because it is materially/economically the most sustainable. By 2025, it should be generally accepted that happy people are both cheaper and more productive for a society, and that the immaterial wealth (popularly called *happiness or well-being*) is a precondition for lasting material wealth. Therefore, in 2025 all over the world, political leaders will face the conclusion of positive psychology – namely, that the single most important source for human happiness is *for people to live in*

circumstances enabling them to be wholeheartedly engaged in both their imme-
diate goals and in a greater purpose. Both the welfare system and the free market
forces will therefore have been "humanized" according to this ideal: In 2025, the
welfare system should fully live up to its name by de facto helping people "fare," in
the original sense of being "on their way," rather than pacifying them as stigma-
tized victims to be monitored closely by external authorities, and the free market
forces should function so that people in general primarily compete for the sake of
demonstrating their excellence and only secondarily for the sake of winning – this
is because it has become clear that a school or a society where the great majority
lose every time a few win will never prevail against schools or societies where all
experience the joy of winning because everyone has a chance of doing their best.

NOTE

1 An important note of caution when creating a list like this is that, evidently, almost all
   good things can degenerate into excess. However, since very few, if any, of the single
   points in focus here appear to be even close to excess in standard education, this author
   has refrained from specifying any criteria that could indicate something becoming "too
   much" in this context, with the exception of hypothesis 5, where a specific ratio between
   positive and negative is important.

APPENDIX 7.1

Illustrations from VISIONS 2020 Transforming Education and
Training Through Advanced Technologies (U.S. Department of
Commerce, 2002)

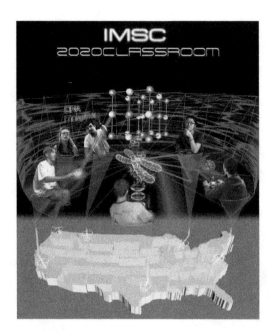

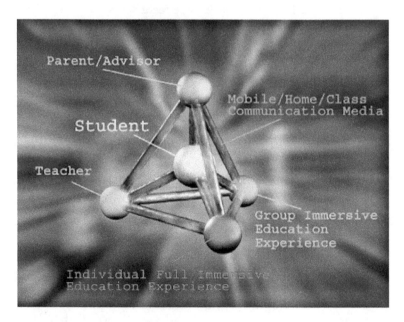

. . . A complete, stable, and individualized learning structure engaging a learner with teachers, parents, advisors, and facilities for group immersion, all connected by portable and stationary media.

. . . A learner enters a Tangitrek. With a force-feedback-sensitive exoskeleton, a moving platform, secured straps, and a three-dimensional display, the learner can travel everywhere and do everything.

. . . In her virtual mobile suit, a learner surfs through a gigantic chemical model whose surfaces and bonds the learner can touch and feel.

. . . A learner observes a prehistoric animal fight its way into life through the egg-shell. The learner can see, hear, smell, and touch the simulated object and the simulated environment.

. . . A learner flies over Acropolis, as it may have looked in ancient Greece, the Antique. The learner can communicate with synthetic Greeks, who can communicate about their lives.

REFERENCES

Allen, M., Witt, P. L., & Wheeless, L. R. (2006). The role of teacher immediacy as a motivational factor in student learning: Using meta-analysis to test a causal model. *Communication Education, 55,* 21–31.

Amabile, T. M. (1996). *Creativity in context.* New York: Westview Press.

Anderson, R., Manoogian, S. T., & Reznick, J. S. (1976). The undermining and enhancing of intrinsic motivation in preschool children. *Journal of Personality and Social Psychology, 34,* 915–922.

Bandura, A. (1986). *Social foundations of thought and action.* Englewood Cliffs, NJ: Prentice Hall.

Bandura, A. (1989). Social cognitive theory. In R. Vasta (Ed.), *Annals of child development, 6. Six theories of child development* (pp. 1–60). Greenwich, CT: JAI Press.

Bandura, A. (1997). *Self-efficacy: The exercise of control.* New York: W. H. Freeman.

Baumeister, R. (2005). *The cultural animal.* New York: Oxford University Press.

Bloom, F. E., & Nelson, C. A. (2001). *Brain, mind, and behavior.* London: Worth.

Bowlby, J. (1979). *The making and breaking of affectional bonds.* London: Tavistock.

Bransford, J. D., Brown, A. L., & Cocking, R. R. (1999). *How people learn – brain, mind, experience, and school.* Washington, DC: National Academy of Sciences.

Brown, D. E. (1991). *Human universals.* Boston: McGraw-Hill.

Camazine, S., Deneubourg, J., Franks, N. R., Sneyd, J., Theraulaz, G., & Bonabeau, E. (2001). *Self-organization in biological systems.* Princeton, NJ: Princeton University Press.

Chaisson, E. (2001). *Cosmic evolution: The rise of complexity in nature.* Cambridge, MA: Harvard University Press.

Csikszentmihalyi, M. (1990). *Flow: The psychology of optimal experience.* New York: Harper & Row.

Csikszentmihalyi, M. (1993): *The evolving self.* New York: Harper Collins.

Csikszentmihalyi, M. (1996). *Creativity: Flow and the psychology of discovery and invention.* New York: Harper Collins.

Csikszentmihalyi, M. (2009). *Learning in 2005.* 125th Anniversary of Folkeskolen, Copenhagen.

Csikszentmihalyi, M., Abuhamdeh, S., & Nakamura, J. (2005). Flow. In A. J. Elliot & C. S. Dweck (Eds.), *Handbook of competence and motivation* (pp. 598–608). New York: Guilford Press.

Csikszentmihalyi, M., & Knoop, H. H. (2008). Kompleksitet: Universelt ideal og global trussel. In J. Lyhne & H. H. Knoop (Eds.), *Positiv psykologi: Positiv pædagogik* (pp. 243–263). Copenhagen: Dansk Psykologisk Forlag.

Csikszentmihalyi, M., & Rathunde, K. (1993). The measurement of flow in everyday life: Towards a theory of emergent motivation. In J. E. Jacobs (Ed.), *Nebraska symposium on motivation, Vol. 40: Developmental perspectives on motivation* (p. 60). Lincoln: University of Nebraska Press.

Damasio, A. R. (2000) *The feeling of what happens: Body and emotion in the making of consciousness.* New York: Harvest Books.

Damon, W. (2003). *The moral advantage: How to succeed in business by doing the right thing.* San Francisco: Berrett-Koehler.

Deci, E. L., & Ryan, R. M. (1991). A motivational approach to self: Integration in personality. In R. Dienstbier (Ed.), *Perspectives on motivation* (pp. 237–288). Lincoln, NE: University of Nebraska Press.

Deci, E. L., & Ryan, R. M. (2000). The "what" and "why" of goal pursuits: Human needs and the self-determination of behavior. *Psychological Inquiry, 11,* 227–268.

Dingfelder, S. (2003). Creativity killers. *APA Monitor, 34*, 57.

Dunn, R., & Dunn, K. (2005). Thirty-five years of research on perceptual strengths. *The Clearing House, 78*, 273–276.

Dunn, R., & Dunn, K. (2008). Teaching to at-risk students' learning styles: Solutions based on international research. *Insights on Learning Disabilities: From Prevailing Theories to Validated Practices, 5*, 89–101.

Elliot, A. J., & Dweck, C. S. (2005). *Handbook of competence and motivation.* New York: Guilford Press.

Frankl, V. E. (1985). *Man's search for meaning: Revised and updated.* New York: Washington Square Press.

Fredrickson, B. L. (1998). What good are positive emotions? *Review of General Psychology, 2*, 300–319.

Fredrickson, B. L. (2001). The role of positive emotions in positive psychology: The broaden-and-build theory of positive emotions. *American Psychologist, 56*, 218–226.

Fredrickson, B. L. (2009). *Positivity: Groundbreaking research reveals how to embrace the hidden strength of positive emotions, overcome negativity, and thrive.* New York: Crown.

Fredrickson, B. L., & Losada, M. (2005). Positive affect and the complex dynamics of human flourishing. *American Psychologist, 60*, 678–686.

Gallup (2002, November 7). *Survey on trust.* Report on trust for the World Economic Forum, New York.

Gardner, H. (1999). *The disciplined mind.* New York: Simon & Schuster.

Gardner, H. (2000). *Intelligence reframed.* New York: Basic Books.

GFK (2003). *Trust levels: Much room for improvement.* Retrieved December 25, 2009, from www.gfk.hr/press_en/trust.htm

GlobeScan (2005, December 15). *GlobeScan report on issues and reputation.* Report on trust for the World Economic Forum, Davos, Switzerland.

Gopnik, A., Meltzoff, A. N., & Kuhl, P. (2001). *The scientist in the crib.* New York: Harper Collins.

Grigorenko, E. L., Jarvin, L., & Sternberg, R. J. (2002). School-based tests of the triarchic theory of intelligence: Three settings, three samples, three syllabi. *Contemporary Educational Psychology 27*, 167–208.

Harter, S. (1978). Effectance motivation reconsidered: Toward a developmental model. *Human Development, 1*, 661–669.

Hauser, M. (2006). *Moral minds: How nature designed our universal sense of right and wrong.* New York: Ecco.

Institute of Medicine (U.S.), Committee on Health and Behavior: Research, Practice and Policy (2001). *Health and behavior: The interplay of biological, behavioral, and societal influences.* New York: National Academy Press.

Joy, B. (2000). Why the future doesn't need us. *Wired Magazine, 4*, 1–11.

Kahneman, D. (2008). Grænser for rationel tænkning i forbindelse med vurderinger og valg. In J. Lyhne & H. H. Knoop (Eds.), *Positiv psykologi: Positiv pædagogik* (pp. 139–188). Copenhagen: Dansk Psykologisk Forlag.

Kashdan, T. (2009). *Curiosity: Discover the missing ingredient to a fulfilling life.* New York: William Morrow.

Kauffman, S. A. (2000). *Investigations.* New York: Oxford University Press.

Knoop, H. H. (2002). *Play, learning and creativity: Why happy children are better learners.* Copenhagen: Aschehoug.

Knoop, H. H. (2005): Kompleksitet: Voksende orden ingen helt forstår. *Kognition & Pædagogik, 57*, 6–24.

Knoop, H. H. (2007a). Control and responsibility: A Danish perspective on leadership. In H. Gardner (Ed.), *Responsibility at work* (pp. 221–245). San Francisco: Jossey-Bass.

Knoop, H. H. (2007b). Wise creativity and creative wisdom. In A. Craft, H. Gardner, & G. Claxton (Eds.), *Creativity and wisdom in education* (pp. 119–132). London: Sage Publications.

Knoop, H. H. (2008). *Folkeskolen år 2025*. Copenhagen: Folkeskolen.

Knoop, H. H., & Lyhne, J. (2005). *Et nyt læringslandskab: Flow, intelligens og det gode læringsmiljø*. Copenhagen: Dansk Psykologisk Forlag.

Kolb, D. (1984). *Experiential learning: Experience as the source of learning and development*. Englewood Cliffs, NJ: Prentice Hall.

Kurzweil, R. (2006). *The singularity is near: When humans transcend biology*. London: Viking Penguin.

Linley, A. (2008). *Average to A+: Realising strengths in yourself and others*. Warwick, UK: CAPP Press.

Lyhne, J., & Knoop, H. H. (2008). *Positiv psykologi: Positiv pædagogik*. Copenhagen: Dansk Psykologisk Forlag.

Massimini, F., & Delle Fave, A. (1991). Religion and cultural evolution. *Zygon, 16*, 27–48.

Myers, D. G. (1993). *The pursuit of happiness*. New York: Avon.

Nakamura, J. (1988). Optimal experience and the uses of talent. In M. Csikszentmihalyi & I. Csikszentmihalyi (Eds.), *Optimal experience: Psychological studies of flow in consciousness* (pp. 319–326). New York: Cambridge University Press.

Peterson, C. (2006). *A primer in positive psychology*. New York: Oxford University Press.

Peterson C., & Seligman, M. E. P. (2004): *Character strengths and virtues: A handbook and classification*. New York: Oxford University Press.

Pinker, S. (1997). *How the mind works*. New York: W. W. Norton.

Pinker, S. (2002). *The blank slate: The modern denial of human nature*. London: BCA.

Pinker, S. (2009). *How the mind works*. New York: W. W. Norton.

Rathunde, K. (1992). Serious play: Interest and adolescent talent development. In A. Krapp & M. Prenzel (Eds.), *Interesse, lerner, leistung* (pp. 137–164). Munster: Aschendorff.

Rathunde, K. (1996). Family context and talented adolescents' optimal experience in school-related activities. *Journal of Research in Adolescence, 6*, 603–626.

Rees, M. (2003). *Our final hour: How terror, error, and environmental disaster threaten humankind's future in this century – on earth and beyond*. New York: Basic Books.

Robinson, K. (2001). *Out of our mind: Learning to be creative*. London: Capstone.

Robinson, K. (2009). *The element: How finding your passion changes everything*. London: Viking Adult.

Runco, M. A. (2004). Creativity. *Annual Review of Psychology, 55*, 657–687.

Ryan, R. M. (1995). Psychological needs and the facilitation of integrative processes. *Journal of Personality, 63*, 397–427.

Ryan, R. M., & Deci, E. L. (2000). Self-determination theory and the facilitation of intrinsic motivation, social development, and well-being. *American Psychologist, 55*, 68–78.

Schmuck, P., & Sheldon, K. M. (2001). *Life-goals and well-being*. Gottingen: Hogrefe & Huber.

Seligman, M. E. P. (2002). *Authentic happiness*. New York: Free Press.

Senge, P. M. (1990). *The fifth discipline: The art and practice of the learning organization*. London: Century Business.

Senge, P., Kleiner, A., Roberts, C., Ross, R., & Smith, B. (1994). *The fifth discipline: Field book. Strategies and tools for building a learning organization*. London: Nicholas Brealey.

Sheldon, K. M., Ryan, R. M., Rawsthorne, L. J., & Ilardi, B. (1997). Trait self and true self: Cross-role variation in the Big-Five personality traits and its relations with psychological authenticity and subjective well-being. *Journal of Personality and Social Psychology, 73*, 1380–1393.

Shernoff, D. J., & Hoogstra, L. (2001). Continuing motivation beyond the high school classroom. *New Directions in Child and Adolescent Development, 93*, 73–87.

U.S. Department of Commerce (2002). *VISIONS 2020 Transforming education and training through advanced technologies*. Retrieved December 25, 2009, from www.technology.gov/2020MM/p_Pht040916.htm

Wilson, D. S. (2002). *Darwin's cathedral: Religion and the nature of society*. Chicago: University of Chicago Press.

Wilson, E. O. (1998). *Consilience: The unity of knowledge*. New York: Alfred A. Knopf.

Wong, P. T. P., & Fry, P. S. (1998). *The human quest for meaning: A handbook of psychological research and clinical applications*. Mahwah, NJ: Lawrence Erlbaum Associates, Inc.

World Economic Forum (2007, January 15). *Worldwide survey highlights lack of faith in leaders in an uncertain world*. Retrieved December 25, 2009, from www.weforum.org/en/media/Latest%20Press%20Releases/voiceofthepeoplesurvey

Wright, R. (2001). *Non-zero: The logic of human destiny*. New York: Vintage Books.

Wright, R., Pinker, S., & Seligman, M. (2002). *Debating human happiness*. Online discussion at http://www.slate.com/?id=2072079&entry=2072402

Zimbardo, P. (2007). *The Lucifer effect: Understanding how good people turn evil*. New York: Random House.

8

Gallup Student Poll: Measuring and Promoting What is Right with Students

SHANE J. LOPEZ and VALERIE J. CALDERON

The graduating students marched proudly into the auditorium to the applause of their friends and family. After acknowledging the teachers and giving a quick speech, the school's head honcho, Dr. Reckmeyer, invited each student to join her on stage – one by one. She then shared what each student did best, she recognized their talents, their skills, and their hard work.

Dr. Reckmeyer described Eva as a creative visionary. "You have great artistic talent. You have an incredible ability to see things in a new and unique way. I hope you continue to enjoy and nourish your love of art throughout your life." Anna was described as a strong student with a warm personality. "You show great determination with each task you do. You work hard to complete each and every project to the best of your ability and love being praised for a job well done." In parting, Dr. Reckmeyer said, "[Anna] I will miss . . . your kindness . . . and your . . . smile. You have had an incredible journey and I feel blessed to have shared it with you." These students and the rest of their peers were truly known by those who taught them. And what was right with them was celebrated.

We learned from some of the parents that all of the students in the graduating class were going to the Happiest Place on Earth. You may be thinking, why would these students plan a group trip to Disneyland? Well, their destination was not Disney. They were going to a place where they could learn new things from smart people who cared about them, laugh with their friends, and dream about the future. These 17 preschoolers from the Donald O. Clifton Child Development Center were headed to kindergarten, the Happiest Place on Earth.

We (SJL & VJC) are very fortunate as we have seen the benefits of the world's only strengths-based preschool first hand. At the Donald O. Clifton Child Development Center, Parrish Lopez and Gabriela and

Nick Calderon are known by name, by what they do best, and by what they want to do in the future. They will build on positive experiences and take what they have learned in preschool to their next stop, the Happiest Place on Earth. They will progress onward through their grammar, secondary, and post-secondary education. Our hope is that *teachers at all levels will really know our children. The good teachers will study what is right with each child and propel each one toward their unique and special future. Healthy communities will not only clear the path but will help forge one for our children to succeed. Our children, all children, deserve nothing less.*

The Gallup Student Poll was developed to tell the stories of American students. What is right about them receives little press coverage. Furthermore, their voice, to a large extent, has not been considered when reforming education, strengthening families, and rebuilding communities. In this chapter, we describe the inaugural poll and its results and discuss the policy implications associated with data on what is right with students.

DEVELOPING AND LAUNCHING THE GALLUP STUDENT POLL

The Gallup Student Poll is a landmark new measure that will track for 10 years the hope, engagement, and well-being of students across the USA. Through a Web-based survey administered in America's schools, cities and school districts are partnering with Gallup and America's Promise Alliance to gather sound, actionable data that can explain and address the high school dropout crisis. The youth voice is a critical missing part of the national dialogue about the dropout crisis and educational and community reform that improves the overall quality of life. The Gallup Student Poll gives America's young people a voice to convey their daily experiences and aspirations for the future. Research has shown that hope, engagement, and well-being are positioned as actionable targets and indicators of success, with links to grades, achievement scores, retention, and employment. Poll data facilitate new family, school, and community conversations and solutions that lead to community engagement and school and student success.

Measuring the Hope, Engagement, and Well-Being of America's Students

The conversation about the future of American youth starts with a shared understanding of what is right with our students, rather than what is wrong. Through a review of social science and educational research, Gallup researchers chose three variables (hope, engagement, and well-being) as the target of the Gallup Student Poll because they met the following four criteria: (1) they can be reliably measured, (2) they have a meaningful relationship with or impact on educational outcomes, (3) they are malleable and can be enhanced through deliberate action, and (4) they are not measured directly by another large-scale survey or testing program. After an extensive literature review, pilot testing of engagement items with 97,000 students and well-being items with 48,000 students, and a predictive and intervention study examining academic achievement and attendance data of 198 high school freshmen (see Appendix 8.1), here are the fundamental findings that are incorporated into the Gallup Student Poll project.

- Hope – the ideas and energy we have for the future. Hope drives attendance, credits earned, and the grade point average (GPA) of high school students. Hope predicts GPA and retention in college, and hope scores are more robust predictors of college success than are high school GPA, SAT (Scholastic Aptitude Test), and ACT (American College Testing) scores.
- Engagement – the involvement in and enthusiasm for school. Engagement distinguishes between high-performing and low-performing schools.
- Well-being – how we think about and experience our lives. Well-being tells us how our students are doing today and predicts their success in the future. High school freshmen with high well-being earn more credits with a higher GPA than peers with low well-being.

Launching the Gallup Student Poll

The inaugural Gallup Student Poll surveyed 70,078 students in grades 5–12 from 335 schools and 59 districts located in 18 states and the District of Columbia. (Gallup, America's Promise Alliance, and the American Association of School Administrators invited 130+ school districts to participate in the March 2009 poll. A wide range of school districts were included in this invitation, from America's Promise 100 Best Communities for Youth and America's Promise 24 Dropout Prevention Summit cities to Gallup Education client districts.) The on-line poll was completed on school computers during one of four fielding options. Polls were open Tuesday to Friday during school hours. See Appendix 8.1 for a summary of data from the first school in the nation participating in the Gallup Student Poll.

HOPE, ACADEMIC SUCCESS, AND THE GALLUP STUDENT POLL

Intelligence and aptitude are not the only determinants of a student's academic success (Dweck, 1999) and future success in the job market, therefore it is important to understand the many factors that keep students on track and in pursuit of their educational and vocational goals. Hope – the ideas and energy for the future – is one of the most potent predictors of the success of our youth.

Hope and Academic Success

Hope is not significantly related to native intelligence (Snyder, McDermott, Cook, & Rapoff, 2002a) or income (Gallup, 2009a), but instead is linked consistently to attendance and credits earned (Gallup, 2009b) and academic achievement. Specifically, hopeful middle school students have better grades in core subjects

(Marques, Pais-Ribeiro, & Lopez, 2009) and scores on achievement tests (Snyder et al., 1997). Hopeful high school students (Gallup, 2009a; Snyder et al., 1991; Worrell & Hale, 2001) and beginning college students (Gallagher & Lopez, 2008; Snyder, Shorey, Cheavens, Pulvers, Adams, & Wiklund, 2002b) have a higher overall GPA. In these studies, the predictive power of hope remained significant even when controlling for intelligence (Snyder et al., 1997), prior grades (Gallagher & Lopez, 2008; Snyder et al., 1991, 2002b), self-esteem (Snyder et al., 2002b), and entrance examination scores (Gallagher & Lopez, 2008; Snyder et al., 2002b).

Hopeful students see the future as better than the present, and believe they have the power to make it so. These students are energetic, full of life. They are able to develop many strategies to reach goals and plan contingencies in the event that they are faced with problems along the way. As such, obstacles are viewed as challenges to be overcome and are bypassed by garnering support and/or implementing alternative pathways. Perceiving the likelihood of good outcomes, these students focus on success and therefore experience greater positive affect and less distress. Generally, high-hope people experience less anxiety and less stress specific to test-taking situations.

Stuck or discouraged students (i.e., low-hope students) may lack the energy to get things done. These students may give up when encountering barriers to goals simply because they cannot think of other pathways around the obstacles or cannot get the support they need. This often results in frustration, a loss of confidence, and lowered self-esteem (see Snyder, 1994). Students with low hope experience high anxiety, especially in test-taking situations. Stuck or discouraged students do not use feedback from failure experiences in an adaptive manner so as to improve performances in the future (Onwuegbuzie, 1998).

Hope and Findings from the March 2009 Gallup Student Poll

The following items, which constitute an internally consistent scale (alpha = .76), were used to measure hope in the Gallup Student Poll:

- I know I will graduate from high school.
- There is an adult in my life who cares about my future.
- I can think of many ways to get good grades.
- I energetically pursue my goals.
- I can find lots of ways around any problem.
- I know I will find a good job after I graduate.

Based on the convenience sample of 70,078 young people, half of American students are hopeful; these students possess numerous ideas and abundant energy for the future. The other half of students are stuck (33%) or discouraged (17%), lacking the ideas and energy they need to navigate problems and reach goals. Hope varies little across the grade levels. Across participating schools, class size was negatively associated with hope (the larger the class, the lower the hope) and the percentage of students on free and reduced lunch was not associated with hope.

Increasing Hope

Hope is malleable (Gallup, 2009c; Lopez, Rose, Robinson, Marques, & Pais-Ribeiro, 2009) and 50% of American students need support from parents, school, and the community to build their energy and ideas for the future. Through a focused effort from people who care about the future of youth, we can double hope in America. Student-centered, hope-enhancing policies involving schools, communities, and families are discussed in a subsequent section of this chapter.

ENGAGEMENT, PERFORMANCE ON STANDARDIZED TESTS, AND THE GALLUP STUDENT POLL

Being engaged promotes productivity and retention (Harter, Schmidt, & Hayes, 2002). This research on employee engagement is clear and the latest research on student engagement (Gallup, 2009d; Gordon, 2006) and student achievement makes a strong case for building engaged schools.

Engagement and Performance on Standardized Tests

Engagement data provide school leaders with information about the conditions that keep students and staff involved in and enthusiastic about school. These data provide a leading indicator of future performance. In a series of studies, Gallup research has demonstrated that student and teacher engagement is associated with future performance on high-stakes tests. For example, engaged students are more than twice as likely to outperform a comparison group of randomly selected students on standardized tests (Gallup, 2009d). Furthermore, in a study of three Texas districts, schools with an engaged professional staff passed more students on standardized tests than did schools with a less engaged staff (Gallup, 2009d).

Engagement and Findings from the March 2009 Gallup Student Poll

The following items, which constitute an internally consistent scale (alpha = .71), were used to measure engagement:

- I have a best friend at school.
- I feel safe in this school.
- My teachers make me feel my schoolwork is important.
- At this school, I have the opportunity to do what I do best every day.
- In the last seven days, I have received recognition or praise for doing good schoolwork.

Based on the convenience sample of 70,078 young people, half of students are engaged. Engaged students are highly involved with and enthusiastic about school. These students arrive at school prepared and eager to learn; they are likely to promote learning readiness in those around them. The other half of students are not engaged, with some just going through the motions at school (30%). These students, while not overtly negative, may blend into the learning landscape and may not be maximizing their own learning potential or facilitating the learning process in others. Those students who are actively disengaged are likely to undermine the teaching and learning process for themselves and others (20%). They require many resources and particular attention from teachers and administrators.

Student engagement peaks during elementary school, decreases through middle school and 10th grade, and plateaus through the rest of high school – seemingly after some of the most actively disengaged students drop out of school. This downward trend suggests that we may be losing the hearts and minds of some students in middle school, with involvement in and enthusiasm for school declining from 5th through to 10th grade. Student responses to "My teachers make me feel my school work is important" account for some of the engagement decline across the grade levels, suggesting that students see school as less important and relevant as they advance through grades. Student responses suggest that praise and recognition contribute significantly to student engagement. The percentage of students who agreed they had received praise and recognition for doing good schoolwork in the last seven days declined over 20 points from 5th through to 10th grade. Less than half of 10th graders agreed with this item. Data also suggest that having too few opportunities to do what they do best also contributed to the definitive and disturbing slide in engagement.

The Gallup Student Poll revealed that a school's commitment to strengths is associated with higher student engagement. Of students who strongly agreed with "My school is committed to building the strengths of each student," 79% were engaged at school, compared to 11% of students who disagreed or strongly disagreed with this statement. Poll data also demonstrated a strong link between experienced well-being, measured by the Positive Yesterdays Index, and engagement. Of students who had a positive yesterday (experienced respect, interest, smile/laugh, energy), 73% were engaged at school, compared to 12% who had a negative yesterday.

Student engagement is not associated with class size or income (Gallup, 2009b).

Increasing Engagement

What is the one intervention that will most positively influence engagement and, in turn, student achievement? Principals engage the staff by getting them excited about the future. When Gallup studied the impact that leaders have throughout an organization, the single most powerful question was whether their leadership made them "feel enthusiastic about the future." Sixty-nine percent of employees who strongly agreed with this statement were engaged in their jobs, compared to a mere 1% of employees who disagreed or strongly disagreed. In turn, engaged teachers get students excited about their future. Together, engaged students, teachers, and principals build engaged schools. Policies directed at driving teacher and student engagement and involving members of the community in building engaged schools are discussed in a subsequent section of this chapter.

WELL-BEING, SUCCESS, AND THE GALLUP STUDENT POLL

Some people think that well-being is a byproduct of scholastic and work success, but recent research suggests that well-being *leads* to success in both school (Lyubomirsky, King, & Diener, 2005) and work (Boehm & Lyubomirsky, 2008; Judge & Hurst, 2008).

The Gallup Student Poll items that measure well-being reflect a broad view of the concept. Nobel laureate Daniel Kahneman makes note of the distinction between evaluative well-being and experienced well-being. As described by Kahneman, evaluative well-being is the way people remember their experiences after they are over, whereas experienced well-being is concerned with momentary affective states and the way people feel about experiences in real-time. Evaluative well-being is rooted in the remembering of self and includes individual assessments of life. On the other hand, experienced well-being seeks to bypass the effects of judgment and memory and capture emotions as close to the subject's immediate experience as possible.

Well-Being and Success

Well-being – how we think about and experience our lives – tells us how our students are doing today and predicts their success in the future.

In an examination of evaluative well-being, high school freshmen with high well-being earned more credits with a higher GPA than peers with low well-being. Specifically, the typical student with high well-being earns 10% more credits and a 2.9 GPA (out of 4), whereas a student with low well-being, completing fewer credits, earns a 2.4 GPA (Gallup, 2009a).

Regarding experienced well-being, most directly measured as positive affect, Lyubomirsky (Boehm & Lyubomirsky, 2008; Lyubomirsky et al., 2005) reviewed cross-sectional, experimental, and longitudinal evidence and found that reports of feeling joyful, excited, or pleasant among other positive emotions are predictors of success and numerous behaviors associated with success. In an exploratory study of the experienced well-being of high school freshmen, those students who reported that they experienced joy and interest yesterday (versus those who had not) had better academic records (Gallup, 2009a).

Well-Being and Findings from the March 2009 Gallup Student Poll

Evaluative well-being – how we think about our lives – is measured by the Gallup Student Poll Well-Being Index. The following items comprise the index:

- Please imagine a ladder with steps numbered from zero at the bottom to ten at the top. The top of the ladder represents the best possible life for

you and the bottom of the ladder represents the worst possible life for you. On which step of the ladder would you say you personally feel you stand at this time? (Item is presented with an interactive ladder graphic.)
- On which step do you think you will stand about five years from now?

When students were asked to respond to the questions based on the classic Cantril Self-Anchoring Striving Scale (ladder questions presented previously), the average response was 7.32. When asked "On which step do you think you will stand about five years from now?" the students' average response was 8.42. Evaluative well-being varies little across grade levels.

The well-being classification system of Thriving, Struggling, and Suffering is used to summarize a student's responses to both items. Based on the convenience sample, nearly two-thirds of students are thriving; they think about their present and future life in positive terms, generally have their basic needs met, and they tend to be in good health and have strong social support. Just over one-third of students are struggling or suffering. Those individuals with low well-being tend to lack adequate personal and social resources.

Experienced well-being – how we feel about our lives – is measured by the Gallup Student Poll Positive Yesterdays Index, composed of the following items:

- Were you treated with respect all day yesterday?
- Did you smile or laugh a lot yesterday?
- Did you learn or do something interesting yesterday?
- Did you have enough energy to get things done yesterday?

According to the convenience sample of youth, over half of respondents (52%) indicated that they were treated with respect all day yesterday. A strong majority of students (80%) indicated that they smiled or laughed a lot yesterday and 70% reported that they learned or did something interesting yesterday. Most students (72%) had enough energy to get things done yesterday. Only 30% of the March 2009 students who completed the poll answered "yes" to all four items, indicating that they had a positive yesterday.

Additional analyses on these four items suggested that there is a downward well-being trend by grade; students experience fewer positive yesterdays as they advance from elementary school to high school. Additionally, class size is negatively associated with the Positive Yesterdays Index – a larger class size generally means lower well-being.

Neither the Well-Being Index nor the Positive Yesterdays Index for schools was associated with a rough indicator of income – the percentage of students who received free or reduced lunch within a school.

Increase Well-Being

Well-being is malleable (Sin & Lyubomirsky, 2009; Suldo, Huebner, Michalowski, & Thalji, 2011). We can boost well-being in America by intentionally targeting students' thoughts and feelings. Student-centered policies aimed at boosting well-being that involve schools, communities, and families are discussed in the subsequent section of this chapter.

POLICY IMPLICATIONS

The subtleties of an inadequate educational experience can rob students of their enthusiasm as they transition from one grade or school to another. Small behaviors make them less engaged and less energetic year after year – from 5th grade to senior year in high school. Shabby, unfocused, and unintentional practices can transform a thriving adolescent, full of vim and vigor, into a struggling young adult. Nothing short of psychological reform of the educational system, including educational pedagogy and intentional development of strengths, hope, engagement, and well-being, will make schools, colleges, and universities what they all should be – some of the happiest places on earth.

The effort to help students simply requires that all community members do more of what they already do best (Figure 8.1). Here we make nine recommendations. We target psychological reform of our schools with four ideas that could promote hope, engagement, or well-being. The remaining five recommendations require the development and marshalling of community resources for the benefit of youth.

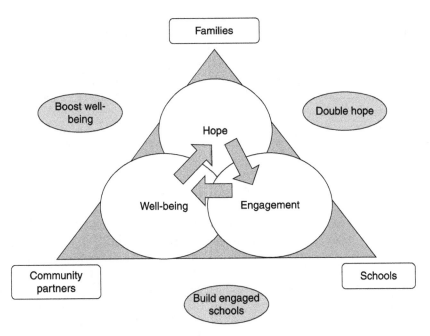

FIGURE 8.1   Partnerships for impacting student hope, engagement, and well-being.

Doubling Hope

Strengths-Based Education   Implementing strengths-based education (Lopez & Louis, 2009) can enhance hope (see Appendix 8.1). It begins with educators discovering what they do best and developing and applying their own strengths while they help students to identify and apply their strengths in the learning process so that they can reach previously unattained levels of personal excellence. Strengths-based education, though grounded in historical tenets and practices, is also built on five modern-day educational principles: (1) the *measurement* of strengths (Liesveld & Miller, 2005; Rath, 2007), achievement (Carey, 2004; U.S. Department of Education, 2004), and determinants of positive outcomes (Lopez, 2004; Rettew & Lopez, 2009), (2) *individualization*, which requires a tailoring of the teacher's/advisor's methods to student needs and interests (Gallup, 2003; Levitz & Noel, 2000), (3) *networking* with friends, family, and professionals who affirm strengths (Bowers, 2009), (4) *deliberate application* of strengths in and out of the classroom (Rath, 2007; Seligman, Steen, Park, & Peterson, 2005), and (5) *intentional development* of strengths through novel experience or focused practice across a period such as a semester, academic year, or an internship (Louis, 2008). Through a parallel process, educators practice the principles of strengths-based education when advising and teaching while students learn to put their strengths to work in learning and social situations.

HopeBanks   Opening local HopeBanks would create opportunities for community members to invest in the future of local youth. A HopeBank secures and provides resources from community members and appropriates them for young people so that they may set and attain their goals for the future. Community members invest in young people and their ideas by linking personal resources (specifically time, talent, knowledge, and skills) to the needs of the youth. As a member of a HopeBank, an individual or a small group of committed adults opens a HopeBank and solicits investment ideas, or goals for the future, from youth through schools and youth organizations. A representative of the HopeBank works with youth to refine these goals in order to make them specific and additive, with defined marks of progress and an attainment timeline. The goal and a list of resources needed are then posted on the HopeBank website, reviewed periodically by members.

Imagine that a company of 2000 people open a HopeBank in their community, and 50 employees sign up as members of the bank. They solicit investment ideas from youth in schools within a few miles of the workplace. Dozens (maybe hundreds) of accounts are opened by youth who submit goals that are refined with the help of the bank manager to make them more attainable; the revised goals are posted. At that point, bank members (i.e., the investors) attempt to match their resources with the needs of local youth. For example, imagine a student submits the proposal "Soon-to-be first generation college student needs help preparing for entrance exams and writing college essays." The HopeBank manager can help the student to clarify the goals, the timeline, and the assistance needed. Upon posting, members work through the bank manager to offer the time, talent, knowledge, and skills needed to help the student get into college. Accounts would be updated on-line (for members and account holders to see) and the return on investment in youth will be tracked over time with updates from young people and members.

Building Engaged Schools

Talented Teachers Schools that select for talent have more engaged teachers. Engaged teachers have engaged students. Engaged schools, made up of engaged leadership, teachers, and students, perform better on standardized tests (Gallup, 2009d; Gordon, 2006).

As teacher candidates graduate from colleges and universities, schools do their best job of hiring the most talented, using proven assessment tools and interviews. It is unclear, however, how successful we are as a nation at recruiting the people who could be the most talented teachers into teacher education programs. The great teacher discussion, which currently focuses on the quality of teachers in the ranks, could begin during the recruitment and education of highly motivated, talented students into quality schools and colleges of education.

Engagement Education Teaching talented soon-to-be teachers how to cultivate the elements of engagement also could increase students' involvement with and enthusiasm for school. Engagement-centered educational pedagogy can provide opportunities during student-teaching and curriculum design courses for teachers-in-training to think critically about ways to facilitate specific behaviors associated with increased student engagement (e.g., providing consistent and meaningful praise and recognition for good schoolwork).

Teachers can practice developing specific, classroom-level action plans aimed at facilitating behaviors that drive engagement in *their* students. Intentional methods for tracking and tailoring student recognition for good schoolwork (learning how to identify and then praise the good work that students do) can be emphasized in current achievement/grade management courses.

The need for highly talented (not only highly educated) teachers is of particular importance when helping teachers find creative, imaginative, tangible ways to free students to do what they do best, while meeting key curriculum goals. Engaged students add learning value to the classroom, as they are infectious in their enthusiasm. Teachers can be encouraged to unleash that energy by fostering a sense of freedom in the learning process. Teachers can acknowledge and highlight what students do best, facilitating the student's engagement level.

Teachers less adept at creative, individualized lesson planning, which allows students the opportunity to practice using their strengths while simultaneously achieving specific learning outcomes, will require collaboration and teamwork among educators to best serve student interests. Individualized learning within engagement education is provided not only with an emphasis on improved cognition, but also to encourage positive learning affect.

Engagement education can include building and sharing student talent portfolios that highlight particular student strengths leveraged for conceptual learning success. Imagine teachers documenting and sharing success stories internally and with the community that not only highlight concepts learned by the student but share how a student got to do what they do best all at the same time, facilitating an engaging learning experience for both student and teacher. Sharing creative ways to help students exercise their greatest talents while facilitating specific learning goals and challenges may often require teamwork, to share with others how a teacher successfully taught a student who had a particular talent a particular concept (Gallup, 2003; Levitz & Noel, 2000). A reference portfolio of talent-enhancing tricks-of-the-teaching-trade could be amassed that benefits scores of students and builds energetic and engaged schools! Since engagement is not necessarily contingent on class size, it is necessary not only to have enough teachers, but also to have enough of the *right* teachers.

Engaged Leadership – Principal Talent   Highly talented principals are leaders who know how to engage their teachers and employees, setting a strong framework for an engaged school. Principals with highly engaged teachers have highly engaged students and higher performing schools. Principals can measure their level of teacher and employee engagement and strategize ways to build engaged teachers and staff.

Principals must not only keep abreast of emerging research, the latest curriculum trends, and how to construct safe environments for teachers and students, but they must be effective organizational leaders and people managers adept at facilitating those things most needed by followers – trust, compassion, stability, and of course hope (Rath & Conchie, 2008). As principals intentionally invest in the engagement of their teachers, this will spill out all over students. Recognizing and praising students will come more naturally to those teachers who have themselves done good work and been recognized (Rath & Clifton, 2004).

Engaged Communities   With Gallup Student Poll data revealing such a definitive and disturbing downward trend in engagement over time in students, the community is responsible for providing reinforcements for building engagement in our schools. With nearly a third of students dropping out of school annually, most during the early high school years, it is unacceptable to assign declining trends in engagement to mood swings or rebellion. We must collectively flip the switch on student engagement during the middle school years and aim intentionally and proactively toward engaged young adults who envision a positive future for themselves and also for their peers. Teachers and principals can leverage relationships not only with involved parents but also with business and community leaders, in specific ways, to build engaged schools.

Schools may extend invitations to area leaders to assign an Engagement Ambassador to the school and build a network of engagement advocates in the community. Each Engagement Ambassador may be invited to facilitate engagement outcomes in students. They may focus on student recognition for schoolwork relevant to their industry or workplace, praise student talents needed for particular business tasks, or volunteer time to work side-by-side with students to clean and clear streets and lots in close vicinity to the school to help make a safe environment for student learning.

Boosting Well-Being

Mandated Reporting for Student Well-Being Scores   Over the last decade, in an era of increased accountability, schools have customarily provided parents of students and the general public with state assessment results. Often, assessment results from local schools appear in the daily newspaper and are reported on by local television news. These reports provide community members with one marker of school quality and some information about how local students, as a group, are doing academically. Such data largely fail to reveal *why* students may be performing the way they are.

The report of additional student data, such as that summarizing the well-being of a student body (disaggregated by grade level), would demonstrate that the schools and the communities are concerned with the well-being of youth and not just their level of achievement. It would broadly acknowledge that academic reporting tells a portion of the student story. Annual reporting would allow for the examination of well-being trends for cohorts of young people. Civic leaders and youth organizations can respond to ebbs and flows in well-being with targeted programming.

Community Well-Being Audits   Historically, community audits focused on aspects of ill-being such as premature births and murders. Now, as a product of the collaboration between Gallup, Healthways, and America's Health Insurance Plans, we have representative well-being data for adult Americans living in each of the 435 congressional districts (see http://www.ahiphiwire.org/wellbeing/). Given coverage of all communities and the breadth of well-being domains measured (life evaluation, emotional health, physical health, healthy behaviors, work environment, basic access), community leaders can begin discussions of what is working for adults and how that could affect the lives of young people.

With the data in hand, leaders can structure a well-being audit and discussion that addresses how community well-being findings translate into local conditions, practices, and regulations conducive to youth well-being, as measured by the Gallup Student Poll. Then, existing community organizations examine their efforts to promote quality of life and to guarantee that students are treated with respect every day, learn or do something interesting every day, have enough energy to get things done every day, and smile and laugh a lot every day, and then coordinate with community and school leaders to refine and create programs that boost well-being. By trading the goal of reducing ill-being for the goal of promoting well-being, leaders may be better able to make communities better places to live. The audit, however, is the launching point for action. Community leaders must move from capturing and analyzing the data to effectively impacting it.

Community Round Tables   A table is an often-used but fitting image for facilitating health, friendship, hospitality, listening, and action. As community leaders initiate friendship with leaders outside of their sphere of influence and focus, the collage of ideas and interests will generate the needed ingenuity and bring to life both complex and simplistic solutions.

Focused, successful action planning born out of an understanding of the well-being data will be successful when leaders from different spheres of interest collaborate around the common goal of healthy, vital, future-focused communities.

Community Round Tables have a vision to boost student well-being and may be chaired and facilitated by: elected or appointed officials; small, medium, and large business owners; youth advocates; superintendents and higher education leaders; parents; healthcare professionals; and leaders of faith communities.

Action plans created by Community Round Tables must be:

- focused on key metrics that matter to youth health and the long-term vitality of the community (e.g., respect, laughter, interest, and energy);
- owned by small groups but facilitated by everyone (this requires leadership to mobilize others and appoint talented communicators to diffuse information to all levels of the community);
- actionable;
- focused on what is right with students (multiply those things helping students to thrive).

Community Round Tables focused on the right metrics will have the short-term effect of improving individual student lives, giving them positive yesterdays and hopeful tomorrows, but it will have the long-term effect of building strong, vibrant communities where human beings live, work, and learn, intent on providing themselves and others with a dignified life and more opportunities to laugh.

CONCLUSION

What would happen if we measure and promote what is right with students? For starters, with the data and resources we have today, we could bring psychological reform to our schools and more vitality to our communities. By doubling hope, building engaged schools, and boosting well-being, we could turn *every* school into a magic kingdom and *every* neighborhood into a great place to grow up. We know that hope is measurable and malleable, engaged schools are attainable, and well-being is predictive. Now we can focus people on what is right, and multiply that by the 34 million 10–18-year-olds in this nation. We need to serve students a healthy dose of tomorrow, and everyone is invited to the table.

APPENDIX 8.1

Gallup Student Poll and Strengths Development in the All American High School (Gallup, 2009c)

The American dream is alive and well at an urban high school in the heartland. The All American High School student body, as diverse as America itself, is unified in its desire to have good jobs, strong families, and happy lives. Their demographics mirror the census of the nation and their goals reflect the hopes of youth around the world.

The Gallup Student Poll The All American High School was the first school in the country to participate in the Gallup Student Poll, a landmark new measure that will track the hope, engagement, and well-being of students across the USA over the next 10 years. Through a secure Web-based survey, 198 freshmen completed the poll.

Overall, 48% of the students were hopeful (15% discouraged), 42% were engaged (17% actively disengaged), and 57% were thriving (3% suffering). Also, 27% of the students reported that they had positive yesterdays (were treated with respect, smiled or laughed a lot, learned or did something interesting, had enough energy to get things done).

The data from the Gallup Student Poll were combined with student performance data, including attendance, credits earned, and the GPA. Hope, engagement, and well-being each played an important role in predicting student behavior.

The hope, ideas, and energy we have for the future predict attendance, credits earned, and the GPA of the All American High School freshmen. Engagement – the involvement in and enthusiasm for school – accounts for a small amount of unique variance in the GPA, with the "praise and recognition" item exhibiting the strongest link (.19) between an engagement item and the GPA.

Well-being – how we think about and experience our lives – tells us how our students are doing today and predicts their success in the future. High school freshmen with high evaluative well-being (how we think about our lives) earn more credits with a higher GPA than peers with low well-being. Specifically, the typical student who is thriving earns 10% more credits and a 2.9 GPA (out of 4), whereas a student with low well-being and completing fewer credits earns a 2.4. Regarding experienced well-being, the two positive emotions of joy (smiling and laughing a lot yesterday) and interest (learning or doing something interesting yesterday) are associated with more credits earned and a higher GPA.

Strengths Development Over the course of the 2008–2009 academic year, freshmen completed StrengthsQuest and were mentored by faculty trained to be strengths-based educators. The strengths development program involved the students participating in weekly activities that include strengths feedback, exploration of Top 5 themes, creation of a strengths display (nametag or poster), small group strengths discussions (linking strengths to life goals, to one personal success story, and to one moment of inspiration shared with someone else at school), and 15-minute individualized strengths conferences.

After finishing the strengths development program, participating students completed a second administration of the Gallup Student Poll. Over the course of the strengths development program, hope increased significantly from pre- to post-testing.

All American High: Four Years Later As students progress through the All American High School, their hope, engagement, and well-being will be tracked via the Gallup Student Poll. Strengths development programming will continue with the support of local strengths-based educators. Educational outcomes for this cohort of students will be compared to those students who preceded them from now until they graduate in 2012.

REFERENCES

Boehm, J. K., & Lyubomirsky, S. (2008). Does happiness promote career success? *Journal of Career Assessment, 16,* 101–116.

Bowers, K. (2009). Making the most of human strengths. In S. J. Lopez (Ed.), *Positive psychology: Exploring the best in people: Discovering human strengths* (pp. 23–36). Westport, CT: Praeger.

Carey, K. (2004). *A matter of degrees: Improving graduation rates in four-year colleges and universities.* Washington, DC: Education Trust.

Dweck, C. S. (1999). *Self-theories: Their role in motivation, personality, and development.* Philadelphia: Psychology Press.

Gallagher, M. W., & Lopez, S. J. (2008). *Hope, self-efficacy, and academic success in college students.* Poster presented at the annual convention of the American Psychological Association, Boston.

Gallup (2003). *Teaching and leading with individualization.* Retrieved June 26, 2007, from http://media.gallup.com/EDUCATION/pdf/TeachingAndLeadingWith Individualization20030508.pdf

Gallup (2009a). *Hope, engagement, and well-being as predictors of attendance, credits earned, and GPA in high school freshmen.* Unpublished raw data, Omaha, NE.

Gallup (2009b). *Relationships between hope, income, and teacher–student ratio in March 2009 Gallup Student Poll.* Unpublished raw data, Omaha, NE.

Gallup (2009c). *Hope as an outcome of strengths development in freshmen in high school.* Unpublished raw data, Omaha, NE.

Gallup (2009d). *Building engaged schools: A scientific method for improving school performance.* Omaha, NE: Gallup Press.

Gordon, G. (2006). *Building engaged schools: Getting the most out of America's classrooms.* New York: Gallup Press.

Harter, J. K., Schmidt, F. L., & Hayes, T. L. (2002). Business-unit-level relationship between employee satisfaction, employee engagement, and business outcomes: A meta-analysis. *Journal of Applied Psychology, 87,* 268–279.

Judge, T. A., & Hurst, C. (2008). How the rich (and happy) get richer (and happier): Relationship of core self-evaluations to trajectories in attaining work success. *Journal of Applied Psychology, 83,* 849–863.

Liesveld, R., & Miller, J. A. (2005). *Teach with your strengths: How great teachers inspire their students.* New York: Gallup Press.

Levitz, R., & Noel, L. (2000). *The earth-shaking, but quiet revolution, in retention management.* Retrieved August 6, 2004, from www.noellevitz.com

Lopez, S. J. (2004). *Naming, nurturing, and navigating: Capitalizing on strengths in daily life.* Paper presented at the National Conference on Building a Strengths-Based Campus: Best Practices in Maximizing Student Performance, Omaha, NE.

Lopez, S. J., & Louis, M. C. (2009). The principles of strengths-based education. *Journal of College and Character, 10,* 1–8.

Lopez, S. J., Rose, S., Robinson, C., Marques, S., & Pais-Ribeiro, J. (2009). Measuring and promoting hope in schoolchildren. In R. Gilman, E. S. Huebner, & M. Furlong

(Eds.), *Promoting wellness in children and youth: Handbook of positive psychology in the schools* (pp. 37–51). Mahwah, NJ: Lawrence Erlbaum Associates, Inc.

Louis, M. C. (2008). A comparative analysis of the effectiveness of strengths-based curricula in promoting first-year college student success. *Dissertation Abstracts International*, 69(06A). (UMI No. AAT 3321378)

Lyubomirsky, S., King, L., & Diener, E. (2005). The benefits of frequent positive affect: Does happiness lead to success. *Psychological Bulletin, 131,* 803–855.

Marques, S. C., Pais-Ribeiro, J., & Lopez, S. J. (2009). Validation of a Portuguese version of the Children's Hope Scale. *School Psychology International, 30,* 538–551.

Onwuegbuzie, A. J. (1998). Role of hope in predicting anxiety about statistics. *Psychological Reports, 82,* 1315–1320.

Rath, T. (2007). *StrengthsFinder 2.0.* New York: Gallup Press.

Rath, T., & Clifton, D. O. (2004). *How full is your bucket,* New York: Gallup Press.

Rath, T., & Conchie, B. (2008). *Strengths-based leadership.* New York: Gallup Press.

Rettew, J. G., & Lopez, S. J. (2009). Discovering your strengths. In S. J. Lopez (Ed.), *Positive psychology: Exploring the best in people: Discovering human strengths* (pp. 1–21). Westport, CT: Praeger.

Seligman, M. E. P., Steen, T., Park, N., & Peterson, C. (2005). Positive psychology progress: Empirical validation of interventions. *American Psychologist, 60,* 410–421.

Sin, N. L., & Lyubomirsky, S. (2009). Enhancing well-being and alleviating depressive symptoms with positive psychology interventions: A practice-friendly meta-analysis. *Journal of Clinical Psychology: In Session, 65,* 467–487.

Snyder, C. R. (1994). *The psychology of hope: You can get there from here.* New York: Free Press.

Snyder, C. R., Harris, C., Anderson, J. R., Holleran, S. A., Irving, L. M., Sigmon, S. T., et al. (1991). The will and the ways: Development and validation of an individual-differences measure of hope. *Journal of Personality and Social Psychology, 60,* 570–585.

Snyder, C. R., Hoza, B., Pelham, W. E., Rapoff, M., Ware, L., Danovsky, M., et al. (1997). The development and validation of the Children's Hope Scale. *Journal of Pediatric Psychology, 22,* 399–421.

Snyder, C. R., McDermott, D., Cook, W., & Rapoff, M. (2002a). *Hope for the journey* (Rev. ed.). Clinton Corners, NY: Percheron Press.

Snyder, C. R., Shorey, H. S., Cheavens, J., Pulvers, K. M., Adams III, V. H., & Wiklund, C. (2002b). Hope and academic success in college. *Journal of Educational Psychology, 94,* 820–826.

Suldo, S. M., Huebner, E. S., Michalowski, J., & Thalji, A. (2011). Promoting subjective well-being. In M. Bray & T. Kehle (Eds), *Oxford handbook of school psychology.* New York: Oxford University Press.

U.S. Department of Education (2004). *Performance measure and accountability.* Available at http://www.ed.gov/about/offices/list/ovae/pi/cte/perfmeas.html

Worrell, F. C., & Hale, R. L. (2001). The relationship of hope in the future and perceived school climate to school completion. *School Psychology Quarterly, 16,* 370–388.

Part IV

Improving Institutions, Organizations, and the World of Work

9

Applied Positive Organizational Psychology: The State of the Science and Practice

IA KO and STEWART I. DONALDSON

During the past decade, an increasing number of organizational scholars have mulled over how positive psychology can be used to improve organizational effectiveness and employee well-being. These musings and related research efforts have resulted in an emerging literature that suggests a number of ways in which the world of work can be improved by the science of positive psychology.

Positive organizational behavior (POB) and positive organizational scholarship (POS) have emerged as areas of study and have garnered considerable attention in recent years. POB refers to "the study and application of positively oriented human resource strengths and psychological capacities that can be measured, developed, and effectively managed for performance improvement in today's workplace" (Luthans, 2002a, p. 59). POB capacities such as hope, optimism, resiliency, and self-efficacy are something one can measure, develop, and use to improve performance (Luthans, 2002b; Luthans & Avolio, 2003; Luthans & Youssef, 2004; Nelson & Cooper, 2007; Youssef & Luthans, 2007). POS is "concerned primarily with the study of especially positive outcomes, processes, and attributes of organizations and their members" (Cameron, Dutton, & Quinn, 2003, p. 4). The basic idea of POS is that understanding the drivers of positive behavior in the workplace would enable organizations to rise to new levels of achievement (Roberts, Spreitzer, Dutton, Quinn, Heaphy, & Barker, 2005). POS seeks to study organizations characterized by "appreciation, collaboration, virtuousness, vitality, and meaningfulness where creating abundance and human well-being are key indicators of success" (Bernstein, 2003, p. 267).

POB and POS share the common root of positive psychology and highlight the importance of scientific process in the development of knowledge. However, they are distinguishable in their core topics of interest, the degree of emphasis on performance improvement, and the level of analysis. In terms of core topics, POB has been mainly concerned with individual psychological qualities and their impact on performance improvement, whereas POS has been mostly concerned with the positive aspects of the organizational context (Bakker & Schaufeli, 2008; Cameron, 2005; Luthans, 2002b). The emphasis on performance improvement is central to POB, but not necessarily to POS. Furthermore, regarding the level of analysis, POB studies have been conducted primarily at the micro- and meso-levels of analysis using survey research, while POS studies have usually been conducted at the organizational level of analysis using diverse qualitative and quantitative research methods (Luthans & Avolio, 2009a, 2009b; Luthans & Youssef, 2007). Of course, this is not to say that POB studies are only at individual level and POS studies are only at organizational level. In fact, they both consider constructs at multiple levels; they do so differently. POB has tended to develop in an inductive way (i.e., from individual to group to organizational levels of analysis), while POS has developed in the opposite direction (Luthans & Avolio, 2009a).

Besides POB and POS, other terms have been used to refer to positive organizational studies or positive psychology applied in the work and organizational settings. They include positive psychology at work, positive workplace, and positive organization (Martin, 2005; Turner, Barling, & Zacharatos, 2002; Wiegand & Geller, 2005). Donaldson and Ko (2010) suggested positive organizational psychology (POP) as an umbrella term that covers POB, POS, and other related labels with regard to their research topics, foci, and the level of analysis. They define POP as "the scientific study of positive subjective experiences and traits in the workplace and positive organizations, and its application to improve the effectiveness and quality of life in organizations" (Donaldson & Ko, 2010, p. 178). The goal of this chapter is to provide an overview of POP, describe its importance, and to review how POP can be applied to improve work life and organizations.

GROWTH AND IMPORTANCE OF POSITIVE ORGANIZATIONAL PSYCHOLOGY

Several factors seem to indicate that POP has grown considerably over the last decade. Increasing numbers of books, book chapters, and journal articles are published, and more professional meetings are held around POP topics. Does this mean that the field of POP has actually grown? A recent study by Donaldson and Ko (2010) provides more concrete evidence of a growing body of POP scholarly literature and an emerging empirical evidence base. Donaldson and Ko examined the POP peer-reviewed journal articles published between 2001 and 2009, to provide a detailed picture of the current state of the field. In particular, they sought to discover the overall growth rate, trends, prevalent topics, and empirical evidence for each topic in the literature. They identified 172 peer-reviewed journal articles (106 conceptual and 66 empirical) that met one or more of the following criteria: (1) the article was linked to the POB or POS literature; (2) the article reported a study that applied positive psychology topics in an organizational setting; and (3) the article reported organizational studies that revisited established/pre-existing topics from positive psychology perspectives. Figure 9.1 illustrates how the number and type of publications have changed since 2001.

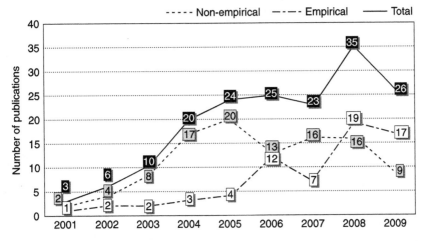

FIGURE 9.1 Positive organizational psychology peer-reviewed journal articles from 2001 to 2009.

Empirical studies have shown that organizations can benefit from facilitating positive organizational behaviors and processes. For example, organizations may increase employee engagement by promoting their strengths (Clifton & Harter, 2003) or psychological capital (Avey, Wernsing, & Luthans, 2008). Organizational performance may be improved through facilitating authentic leadership or organizational virtuousness (Cameron, Bright, & Caza, 2004).

Table 9.1 summarizes some of the benefits of POP that have been found in recent research projects. We will discuss some of the research on these topics in greater detail later in this chapter.

Donaldson and Bligh (2006) explored how POP can be used to enhance more traditional topic areas and applications of organizational psychology, such as maximizing person–job–organization fit, building optimal team performance, mentoring and coaching, optimizing work and family balance, promoting organizational learning and continuous improvement, and the like. Furthermore, Preskill and Donaldson (2008) provided a detailed example of how positive psychology can help to improve the development and evaluation of career development programs. These examples illustrate that positive psychology is providing new insights and approaches for enhancing organizational and employee functioning and well-being. A range of training and career opportunities for positive organizational psychologists have now been identified and offer great promise for the continued expansion of applications of positive psychology in the workplace (see Donaldson & Bligh, 2006).

KEY POP CONCEPTS AND APPLICATIONS

We are now going to review some of the key POP concepts. These topics have been selected based on the extant and future application implication, as well as the amount of literature (both theoretical and empirical) aggregated thus far. For

TABLE 9.1   Examples of potential benefits of POP

Strengths-based approach

- Higher productivity, lower turnover, and higher customer loyalty at both employee and work unit levels (Harter et al., 2002)
- Decreased turnover rate and increased employee engagement, state hope, and life satisfaction (Black, 2001; Hodges & Clifton, 2004)
- Increased employee engagement (Clifton & Harter, 2003)
- Increased employee and team productivity (Connelly, 2002)

Authentic leadership
- Higher OCB, higher organizational commitment, better organizational performance, higher follower satisfaction with supervisor, higher job satisfaction, and better job performance (Walumbwa et al., 2008)

Positive organizational development and change
- Higher future success expectancy, better coping with stress, better job performance, and higher job satisfaction (Armstrong-Stassen & Schlosser, 2008)
- Increase in stock prices, better customer relations, better employee relationships, higher quality product, and innovative union–management partnership (Cooperrider & Whitney, 1999; Whitney & Cooperrider, 2000)

Organizational virtuousness
- Better objective and perceived organizational performance: higher profit margin, innovation, customer retention, employee turnover, and quality (Cameron et al., 2004)

Psychological capital
- Better job performance, higher job satisfaction, and higher organizational commitment (Larson & Luthans, 2006; Luthans et al., 2008b)
- More engagement, higher OCB, lower voluntary and involuntary absenteeism, and lower cynicism and deviance (Avey et al., 2008)

Flow
- Extra-role job performance (Eisenberger et al., 2005)
- Better in-role and extra-role job performance (Demerouti, 2006)
- More organizational and personal resources (Salanova et al., 2006)
- Higher motivation, enjoyment, participation, aspirations, and buoyancy (Martin & Jackson, 2008)

each topic, we will provide definitions, theories, empirical evidence, and existing or potential applications, whenever the relevant information is available. It should be noted that we intend to provide a brief description – rather than a comprehensive explanation – to serve as a roadmap for future exploration of the topics presented.

Strengths

Clifton and Harter (2003) define strength as "the ability to provide consistent, near-perfect performance in a given activity" (p. 114). The basic premise of the strengths-based approach is that all people have talents, on which strengths are built, and the roles in the organization must play to strengths. Weaknesses should not be ignored, but addressed in a constructive manner. Several researchers assert that focusing and building on employees' strengths and investing in what people do best naturally can help organizations to achieve excellence and experience the greatest gains in human development (e.g., Clifton & Harter, 2003; Roberts et al., 2005).

Identifying and fostering individuals' strengths at work may be done through at least three ways. One is using the Values in Action (VIA) Classification of Character Strengths (www.viacharacter.org). Since Peterson and Park provide detailed explanation on the VIA Classification in their chapter in this book (see Chapter 4), we instead focus on other two methods of fostering strengths: the Clifton StrengthsFinder and the Reflected Best Self (RBS) exercise.

The Clifton StrengthsFinder (www.strengthsfinder.com) is a Web-based assessment developed by the Gallup Organization in 1998. There are 34 themes of talents (e.g., achiever, activator, deliberative, empathy, positivity) and each individual is provided with a report on his/her top five talents (Buckingham & Clifton, 2001). This instrument is not free; however it has been widely used in many organizations and in different languages, as the book *Now, Discover Your Strengths* became a bestseller. Applying the StrengthsFinder talent themes requires support from supervisors or the organization as a whole. Once employees identify their themes of talent, they should be given opportunities to use their talent to develop strengths. Also, it is important for working groups and teams to coordinate each member's strengths to maximize the organizational outcome. Usually managers or leaders take the coordinator role and provide their employees with relevant support. In order to effectively coordinate employees' strengths, managers are often trained as strengths coaches (Hodges & Clifton, 2004).

The RBS exercise is a tool to help people understand and develop their individual talents. It allows employees to develop a sense of their personal best in order to increase their future potential (Roberts et al., 2005). There are four steps in this exercise. Individuals first identify from whom they want to receive feedback, either people at work or outside of the work, and ask for feedback. Once they collect feedback from various sources, individuals recognize patterns by searching for common themes, which may or may not confirm one's sense of his or herself, depending on the previous awareness of one's own strengths. Then, individuals compose their own self-portrait – "an insightful image that [one] can use as a reminder of [one's] previous contributions and as a guide for future action" (Roberts et al., p. 77) – by writing a description (of oneself) that reviews and refines the accumulated information. This process helps to create a more vivid sense of the possible self – the person one might be in totally different contexts. Finally, based on the description, individuals redesign the job to build on what they are good at. This starts with making small changes in the way one works and spends one's time at work. These four steps of the RBS exercise can help people to uncover their unrecognized areas of potential.

Empirical studies show that strengths-based employee development may indeed lead to positive business outcomes (i.e., increase in profitability, safety, and satisfaction, decrease in turnover), an increase in employee engagement, and an increase in other positive experiences in the workplace (Black, 2001; Clifton & Harter, 2003; Connelly, 2002; Hodges & Clifton, 2004).

First, regarding positive business outcomes, Black (2001) discovered that strengths-based development helped a hospital to achieve a dramatic decrease in turnover. The hospital's annual turnover rate of 35% declined by 50% after the hospital conducted structured talent inventory interviews and built teams that let each member use their strengths. Moreover, Connelly (2002) found that strengths-based team intervention increased per-person-productivity by 6% in the study of the Toyota North American Parts Center (California), which is composed of 400 employees on 54 teams. The team members used StrengthsFinder to identify their talents, and the managers attended a special four-day course to learn how to manage teams and optimize each member's strengths and relationships among the members. Two teams that went through a more intensive strengths-based development program experienced a 9% productivity increase in six months. In addition, Harter, Schmidt, and Hayes (2002) discovered that employees who had the opportunity to use their strengths every day were more productive, had lower turnover, and showed higher customer loyalty. Also, the work units composed of such employees yielded significantly higher performance.

Second, with regard to employee engagement, Black (2001) found that strengths-based development not only impacted business outcomes but also employee engagement in the case of the hospital introduced earlier. The hospital was experiencing low employee engagement (i.e., ranked in the bottom quartile of Gallup's worldwide employee engagement database). Two years later the employee engagement dramatically increased (i.e., moved to the top quartile of Gallup's database). Clifton and Harter (2003) also revealed increased employee engagement as a result of the strengths-based approach. In their review of data related to employee engagement interventions from 65 organizations, companies who utilized strengths-based development experienced a dramatic increase in employee engagement in two years.

Lastly, strengths-based interventions can promote other positive experiences at work, such as hope, subjective well-being, and self-efficacy. In Black's (2001) study, a strengths-based intervention increased hospital employees' levels of state hope – "an individual's present goal-directed thinking" (Snyder, Sympson, Ybasco, Borders, Babyak, & Higgins, 1996; as cited in Hodges & Clifton, 2004, p. 263) – and life satisfaction. Also, Hodges and Clifton's (2004) pre-test–post-test study reported that the strengths-based intervention increased hospital employees' state hope level. The employees completed StrengthsFinder and received action statements, and 24 employees were trained as strengths coaches and helped other employees to build their strengths. One year after the intervention, 40% who stated that they maximally participated in the intervention reported a significantly higher increase in their hope. In addition, a strengths-based approach may increase the employees' self-efficacy. In a study of 212 UCLA students, a strengths-based developmental intervention conducted throughout a semester increased the students' awareness of strengths, direction about the future, and level of confidence (Hodges & Clifton, 2004).

In summary, the extant literature provides evidence that strengths-based interventions can increase organizational effectiveness and employee well-being. Although there is a need for more empirical research, especially studies comparing the impact of focusing on strengths and managing weakness versus focusing on weakness (Clifton & Harter, 2003), the research findings thus far seem promising.

Coaching

Coaching is "a service provided to those in business who want individual assistance to enhance their performance, skills, and achievement (Douglas & McCauley, 1999; cited in Kauffman & Scoular, 2004, p. 288). Most of the coaching literature focuses on leadership or executive coaching (Grant, Curtayne, & Burton, 2009; Linley, Woolston, & Biswas-Diener, 2009; Wood & Gordon, 2009). Some highlight the similarities between positive psychology and coaching psychology, and contend that coaching psychology is a form of applied positive psychology (Grant & Cavanagh, 2007; Linley et al., 2009). Grant and Cavanagh assert that both positive psychology and coaching psychology are abundance based and solution focused, and assume that people have a natural tendency to want to grow and develop their potential and that they thrive within the supporting environment. Kauffman and Scoular (2004) state that positive psychology and a strengths-based orientation provide a more appropriate model for executive coaching since both are based on the assumption that individuals have everything they need to address the challenge.

Grant and Cavanagh (2007) provide some insight into the growth and the current status of the coaching literature. In terms of quantity, the coaching literature has clearly grown fast recently. Since 1937, 355 papers on coaching have been published, but 74% (262) of these were published between 2000 and July 2007. Moreover, between 1980 and July 2007, 69 psychological coaching outcome papers that examined the effect of an intervention on specific variables (e.g., goal attainment, performance, well-being) were published. In terms of quality, the development of the coaching literature may not be as clear as quantitative growth. Among the 69 papers, 8 randomized controlled studies indicate that coaching may improve performance in various ways (e.g., Gattellari, Donnelly, Taylor, Meerkin, Hirst, & Ward, 2005; Taylor, 1997). Nonetheless, only one of those eight was conducted in the workplace and no significant impact of coaching on the outcomes was found (i.e., supervisors' feedback skills in this study). Furthermore, Grant and Cavanagh maintain that it is difficult to develop a common knowledge base of coaching outcomes because 46 within- or between-subject outcome studies inconsistently used outcome measures and often did not measure goal attainment, which is an important coaching outcome measure. Based on these findings, Grant and Cavanagh argue that coaching psychology is still in the early stages of development and they call for improving both the quality and quantity of research as well as engaging in the development of the wider coaching industry.

In a more recent study, Grant and his colleagues (2009) examined the effects of coaching programs among executives and senior managers and used a randomized control waitlist design. They compared the coaching group that received coaching immediately after the initial workshop (Time 1) and finished it 10 weeks later (Time 2) to a waitlist control group that received coaching 10 weeks (Time 2) after a training workshop (Time 1) and finished it in another 10 weeks (Time 3). At Time 2 (when only the coaching group had finished coaching), the coaching group reported higher goal attainment, lower depression, and higher workplace well-being than the control group. At Time 3 (when the control group also had finished coaching), the control group reported increased levels of goal attainment and workplace well-being compared to their own levels at Time 2. The coachees also reported other benefits of coaching, such as increased confidence, the gaining of applied management skills, being better able to deal with organizational change or stress, personal or professional insights, and feeling helped with finding ways to develop their career.

Overall, the existing coaching literature shows that coaching, even if it is short term, can be effective. As more researchers are becoming involved, coaching is developing a more solid theoretical and scientific foundation. With more empirical research support, coaching as applied positive psychology can play an important role in helping people cope with the uncertainty and challenges during organizational change.

Positive Leadership

A positive approach to leadership produced studies on different types of positive leadership, including authentic (Avolio, Luthans, & Walumbwa, 2004; Gardner & Schermerhorn, 2004; May, Chan, Hodges, & Avolio, 2003; Walumbwa, Avolio, Gardner, Wernsing, & Peterson, 2008), transformational (Walumbwa et al., 2008), ethical (Brown & Treviño, 2006), and spiritual (Panday & Gupta, 2008) leadership. These different types of positive leadership do share similarities in that they all possess such attributes as concern for others, integrity, and role modeling (Brown & Treviño, 2006). In this chapter, we focus on authentic leadership (AL), as it is considered the root construct of positive forms of leadership (Avolio & Gardner, 2005).

Authentic leaders are "individuals who are deeply aware of how they think and behave and are perceived by others as being aware of their own and others' values/ moral perspective, knowledge, and strengths; aware of the context in which they operate; and who are confident, hopeful, optimistic, resilient, and high on moral character" (Avolio, Gardner, Walumbwa, Luthans, & May, 2004, p. 802). AL refers to "a process that draws from both positive psychological capacities and a highly developed organizational context, which results in both greater self-awareness and self-regulated positive behaviors on the part of leaders and associates, fostering positive self-development" (Luthans & Avolio, 2003, p. 243). At the core of AL is leader self-awareness. Leader self-awareness requires a focus on learning about one's own leadership capabilities, such as strengths, limitations, and developmental goals (Avolio, Wernsing, Chan, & Griffith, 2007).

Authentic leaders are similar to transformational leaders, such that both are moral and self-aware (Brown & Treviño, 2006). Transformational leaders are leaders who "stimulate and inspire followers to both achieve extraordinary outcomes and, in the process, develop their own leadership capacity" (Bass & Riggio, 2006, p. 3). One big difference is that transformational leaders actively set out to transform the follower into a leader, whereas authentic leaders *model* positive attributes such as hope, optimism, and resiliency (Avolio, 2005; Avolio & Gardner, 2005; Brown & Treviño, 2006).

Gardner, Avolio, Luthans, May, and Walumbwa (2005) proposed a self-based model of authentic leader and follower development. Their model includes two antecedents of authentic leadership development (ALD): personal history (e.g., family influences, early life challenges); and trigger events (i.e., dramatic or subtle changes in the individual's circumstances that facilitate personal growth and development). These antecedents serve as positive forces in developing leader self-awareness, which is one of two core elements of the ALD process. In particular, authentic leaders are aware of their own values, identity, emotions, motives, and goals. The other core element is self-regulation, which includes internalized regulation, balanced processing of information, authentic behavior, and relational transparency. By modeling positive values, psychological states, behaviors, and self-development, authentic leaders develop authentic followers who exhibit the parallel qualities of their leaders and "develop an engaged, highly positive, ethical organizational climate" (Avolio, Griffith, Wernsing, & Walumbwa, 2010, p. 42).

Empirical research on AL is growing and seems promising. Yammarino, Dionne, Schriesheim, and Dansereau (2008) conducted a review and analysis of the AL literature. They identified a total of 27 publications (i.e., book chapters and journal articles), and 4 out of those were empirical in nature. Walumbwa et al. (2008) revealed that AL was linked to positive consequences such as organizational citizenship behavior, organizational commitment, follower satisfaction with supervisor, and follower job satisfaction and performance. Based on these findings they assert that organizations may garner positive returns on the investment by training leaders to be more authentic. Walumbwa, Luthans, Avey, and Oke (2009) found that authentic leadership was positively related to group-level psychological capital and trust, which in turn contributed to two desired group outcomes: group citizenship behavior and performance. Clapp-Smith, Vogelgesang, and Avey (2009) also revealed that group-level trust in management mediated the relationship between authentic leadership and performance (i.e., unit sales growth) as well as the relationship between follower psychological capital and performance.

ALD intervention is at a very early stage of development. However, there is preliminary evidence suggesting that positive leadership interventions can be effective and produce positive organizational outcomes (e.g., Wernsing, 2010). Moreover, Reichard and Avolio (2005) reviewed leadership intervention studies conducted in the last 100 years (1900–2004). They found that leadership interventions had a positive impact on work outcomes (e.g., ratings of leader performance), regardless of the theory being investigated and the duration of those interventions. This provides a hopeful future for ALD intervention to positively influence organizational outcomes.

To sum up, authentic leaders possess self-awareness, self-regulation, and positive psychological characteristics. Through positive modeling, authentic leaders develop authentic followers and positively influence followers' work attitudes and behaviors, ultimately leading to positive organizational outcomes.

Positive Organizational Development and Change

A positive approach to organizational development and change (ODC) is one of the latest trends in organizational development (Greiner & Cummings, 2004).

Cameron (2008) asserts that although positive organizational change can result from both the positive and the negative, more emphasis should be given to the positive to mitigate negative tendencies and stimulate positive organizational change. He states that "when both the positive and negative are present, the survival benefits of attending to the negative tend to create stronger defensive reactions than inclinations toward the positive" (Cameron, 2008, p. 16).

Empirical studies on positive ODC largely focus on discovering positive aspects and processes that can alleviate stressful organizational change. Organizational downsizing, for example, may become less stressful and more productive when the organization members are more optimistic. A recent study found that managers' generalized optimism is related to positive organizational outcomes (e.g., higher future success expectancy and better coping with stress, job performance, and job satisfaction during and after downsizing; Armstrong-Stassen & Schlosser, 2008). Also, an organizational tragedy such as a school shooting can be recovered from more effectively through an organizational healing process that strengthens organizational relationships and the future capacity for recovery (Powley & Piderit, 2008).

Appreciative inquiry (AI) is perhaps the most widely used positive ODC practice as it has become increasingly popular (Van der Haar & Hosking, 2004). Cooperrider and Whitney (1999) define AI as "the cooperative search for the best in people, their organizations, and the world around them. It involves systematic discovery of what gives a system 'life' when it is most effective and capable in economic, ecological, and human terms" (pp. 247–248). Although it was developed in the 1980s (Appreciative Inquiry Commons, n.d.) – over a decade before the first introduction of positive psychology – AI and positive psychology share the core idea of focusing on positive human experiences and functioning. AI takes four stages ("the 4-D cycle"): (1) discovery (i.e., a systemic or system-wide cooperative inquiry into the best of what is or has been); (2) dream (i.e., exploration of the organization's greatest possibilities); (3) design (i.e., drafting provocative propositions or design statements describing the ideal organization); and (4) destiny (i.e., a series of actions inspired by previous steps to support ongoing learning and innovation) (Whitney & Trosten-Bloom, 2003). Through these phases, AI helps organizations to undergo changes more successfully and achieve positive outcomes such as increase in stock prices, better customer relations, better employee relationships, higher quality product, and an innovative union–management partnership (Cooperrider & Whitney, 1999; Whitney & Cooperrider, 2000). Real-life AI cases, including Avon Mexico, GTE, the city of Chicago, and the United Nations, can be found on the AI Commons website (appreciativeinquiry.case.edu). In summary, these findings suggest that efforts to improve organizations can become more effective and less stressful when organizational development practitioners use positive approaches and processes.

Organizational Virtuousness

Organizational virtuousness refers to "individuals' actions, collective activities, cultural attributes, or processes that enable dissemination and perpetuation of virtuousness in an organization" (Cameron et al., 2004, p. 768), where virtuousness is defined as "what individuals and organizations aspire to be when they are at their very best" (p. 767). As this definition implies, organizational virtuousness can be conceptualized from two levels. Virtuousness in organizations relates to organizational members' transcendent, elevating behavior, whereas virtuousness by organizations refers to organizational features that enable the virtuousness of the organization's members (Cameron et al., 2004). Virtuousness is important to individuals and organizations because it helps them to cope effectively and achieve positive outcomes, even in turbulent conditions, through its amplifying (i.e., self-perpetuating) and buffering effects (Cameron, 2006; Caza, Barker, & Cameron, 2004). Perceptions of organizational virtuousness are associated with objective indicators of organizational performance (i.e., profit margin) as well as perceived organizational performance such as innovation, customer retention, employee turnover, and quality (Cameron et al., 2004). In summary, these studies suggest that organizations can achieve higher levels of desired outcomes when their members display virtuous behaviors, enabled by organizational systems and processes. Kim Cameron's chapter in this book (Chapter 11) provides more detailed explanation of how virtuousness and virtuous leadership can contribute to producing positive organizational outcomes.

Psychological Capital (PsyCap)

PsyCap is a core construct of POB (Luthans, Vogelgesang, & Lester, 2006b; Luthans & Youssef, 2004) and is defined as:

> An individual's positive psychological state of development that is characterized by: (1) having confidence (self-efficacy) to take on and put in the necessary effort to succeed at challenging tasks; (2) making a positive attribution (optimism) about succeeding now and in the future; (3) persevering toward goals, and when necessary, redirecting paths to goals (hope) in order to succeed; and (4) when beset by problems and adversity, sustaining and bouncing back and even beyond (resiliency) to attain success.
> (Luthans, Avey, Avolio, Norman, & Combs, 2006a, p. 388)

Empirical findings from recent studies show the important role that PsyCap may play in yielding positive outcomes: job performance, job satisfaction, and organizational commitment (Larson & Luthans, 2006; Luthans, Norman, Avolio, & Avey, 2008b); engagement and organizational citizenship behavior (Avey et al., 2008); lower voluntary and involuntary absenteeism records (Avey, Patera, & West, 2006); lower cynicism and deviance (Avey et al., 2008); and less stress symptoms, intentions to quit, and job search behavior (Avey, Luthans, & Jensen, 2009). Moreover, a recent study on team-level PsyCap suggests that optimism may be the most functional team-level POB capacity for newly formed teams; optimism was positively linked to cohesion, cooperation, coordination, and satisfaction (West, Patera, & Carsten, 2009). These findings suggest that PsyCap contributes to positive organizational change by promoting positive attitudes and behaviors while countering dysfunctional attitudes and behaviors. Also, PsyCap may provide more insights on positive work attitudes currently being recognized by human and social capital, as it was found to predict job satisfaction and organizational commitment beyond human and social capital (Larson & Luthans, 2006).

Furthermore, PsyCap can be developed with only a small amount of training (Luthans, Avey, & Patera, 2008a; Luthans et al., 2006b). Luthans et al. (2008a) introduced Psychological Capital Intervention (PCI), a short Web-based intervention focused on an integrated developmental strategy for PsyCap capacities. In the first session (45 minutes), the participants learn about resilience and efficacy and how to apply them at work. They also view examples of resilience and efficacy in dramatized settings portrayed in movie clips. Next, the participants think of personal work-related challenging situations and create specific courses of action to deal with the situations. In the next self-reflection exercises they write past thoughts, emotions, and behaviors, as well as future steps and actions to take during challenging situations. Finally, the session ends with a session summary to facilitate the transfer of the training to the participants' jobs. The second session (45 minutes) on hope and optimism is similarly structured. The participants learn the importance of personal values and the challenge of accomplishing tasks and goals. They write down several challenging, appropriate, and personally valuable tasks they want to accomplish, they participate in a discussion, view examples of realistically challenging and personally valuable goals, and practice making goals more attainable. Luthans et al. (2008a) conducted PCI with 364 working adults. Compared to the control group that participated in a decision-making exercise, the treatment group showed a significant increase in PsyCap, even after controlling for pre-PsyCap scores, demographics, and job level.

Overall, the evidence suggests that PsyCap is open to development and may lead to positive employee attitudes and behaviors, which in turn are expected to contribute to positive organizational outcomes.

Flow at Work

Flow refers to "the state in which people are so involved in an activity that nothing else seems to matter; the experience itself is so enjoyable that people will do it even at great cost, for the sheer sake of doing it" (Csikszentmihalyi, 1990, p. 4). Nakamura and Csikszentmihalyi (2002) describe the following characteristics of flow: it involves intense and focused concentration on the activity; action and awareness merge together; the person loses self-consciousness and is no longer aware of self; there is a sense of control over the action; the sense of time is distorted; and the activity is intrinsically rewarding. Flow can be created in any situation as long as certain conditions are met (Csikszentmihalyi, Abuhamdeh, & Nakamura, 2005). The key conditions for flow include: (1) a clear set of goals, (2) a balance between perceived challenges and perceived skills where both exceed the person's average levels so that the challenges stretch the skills, and (3) clear and immediate feedback (Csikszentmihalyi et al., 2005).

Interestingly, flow is experienced more often at work than in leisure (Csikszentmihalyi & LeFevre, 1989; LeFevre, 1988). Individuals more motivated in flow reported more positive experiences at work (Csikszentmihalyi & LeFevre, 1989). Knowledge workers experience, are aware of, and pay attention to flow

(Quinn, 2005). However, the degree to which one experiences flow at work may depend on the individual and structural factors (e.g., job types, task types) and job resources (Bakker & Geurts, 2004; Quinn, 2005; Salanova, Bakker, & Llorens, 2006). Bakker and Geurts (2004) revealed that the most significant predictors of flow were job resources (i.e., autonomy, possibilities development, and performance feedback) among 1090 Dutch workers. Bakker (2005) later discovered that job resources (i.e., social support, supervisory coaching, autonomy, and feedback) positively influenced the balance between challenges and skills, which contributed to flow experience. Salanova et al. (2006) found that both job resources (i.e., social support, innovation, and rules) and personal resources (i.e., self-efficacy) fostered flow among 258 teachers, and this flow experience influenced the future accumulation of job and personal resources eight months later.

Flow at work is important because of two main reasons. First, flow is a positive and intrinsically rewarding experience. The more an employee experiences flow within a particular activity (e.g., work task), the greater the employee's sense of control and enjoyment from the activity (Csikszentmihalyi & LeFevre, 1989; Quinn, 2005). Second, flow has several potential positive organizational outcomes. Flow may decrease anxiety, improve employee effectiveness, and enhance job satisfaction and work relationships (Goodman, 1996). Also, it may produce higher job satisfaction and better job performance (e.g., Csikszentmihalyi & LeFevre, 1989; Demerouti, 2006; Eisenberger, Jones, Stinglhamber, Shanock, & Randall, 2005; Goodman, 1996; LeFevre, 1988; Salanova et al., 2006). Demerouti (2006) revealed that frequent flow experiences were beneficial for both in-role and extra-role performance, but only for employees high in conscientiousness. Eisenberger et al. (2005) discovered that employees' flow experience was significantly related to their positive mood, task interest, and organizational spontaneity (i.e., voluntarily performed extra-role behaviors), among dispositionally achievement-oriented employees.

Despite the empirical evidence suggesting the potential benefits of flow to individuals and organizations, flow intervention seems to be still at a very early stage of development. Heckman (1997) earlier asserted that designing work for flow experience would allow organizations to be more adaptable and adaptive, as well as to achieve creative employee potentials. Moreover, Kauffman and Scoular (2004) stated that flow has high potential for use by executive coaches. Nonetheless, little work has been done to design a job for flow or coaching to create executives' flow experience.

In summary, research on flow at work suggests that organizations may increase the employee flow experience by providing support and resources. Although little work has been done with regard to flow intervention in the workplace, flow has high potential for improving employee job satisfaction, motivation, and job performance.

CONCLUSION

We have provided a broad overview of the emerging science supporting applied positive organizational psychology. Theory, research, and applications have been presented to provide readers with a sense of the current state of science and practice in this area. Positive organizational psychology is now being used to enhance and expand traditional topics and applications of organizational psychology, as well as to open up new training and career opportunities for the next generation. It should be noted, however, that we did not attempt to cover all the important topics in the current literature. For example, we deliberately steered clear of the excellent work being done on positive identity, prosocial practices, and flourishing, as these topics are thoroughly covered by Jane Dutton and her colleagues in Chapter 10. We also gave limited attention to the research on virtuous organizations and mentoring because they are addressed by Kim Cameron in Chapter 11 and by Jeanne Nakamura in Chapter 12. We believe that it will become clear to you, after you read all of these chapters, that improving the world of work and organizations is one of the most fruitful contexts for further development of the science of applied positive psychology.

REFERENCES

Appreciative Inquiry Commons. (n.d.). *AI history and timeline*. Retrieved April 4, 2010, from http://appreciativeinquiry.case.edu/intro/timeline.cfm

Armstrong-Stassen, M., & Schlosser, F. (2008). Taking a positive approach to organizational downsizing. *Canadian Journal of Administrative Sciences, 25*, 93–106.

Avey, J. B., Luthans, F., & Jensen, S. M. (2009). Psychological capital: A positive resource for combating employee stress and turnover. *Human Resource Management, 48*, 677–693.

Avey, J. B., Patera, J. L., & West, B. J. (2006). The implications of positive psychological capital on employee absenteeism. *Journal of Leadership and Organizational Studies, 13*, 42–60.

Avey, J. B., Wernsing, T. S., & Luthans, F. (2008). Can positive employees help positive organizational change? Impact of psychological capital and emotions on relevant attitudes and behaviors. *Journal of Applied Behavioral Science, 44*, 48–70.

Avolio, B. J. (2005). *Leadership development in balance: Made/born*. Mahwah, NJ: Lawrence Erlbaum Associates, Inc.

Avolio, B. J., & Gardner, W. L. (2005). Authentic leadership development: Getting to the root of positive forms of leadership. *Leadership Quarterly, 16*, 315–338.

Avolio, B. J., Gardner, W. L., Walumbwa, F. O., Luthans, F., & May, D. R. (2004). Unlocking the mask: A look at the process by which authentic leaders impact follower attitudes and behaviors. *Leadership Quarterly, 15*, 801–823.

Avolio, B. J., Griffith, J., Wernsing, T. S., & Walumbwa, F. O. (2010). What is authentic leadership development? In P. A. Linley, S. Harrington, & N. Garcea (Eds.), *Oxford handbook of positive psychology and work* (pp. 39–51). New York: Oxford University Press.

Avolio, B. J., Luthans, F., & Walumbwa, F. O. (2004). *Authentic leadership: Theory building for veritable sustained performance*. Working paper. Lincoln, NB: Gallup Leadership Institute, University of Nebraska.

Avolio, B. J., Wernsing, T. S., Chan, A. Y. L., & Griffith, J. L. (2007). *A theory of developing leader self-awareness*. Unpublished manuscript, University of Nebraska, Lincoln.

Bakker, A. B. (2005). Flow among music teachers and their students: The crossover of peak experiences. *Journal of Vocational Behavior, 66*, 26–44.

Bakker, A. B., & Geurts, S. A. E. (2004). Toward a dual-process model of work–home inter-
ference. *Work and Occupations, 31,* 345–366.

Bakker, A. B., & Schaufeli, W. B. (2008). Positive organizational behavior: Engaged
employees in flourishing organizations. *Journal of Organizational Behavior, 29,*
147–154.

Bass, B. M., & Riggio, R. E. (2006). *Transformational leadership* (2nd ed.). Mahwah, NJ:
Lawrence Erlbaum Associates, Inc.

Bernstein, S. D. (2003). Positive organizational scholarship: Meet the movement: An interview with Kim Cameron, Jane Dutton, and Robert Quinn. *Journal of Management
Inquiry, 12,* 266–271.

Black, B. (2001). The road to recovery. *Gallup Management Journal, 1,* 10–12.

Brown, M. E., & Treviño, L. K. (2006). Ethical leadership: A review and future directions.
Leadership Quarterly, 17, 595–616.

Buckingham, M., & Clifton, D. O. (2001). *Now, discover your strengths.* New York: Free
Press.

Cameron, K. S. (2005). Organizational effectiveness: Its demise and re-emergence through
positive organisational scholarship. In K. G. Smith & M. A. Hitt (Eds.), *Great
minds in management: The process of theory development* (pp. 304–330). New
York: Oxford University Press.

Cameron, K. S. (2006). Good or not bad: Standards and ethics in managing change. *Academy
of Management Learning and Education, 5,* 317–323.

Cameron, K. S. (2008). Paradox in positive organizational change. *Journal of Applied
Behavioral Sciences, 44,* 7–24.

Cameron, K. S., Bright, D., & Caza, A. (2004). Exploring the relationships between
organizational virtuousness and performance. *American Behavioral Scientist, 47,*
766–790.

Cameron, K. S., Dutton, J. E., & Quinn, R. E. (2003). Foundations of positive organizational scholarship. In K. S. Cameron, J. E. Dutton, & R. E. Quinn (Eds.), *Positive
organizational scholarship: Foundations of a new discipline* (pp. 3–13). San
Francisco: Berrett-Koehler.

Caza, A., Barker, B. A., & Cameron, K. S. (2004). Ethics and ethos: The buffering and
amplifying effects of ethical behavior and virtuousness. *Journal of Business Ethics,
52,* 169–178.

Clapp-Smith, R., Vogelgesang, G. R., & Avey, J. B. (2009). Authentic leadership and positive
psychological capital. *Journal of Leadership and Organizational Studies, 15,*
227–240.

Clifton, D. O., & Harter, J. K. (2003). Investing in strengths. In K. S. Cameron, J. E. Dutton,
& R. E. Quinn (Eds.), *Positive organizational scholarship* (pp. 111–121). San
Francisco: Berrett-Koehler.

Connelly, J. (2002). All together now. *Gallup Management Journal, 2,* 13–18.

Cooperrider, D. L., & Whitney, D. (1999). Appreciative Inquiry: A positive revolution in
change. In P. Holman, & T. Devane (Eds.), *The change handbook* (pp. 245–261).
San Francisco: Berrett-Koehler.

Csikszentmihalyi, M. (1990). *Flow: The psychology of optimal experience.* New York: Harper
& Row.

Csikszentmihalyi, M., Abuhamdeh, S., & Nakamura, J. (2005). Flow. In A. Elliot & C. S.
Dweck (Eds.), *Handbook of competence and motivation* (pp. 598–608). New York:
Guilford Press.

Csikszentmihalyi, M., & LeFevre, J. (1989) Optimal experience in work and leisure. *Journal
of Personality and Social Psychology, 56,* 815–822.

Demerouti, E. (2006). Job characteristics, flow, and performance: The moderating role of conscientiousness. *Journal of Occupational Health Psychology*, 11, 266–280.

Donaldson, S. I., & Bligh, M. (2006). Rewarding careers applying positive psychological science to improve quality of work life and organizational effectiveness. In S. I. Donaldson, D. E. Berger, & K. Pezdek (Eds.), *Applied psychology: New frontiers and rewarding careers*. Mahwah, NJ: Lawrence Erlbaum Associates, Inc.

Donaldson, S. I., & Ko, I. (2010). Positive organizational psychology, behavior, and scholarship: A review of the emerging literature and evidence base. *Journal of Positive Psychology*, 5, 177–191.

Douglas, C. A., & McCauley, C. D. (1999). Formal developmental relationships: A survey of organizational practices. *Human Resource Development Quarterly*, 10, 203–220.

Eisenberger, R., Jones, J. R., Stinglhamber, F., Shanock, L., & Randall, A. T. (2005). Flow experience at work: For high need achievers alone? *Journal of Organizational Behavior*, 26, 755–775.

Gardner, W. L., Avolio, B. J., Luthans, F., May, D. R., & Walumbwa, F. (2005). "Can you see the real me?" A self-based model of authentic leader and follower development. *Leadership Quarterly*, 16, 343–372.

Gardner, W. L., & Schermerhorn Jr., J. R. (2004). Unleashing individual potential performance gains through positive organizational behavior and authentic leadership. *Organizational Dynamics*, 33, 270–281.

Gattellari, M., Donnelly, N., Taylor, N., Meerkin, M., Hirst, G., & Ward, J. (2005). Does "peer coaching" increase GP capacity to promote informed decision making about PSA screening? A cluster randomised trial. *Family Practice*, 22, 253–265.

Goodman, D. H. (1996). Construction and validation of an instrument designed to assess flow and job satisfaction in occupational settings: Exploratory research. *UMI Dissertation Services*. (UMI No. 9633807)

Grant, A. M., & Cavanagh, M. J. (2007). Evidence-based coaching: Flourishing or languishing? *Australian Psychologist*, 42, 239–254.

Grant, A. M., Curtayne, L., & Burton, G. (2009). Executive coaching enhances goal attainment, resilience and workplace well-being: a randomised controlled study. *Journal of Positive Psychology*, 4, 396–407.

Greiner, L. E., & Cummings, T. G. (2004). Wanted: OD more alive than dead! *Journal of Applied Behavioral Sciences*, 40, 374–391.

Harter, J. K., Schmidt, F. L., & Hayes, T. L. (2002). Business-unit-level relationship between employee satisfaction, employee engagement, and business outcomes: A meta-analysis. *Journal of Applied Psychology*, 87, 268–279.

Heckman, F. (1997). Designing organizations for flow experiences. *Journal of Quality and Participation, March*, 62–71.

Hodges, T. D., & Clifton, D. O. (2004). Strengths-based development in practice. In P. A. Linley & S. Joseph (Eds.), *Positive psychology in practice: From research to application* (pp. 256–268). Hoboken, NJ: John Wiley & Sons.

Kauffman, C. & Scoular, A. (2004). Toward a positive psychology of executive coaching. In P. A. Linley & S. Joseph (Eds.), *Positive psychology in practice* (pp. 287–302). Hoboken, NJ: John Wiley & Sons.

Larson, M., & Luthans, F. (2006). Potential added value of psychological capital in predicting work attitudes. *Journal of Leadership and Organizational Studies*, 13, 75–92.

LeFevre, J. (1988). Flow and the quality of experience during work and leisure. In M. Csikszentmihalyi & I. Csikszentmihalyi (Eds.), *Optimal experience: Psychological studies of flow in consciousness* (pp. 307–318). New York: Cambridge University Press.

Linley, P. A., Woolston, L., & Biswas-Diener, R. (2009). Strengths coaching with leaders. *International Coaching Psychology Review, 4*, 37–48.

Luthans, F. (2002a). Positive organizational behavior: Developing and managing psychological strengths. *Academy of Management Executive, 16*, 57–72.

Luthans, F. (2002b). The need for and meaning of positive organizational behavior. *Journal of Organizational Behavior, 23*, 695–706.

Luthans, F., Avey, J. B., Avolio, B. J., Norman, S. M., & Combs, G. M. (2006a). Positive psychological capital: Toward a micro-intervention. *Journal of Organizational Behavior, 27*, 387–393.

Luthans, F., Avey, J. B., & Patera, J. L. (2008a). Experimental analysis of a web-based training intervention to develop positive psychological capital. *Academy of Management Learning and Education, 7*, 209–221.

Luthans, F., & Avolio, B. J. (2003). Authentic leadership: A positive developmental approach. In K. S. Cameron, J. E. Dutton, & R. E. Quinn (Eds.), *Positive organizational scholarship: Foundations of a new discipline* (pp. 241–261). San Francisco: Berrett-Koehler.

Luthans, F., & Avolio, B. J. (2009a). The "point" of positive organizational behavior. *Journal of Organizational Behavior, 30*, 291–307.

Luthans, F., & Avolio, B. J. (2009b). Inquiry unplugged: Building on Hackman's potential perils of POB. *Journal of Organizational Behavior, 30*, 323–328.

Luthans, F., Norman, S. M., Avolio, B. J., & Avey, J. B. (2008b). The mediating role of psychological capital in the supportive organizational climate–employee performance relationship. *Journal of Organizational Behavior, 29*, 219–238.

Luthans, F., Vogelgesang, G. R., & Lester, P. B. (2006b). Developing the psychological capital of resiliency. *Human Resource Development Review, 5*, 25–44.

Luthans, F., & Youssef, C. M. (2004). Human, social, and now positive psychological capital management: Investing in people for competitive advantage. *Organizational Dynamics, 33*, 143–160.

Luthans, F., & Youssef, C. M. (2007). Emerging positive organizational behavior. *Journal of Management, 33*, 321–349.

Martin, A. J. (2005). The role of positive psychology in enhancing satisfaction, motivation, and productivity in the workplace. *Journal of Organizational Behavior Management, 24*, 113–133.

Martin, A. J., & Jackson, S. A. (2008). Brief approaches to assessing task absorption and enhanced subjective experience: Examining "short" and "core" flow in diverse performance domains. *Motivation and Emotion, 32*, 141–157.

May, D. R., Chan, A. Y. L., Hodges, T. D., & Avolio, B. J. (2003). Developing the moral component of authentic leadership. *Organizational Dynamics, 32*, 247–260.

Nakamura, J., & Csikszentmihalyi, M. (2002). The concept of flow. In C. R. Snyder & S. J. Lopez (Eds.), *Handbook of positive psychology* (pp. 89–105). New York: Oxford University Press.

Nelson, D. L., & Cooper, C. L. (2007). Positive organizational behavior: An inclusive view. In D. L. Nelson & C. L. Cooper (Eds.), *Positive organizational behavior* (pp. 3–8). London: Sage Publications.

Panday, A., & Gupta, R. K. (2008). Spirituality in management: A review of contemporary and traditional thoughts and agenda for research. *Global Business Review, 9*, 65–83.

Powley, E. H., & Piderit, S. K. (2008). Tending wounds. *Journal of Applied Behavioral Science, 44*, 134–149.

Preskill, H., & Donaldson, S. I. (2008). Improving the evidence base for career development programs: Making use of the evaluation profession and positive psychology movement. *Advances in Developing Human Resources, 10*, 104–121.

Quinn, R. W. (2005). Flow in knowledge work: High performance experience in the design of national security technology. *Administrative Science Quarterly, 50,* 610–641.

Reichard, R. J., & Avolio, B. J. (2005). Where are we? The status of leadership intervention research: A meta-analytic summary. In W. L. Gardner, B. J. Avolio, & F. O. Walumbwa (Eds.), *Authentic leadership and practice: Origins, effects, and development* (pp. 203–226). Oxford, UK: Elsevier Science.

Roberts, L. M., Spreitzer, G., Dutton, J., Quinn, R., Heaphy, E., & Barker, B. (2005). How to play to your strengths. *Harvard Business Review, 83,* 74–80.

Salanova, M., Bakker, A. B., & Llorens, S. (2006). Flow at work: Evidence for an upward spiral of personal and organizational resources. *Journal of Happiness Studies, 7,* 1–22.

Snyder, C. R., Sympson, S. C., Ybasco, F. C., Borders, T. F., Babyak, M. A., & Higgins, R. L. (1996). Development and validation of the state hope scale. *Journal of Personality and Social Psychology, 70,* 321–335.

Taylor, L. M. (1997). *The relation between resilience, coaching, coping skills training, and perceived stress during a career-threatening milestone.* Unpublished doctoral dissertation, Georgia State University.

Turner, N., Barling, J., & Zacharatos, A. (2002). Positive psychology at work. In C. R. Snyder & S. J. Lopez (Eds.), *Handbook of positive psychology* (pp. 715–728). New York: Oxford University Press.

Van der Haar, D., & Hosking, D. M. (2004). Evaluating appreciative inquiry: A relational constructionist perspective. *Human Relations, 57,* 1017–1036.

Walumbwa, F. O., Avolio, B. J., Gardner, W. L., Wernsing, T. A., & Peterson, S. J. (2008). Authentic leadership: Development and validation of a theory-based measure. *Journal of Management, 34,* 89–126.

Walumbwa, F. O., Luthans, F., Avey, J. B., & Oke, A. (2009). Authentically leading groups: The mediating role of collective psychological capital and trust. *Journal of Organizational Behavior, 30,* 1–21.

West, B. J., Patera, J. L., & Carsten, M. (2009). Team level positivity: Investigating positive psychological capacities and team level outcomes. *Journal of Organizational Behavior, 30,* 249–267.

Wernsing, T. S. (2010). *Leader self-awareness development: An intervention and test of a theoretical model* (Doctoral dissertation). Available from Dissertations and Theses database. (UMI No. 3390666)

Whitney, D., & Cooperrider, D. L. (2000). The appreciative inquiry summit: An emerging methodology for whole system positive change. *Journal of Organization Development Network, 32,* 13–26.

Whitney, D., & Trosten-Bloom, A. (2003). *The power of appreciative inquiry: A practical guide to positive change.* San Francisco: Berrett-Koehler.

Wiegand, D. M., & Geller, E. S. (2005). Connecting positive psychology and organizational behavior management: Achievement motivation and the power of positive reinforcement. *Journal of Organizational Behavior Management, 24,* 3–25.

Wood, B., & Gordon, S. (2009). Linking MBA learning and leadership coaching. *International Coaching Psychology Review, 4,* 87–104.

Yammarino, F. J., Dionne, S. D., Schriesheim, C. A., & Dansereau, F. (2008). Authentic leadership and positive organizational behavior: A meso, multi-level perspective. *Leadership Quarterly, 19,* 693–707.

Youssef, C. M., & Luthans, F. (2007). Positive organizational behavior in the workplace: The impact of hope, optimism, and resilience. *Journal of Management, 33,* 774–800.

10

Prosocial Practices, Positive Identity, and Flourishing at Work

JANE E. DUTTON, LAURA MORGAN ROBERTS,
and JEFF BEDNAR

When you think of yourself at work, how do you think you are faring? Are you flourishing at work, feeling a sense of engagement, motivation, growth, and learning, or is languishing a better descriptor for your state of well-being? This chapter explores one important way in which organizations shape our ability to flourish at work. As employees we spend more time engaged with our work organizations than we do with our families, friends, or other institutions (Hochschild, 1997). New technologies are quickly blurring the boundaries between work and non-work, amplifying work immersion for the average employee. In such a world, how do work organizations leave their imprint on employees, or, from a positive organizational psychology perspective, how do work contexts cultivate employee flourishing? In this chapter, we explore how work contexts cultivate employee flourishing through the way they shape the identities that employees construct at work.

We address this link between work contexts, identity, and employee flourishing through a focus on organizational practices. Organizational practices refer to the situated, recurrent activities that people engage in at work (Orlikowski, 2002). For example, organizations have distinct socialization practices to assist newcomers to the organization (Van Maanen & Schein, 1979). Organizational researchers have explored how organizational practices affect an organization's strategy (Jarzabkowski, 2004), the design of work (Barley, 1986), organizational learning (Antonacopoulou, 2006), and organizational performance (Cameron, Mora, & Leutscher, 2009). More recently, researchers have been exploring this potentially important link between organizational practices and the construction of employee identity (Carlsen, 2006; Michel, 2007) but there has been a dearth of research on how organizational practices shape work-related identities in ways that foster employee flourishing. A focus on what we call prosocial practices and positive work-related identities permits us to build this important conceptual link.

We build the core arguments of our chapter in four sequential steps. First we introduce the idea of positive work-related identities (Dutton, Roberts, & Bednar, 2010; Roberts & Dutton, 2009). Next we review research suggesting that positive work-related identities are linked to various indicators of flourishing. We note at the outset that few of these studies establish truly causal effects, so additional empirical research is required to validate these links. We then focus on a category of organizational practices – prosocial practices – that seem to have a potent effect on the way employees construct their identities at work. Finally, we outline a research agenda for positive organizational psychology to contribute to society through increasing our understanding of how organizational practices affect employees' identities and their ability to flourish at work.

POSITIVE WORK-RELATED IDENTITIES

Because work is a key domain in people's lives, involvement in work organizations is a critical source of identity (Ashforth & Mael, 1989; Dutton, Dukerich, & Harquail, 1994; Gini, 1998). The term "identity" refers to the way in which an individual constructs or defines him or herself (Gecas, 1982) and "work-related" identities are the meanings that individuals take on through their engagement with aspects of work, including professions, occupations, work-roles, or organizations (Dutton et al., 2010). As employees come to identify with certain aspects of their professions, occupations, work-roles, or organizations, they often infuse their individual identities with the defining characteristics of these collectives or roles. For example, employees who joined Amway began to see themselves as free, family-oriented, altruistic, and successful as they engaged in various practices called "dream-building" (Pratt, 2000). Employees of the Port Authority (PA) of New York and New Jersey saw themselves as talented professionals who were building beautiful edifices and preserving New York City's symbols of global trade (Dutton & Dukerich, 1991). As a result, employees felt personally insulted when the PA was criticized by the media for inhumane treatment of homeless persons who were frequenting PA-run buildings (Dutton & Dukerich, 1991). These examples remind us that employees often take on qualities and characteristics of their work organizations and fuse them with their own self-constructions.

The desire to construct a positive identity is a central assumption in many psychological and sociological theories (Gecas, 1982; Turner, 1982). We build on this assumption by asking: What are the different ways in which an individual's work identity can be positive? A review of research published in organizational psychology reveals that work-related identities can be positive in at least four different ways (Dutton et al., 2010): content (i.e., the attributes or characteristics that one uses to define him or herself include character strengths and virtues); subjective evaluation (i.e., the identity is regarded favorably); development (i.e., a person sees him or herself as growing in ways that promote maturity and adaptation); or structure (i.e., the multiple facets of one's identity are related in harmonious and complementary ways) (Dutton et al., 2010). For example, a professor may find his or her professional identity to be positive because it is endowed with the virtue of wisdom; because it is evaluated positively by students; because it is on a trajectory of constant learning and progression; or because it facilitates compatibility and balance between multiple identities (i.e., researcher, teacher, consultant, parent). Each one of these theoretical perspectives on identity points to several different antecedents that cultivate positive identities and different outcomes that are associated with positive identities.

POSITIVE WORK-RELATED IDENTITIES AND FLOURISHING

Dutton and colleagues argue that as employees' work-related identities become more positive, individuals are strengthened and become more capable of dealing with current challenges while identifying and taking advantage of new opportunities (Dutton et al., 2010). Here, we provide suggestive evidence that cultivating various forms of positive work-related identity also promotes employee flourishing more generally. These potential implications for flourishing help to justify why it is important to cultivate positive work-related identities. A variety of conceptual and empirical studies suggest that as employees' work-related identities become more positive, they experience enhanced psychological functioning, positive feelings, and social functioning (the three components of flourishing identified by Keyes' (1998) typology of mental health). For example, one indicator of healthy psychological functioning at work is work engagement. Work engagement is defined as a positive, fulfilling, personal state characterized by vigor (e.g., high levels of energy and mental resilience while working), dedication (e.g., significance, enthusiasm, inspiration, pride, and challenge), and absorption (e.g., being fully concentrated and happily engrossed in one's work; Hakanen, Perhoniemi, & Toppinen-Tanner, 2008). Research shows that positive self-evaluations of work-related identity are an important predictor of work engagement (Mauno, Kinnunen, & Ruokolainen, 2007; Xanthopoulou, Bakker, Demerouti, & Schaufeli, 2009). Moreover, cultivating an identity at work that is more virtue-based (e.g., understanding and utilizing one's strengths at work) is also related to work engagement (Harter, Schmidt, & Keyes, 2003). Research also shows that work engagement is associated with adaptive behaviors (e.g., personal initiative – see Hakanen et al., 2008) and ultimately affects "bottom line" outcomes (e.g., profits, productivity, employee retention, and customer satisfaction; Harter et al., 2003). Taken together, this research on work engagement suggests that cultivating a positive, work-related identity helps individuals to flourish at work.

Other indicators of enhanced psychological functioning include self-acceptance, personal growth, and environmental mastery, or the capacity to effectively manage one's life and surrounding world (Keyes, 1998; Ryff & Keyes, 1995). Research on identity change during role challenges suggests that positive identities relate to employee flourishing. For example, Ibarra's (2003) study of professionals in major career transitions suggests that individuals who explore new possible selves at work adapt more effectively to the demands of changing work environments and experience more coherence between who they are and what they do.

This research on psychological functioning further strengthens the claim that cultivating positive identities at work helps individuals to flourish.

Positive identities also may link to flourishing through how they cultivate positive emotions. For example, Fine's (1996) work on restaurant cooks shows that individuals draw on different rhetorics to shape how they think of themselves as workers. These different self-views enable cooks to experience positive emotions such as pride, enthusiasm, and honor, which promote occupational satisfaction, creativity, and social cohesion (Fine, 1996). Positive emotions, in general, help individuals to build cognitive and social resources, counteract the impact of negative emotions, and expand the terrain of possibilities for who an individual can become (Fredrickson, 1998, 2009; see also Roberts, Dutton, Spreitzer, Heaphy, & Quinn, 2005, for an organizational application).

A third way in which positive work-related identities promote flourishing is by enhancing social well-being and promoting the adoption of behaviors that build social coherence, social actualization, social integration, social acceptance, or social contribution (Keyes, 1998). For example, a study by Dukerich, Golden, and Shortell (2002) reports that physicians who evaluate their organization's identity (i.e., the health system) more favorably are more willing to engage in cooperative behaviors that will benefit other employees (e.g., extra-role behaviors) as well as the healthcare system as a whole (e.g., referring patients to doctors within the system). The work of Reed and Aquino (2003) suggests that as employees incorporate virtuous attributes and characteristics into their identity (what Reed and Aquino call a moral identity), they will minimize ingroup/outgroup distinctions and show increasing sympathy toward outgroup members. As these ingroup/outgroup distinctions break down, social cohesion can increase in organizations (Reed & Aquino, 2003). These studies on social functioning further substantiate the claim that cultivating more positive identities at work can help employees to flourish.

The preliminary evidence that positive work-related identities may be psychologically and socially beneficial to employees raises the next logical question: How do different workplaces influence the way employees come to understand who they are? How can organizational practices shape or cultivate these forms of positive identity? The next section focuses on a particular kind of work practice that may be a powerful contributor to the construction of a positive identity at work.

PROSOCIAL PRACTICES AND POSITIVE WORK-RELATED IDENTITIES

In organizational studies, there is a rich vein of research that examines organizational practices: the distinctive set of recurrent, patterned activities that characterize an organization (Orlikowski, 2002). These practices are part of an organization's signature, which shapes how the organization's knowledge is organized (Orlikowski, 2002), how resources are created (Feldman, 2004), how organizational learning occurs (Gherardi, 2006), and how organizational change occurs (Feldman & Pentland, 2003). While organizational researchers have focused on how specific human resource-related practices shape employee attitudes and actions (Losey, Meisinger, & Ulrich, 2005; Ulrich & Brockbank, 2005), they have devoted limited attention to how organizational practices impact employees' identities. Yet, because organizational practices are linked to employee doing, and employee doing is linked to employee becoming (Bem, 1972; Carlsen, 2006), it seems logical and productive to ask: What organizational practices are conducive to the cultivation of positive work-related identities?

Our literature search revealed that a certain category of practices – prosocial practices – have a particularly potent influence on the way employees construct their identities. Prosocial practices are designed to protect and/or promote the welfare of other people and provide a conduit for employees to participate in routine helping and giving at work. Research in positive psychology indicates that engaging in helping others and giving to a cause that is larger than oneself promote flourishing (see Piliavin, 2003, for a review of the positive impacts of volunteering on the volunteer). While the direct effects of prosocial behavior outside of the workplace have been examined, such effects within the workplace have received far less attention. A ground-breaking line of research in this vein by Grant (Grant, 2007; Grant, Campbell, Chen, Cottone, Lapedis, & Lee, 2007) and colleagues shows that engaging in prosocial practices at work often increases psychological and social functioning, as indicated by greater persistence, performance, and citizenship behaviors on the job (e.g., Grant, 2008a, 2008b; Grant et al., 2007; Grant & Mayer, 2009).

In this chapter, we expand this line of research by examining organizational practices that cultivate prosocial behavior and, more importantly, locate identity as a central mechanism that can explain why prosocial practices might promote flourishing at work. While a few studies show that engaging in helping behaviors increases self-evaluations (e.g., Newman, Vasudev, & Onawola, 1985), the central role of identity remains underexplored. We suggest that organizations that routinize employees' prosocial thoughts and behaviors through participation in institutionalized practices are more likely to cultivate employees' positive work-related identities. We detail findings from three field studies of employees' identification and/or commitment to their work organizations that provide evidential support for these core claims.

EMPLOYEE SUPPORT PRACTICES AND EMPLOYEES' POSITIVE IDENTITIES

Many work organizations have provided opportunities for employees to participate in different types of employee support practices. Employee support practices include institutionalized procedures and routines that provide emotional, financial, and/or instrumental assistance to employees beyond pay, benefits, or recognition (Grant, Dutton, & Rosso, 2008). For some employee support practices, assistance to employees is provided directly by the organization, such as in childcare or elder care programs (e.g., Cascio, 2003; Goodstein, 1995). Other practices provide opportunities for employee-to-employee helping or giving, such as when organizations allow employees to donate their vacation time to co-workers who need it (e.g., Griffin Hospital, as cited in Cameron, 2008, p. 11). Organizational researchers often examine how these practices shape employees' performance, commitment, or attachment to the organization (Perry-Smith & Blum, 2000; Trice & Beyer, 1984). For our purposes, we are interested in how these practices shape the kinds of identities that individuals construct at work.

Grant et al. (2008) conducted a survey and interview study of a Fortune 500 retail company (called Big Retail) to assess how employee participation in an employee support program (called the Employee Support Foundation, ESF) affected employee commitment. Participants in this program voluntarily granted permission for the company to deduct a dollar from their weekly paycheck. The company matched employee donations at a rate of 50 cents per dollar and donations were pooled in a fund that employees could potentially draw from during crises such as illnesses, family deaths, or financial hardships. The ESF also provided educational scholarships and a bereavement response initiative. Therefore, this form of employee support program allowed employees to both receive and give support to their colleagues when faced with special needs. The 40 interviews and the employee survey revealed that there was a relationship between participation in the ESF and the employees' affective commitment and attachment to the organization. The results also suggested that participation in these programs changed the way individuals viewed the organization's identity and, by association, their own identity as an organizational member (Grant et al., 2008).

First, the interview study (20 store managers and 20 employees) consistently suggested that individuals took on a more positive identity by seeing themselves and the organization as more helpful, caring, and benevolent. While some researchers have called this a prosocial identity (Grant, 2007; Grant, Molinsky, Margolis, Kamin, & Schiano, 2009), this type of identity content implies that people are defining themselves with virtuous strengths or qualities such as kindness, generosity, care, compassion, niceness, and love (Peterson & Seligman, 2004). Several quotes illustrate the connection that employees felt between the ESF program, the company, and their identity. For example, managers discussed how participation in the program changed their capacity to help others:

> I have an employee . . . she was a young single mother . . . During the pregnancy, she switched from part-time to full-time, and in the process lost her insurance because she didn't read the packet completely . . . When we found out, I grabbed the ESF paperwork and started calling the ESF, and it was just the ability to help her through her pregnancy . . . It was good that there was somebody there that I could call and say, "Hey, this is what I've got, and can I help?" and to know that I was going to be able to help my employee . . . Because of the help that they've been to the employees . . . I feel good, because I know that there's somebody out there that it's helping. (Manager #11)
>
> (Grant et al., 2008, p. 903)

The bolstered capacity to help and care for others allowed managers to see themselves as more caring individuals. This connection is clearly evident in the quote below:

I think it will always, I mean for the rest of my life, I will always be a more compassionate person. I always was, but more so now. Definitely nonjudgmental. You know like there's that saying "There but for the grace of God go I," you know, because I could be in their shoes tomorrow, and it doesn't really matter your education level, things happen to people, unexpected things. So they may not be prepared for them properly with insurance or whatever. So I think . . . I don't think a day will go by the rest of my life, that I won't think about the employees that were helped by the Foundation while I was involved. (Manager, K8)

While the interview study suggested that participation in the ESF increased employee commitment by changing how employees defined themselves and the company, the survey study provided an opportunity to test this association more rigorously (Grant et al., 2008). Using structural equation modeling to analyze survey responses from 240 employees, the authors found that the link between employee participation in the ESF and affective commitment to the company was partially mediated by the extent to which employees interpreted their identity and the organization's identity as caring and benevolent. Thus, in both qualitative and quantitative analyses there was evidence of a link between employees' participation in a prosocial practice and defining themselves and their organization in more positive, virtuous terms.

COMMUNITY OUTREACH PRACTICES AND EMPLOYEES' POSITIVE IDENTITIES

Many organizations have also implemented community outreach practices for their employees. Community outreach practices refer to programs and routines that allow employees to provide assistance to groups outside of the employing organization in order to build ties between organizations and their communities (Bartel, 2001). These programs can be highly variable in terms of the kind of work (e.g., mentoring children, building structures, or delivering meals) and the length of time that they engage employees with outside groups (e.g., single-day encounters to year-long commitments). Depending on the organization, these programs may be called corporate citizenship programs, employee involvement programs, or corporate volunteer activities. As with the employee support programs, the practices enable and encourage employees in work organizations to engage in helping and contributing to others. However, for these programs, the recipients of help are individuals outside of the organization's boundaries.

Bartel (2001) was interested in whether employee participation in community outreach practices influenced employee levels of organizational identification, interpersonal cooperation, and effort. She designed a longitudinal field study to examine the impact of participation in outreach activities on employees at Pillsbury Company. The participants in her study completed pretest and posttest surveys along with self-report diaries at regular intervals. Supervisors also filled out surveys at the beginning and end of the employees' participation in the program.

Bartel's (2001) results suggest that employee participation in the program was associated with an increase in levels of identification, cooperation, and effort exerted on the job. When she analyzed what accounted for these changes, three mechanisms related to positive identity construction were apparent. First, interacting with members of other organizations while doing community work facilitated more intergroup comparisons. These intergroup comparisons left employees feeling better off and more fortunate than those with whom they compared themselves. Thus, this downward comparison process enhanced the participants' identities. Second, participation in these programs altered the employees' evaluations of their organization's identity. Participants began to see their organization as more cooperative, socially responsive, and innovative. Third, participation in the programs increased the employees' use of the organization's identity as a source of self-definition (as indicated by stronger levels of employer identification). As a result of these three different mechanisms, participants in community outreach programs developed more positive work-related identities.

BENEFICIARY CONTACT PRACTICES

Finally, some work organizations grant employees exposure to the beneficiaries of their work. Grant and colleagues (Grant 2008a; Grant et al., 2007) have been exploring how this contact with the beneficiaries of work affects motivation and performance. This series of studies suggests that one reason why beneficiary contact practices lead to increased persistence and motivation on the job is because they alter how employees define themselves. In particular, this work implies that practices facilitating awareness and learning about the positive impact that one's work has had on others helps employees to evaluate who they are more positively and can change the content of their identities. While none of these studies was designed to study positive identity mechanisms directly, the set of studies are suggestive that identity may partially account for how and why these practices have their effects.

One field experiment examined the impact of contact with the beneficiaries on call-center workers who were raising money for a university. In the experimental condition, the callers were provided with 10 minutes of contact with a scholarship recipient (the beneficiary) who explained to callers the difference the scholarship had made in his life. There were two control conditions – one with no beneficiary contact and one involving a letter from a beneficiary that described impact. Just 10 minutes of direct contact with the beneficiary resulted in significantly greater persistence (142% increase in phone time) and job performance (171% more money raised) one month later, when compared with individuals in the two control conditions (Grant et al., 2007). In a second study designed to deepen understanding of why the interpersonal contact with beneficiaries was so important, Grant et al. (2007) used an experimental study to explore how interpersonal contact with beneficiaries affected an individual's self-perception (Grant et al., 2007, experiment 2). In this laboratory experiment, the subjects were exposed to the beneficiary of their work through a casual four-minute conversation before the experiment began. Again, the study showed the significant effect of beneficiary contact on task persistence. Importantly, the key mediator of this effect was perceived impact, which involved subjects seeing themselves as a helpful contributor to others. While perceived impact was not measured as an indicator of positive identity, discussions with subjects suggested that participants in the study who were exposed to the beneficiary saw themselves as more generous and helpful. Thus, these studies suggest that beneficiary contact makes prosocial characteristics (i.e., kind, benevolent, helpful, etc.) more accessible for self-definition.

In a related study designed to assess the effects of beneficiary impact on the employees' job dedication and helping, Grant (2008b) conducted a field experiment with lifeguards working at a community pool. In the beneficiary impact condition, Grant exposed lifeguards to stories of rescues performed by other lifeguards as a means of making salient the significance of their impact on others. One month later, supervisors' ratings of the lifeguards showed that lifeguards who received this task significance treatment were more dedicated to their jobs and more helpful to others. Debriefs with the lifeguards in the beneficiary impact condition suggested that these lifeguards had begun to see themselves more positively (what Grant, 2008b, called perceived social worth). Again, this study provides indirect evidence that exposure to the beneficiaries of one's work increases the positivity of an employee's work-related identity.

DISCUSSION

This trio of studies provides suggestive evidence that organizational practices can shape how employees define themselves in ways that might pave the way for employee flourishing. The three studies we reviewed showed a pattern of how prosocial organizational practices cultivate more positive work-related identities. These prosocial practices – employee support, community outreach, and beneficiary impact practices – promote thoughts and actions that influence two aspects of identity: identity content and identity evaluation.

Identity content becomes more positive as individuals who participate in prosocial practices come to define themselves in more virtuous ways. Dutton et al. (2010) introduce the virtue perspective on positive identity to encompass certain qualities that are indicators of what some scholars have called the "master virtues" (Peterson & Seligman, 2004). Drawing from virtue ethics (e.g., Aristotle, 1984; MacIntyre, 1981), and discussed by philosophers and religious leaders across time, virtues are assumed to be morally good qualities that distinguish people of good character (Dahlsgaard, Peterson, & Seligman, 2005). When individuals use or claim these morally good qualities as self-defining features, then an identity becomes more positive. In the studies that we presented here, the individuals came to define themselves as more helpful, caring, generous, and benevolent as a result of engaging in prosocial organizational practices that benefit other employees and the external community.

As individuals engaged in prosocial organizational practices, the changes in identity content were often accompanied by changes in identity evaluations. Dutton et al. (2010) introduce the evaluative perspective to explain that identity evaluations are another important source of positivity in work-related identities.

Identification with favorably regarded social groups such as organizations helps individuals to feel more positively about themselves, which is important for psychological and social functioning (Baumeister, 1999; Branscombe, Ellemers, Spears, & Doosje, 1999; Gecas, 1982; Hogg & Terry, 2001). As such, individuals strive to construct and maintain positively regarded identities at work (Ashforth & Kreiner, 1999; Elsbach & Kramer, 1996; Kreiner, Ashforth, & Sluss, 2006; Pierce & Gardner, 2004). Prosocial organizational practices facilitate behaviors that enhance the esteem in which employees hold their employing organization as a sponsor of such practices and themselves as members of the organization.

The links we have proposed in this chapter open up multiple opportunities for future research. First, research needs to consider and test *how* prosocial practices exert their effects on positive identities. The research we have reviewed suggests that multiple cognitive and behavioral pathways may be important. One pathway is the route of attribute salience. This account suggests that employee participation in certain organizational practices makes certain attributes (such as caring or generosity) more salient and accessible for self-definition (Markus & Kunda, 1986). A different cognitive path suggests that participation in certain prosocial practices makes social group memberships more salient and attractive for self-definition (e.g., I am a member of Big Retail). If the social group has desirable qualities (i.e., generous or caring), individuals will identify more strongly with the social group and incorporate these attributes into their own self-concepts. Prosocial practices can also cultivate positive identities via social comparisons, as we saw in the Bartel study. In this case, intergroup comparisons that are elicited during participation in the programs elevate regard for one's own group, thus creating a more positive work-related identity. Prosocial practices may reinforce ways of doing that create the foundations for ways of being (Carlsen, 2006). Thus, individuals who engage in behaviors that are more caring, generous, and giving actually become more caring, generous, and giving.

Prosocial practices may also engage a different form of motivation that Crocker and colleagues (Crocker, 2008; Crocker & Canevello, 2008) call an ecosystem perspective. These researchers provide evidence about the benefits of taking an ecocentric perspective toward life – placing greater importance on the needs and concerns of others than on the desires and drives of one's own ego. Prosocial practices provide a conduit through which employees can cultivate and exercise this type of ecocentric orientation at work by making compassionate instead of self-image goals more salient (Crocker & Canevello, 2008). When compassionate goals are operational, individuals behave differently towards each other (in terms of giving and providing support: Crocker & Canevello, 2008), which is likely to foster a more positive work identity in terms of defining oneself as being a more caring and generous person.

A final path through which prosocial practices may affect self-definition is suggested by Lyubomirsky (2007), who argues that kindness "can jumpstart a cascade of positive social consequences" (p. 130) by enabling people to take on the identity of someone who is compassionate and altruistic, and enhancing their experience of self-acceptance, self-esteem, and self-efficacy. These claims are supported by our analysis of the impact of organizational prosocial practices on positive work-related identities. Moreover, participating in programs that institutionalize prosocial behaviors (e.g., volunteering) has been shown to have several positive psychological and social benefits, and at times these benefits are more pronounced for those who are giving than for those receiving help (see Piliavin, 2003, for a review).

Future research should also consider a broader range of prosocial practices that may contribute to how employees construct themselves positively. Organizations have institutionalized various developmental practices that shape how employees see and define themselves at work. For example, mentoring practices create opportunities for more seasoned organizational members to facilitate the growth and development of new members (e.g., Ragins & Kram, 2007), thus allowing mentors to see themselves as contributors to others. Organizational evaluation and reward practices could also play a role in encouraging prosocial behavior, and thereby affect the kinds of positive identities that employees construct. For example, some work organizations explicitly encourage and reward co-worker helping (e.g., Southwest Airlines fosters peer-to-peer contributing: Gittell, 2003). Future research might consider which types of prosocial practices have the most potent and/or most enduring impact on employee self-constructions. Future research might also consider whether the mechanisms by which different types of practices shape employees' positive identities are similar or different.

Not all organizational practices designed to have prosocial impact are likely to motivate and engage employees to the same degree. Future research needs to systematically consider factors that limit the capacity of prosocial practices to cultivate positive identities. For example, Grant (2008a) has shown that when employees have choice and discretion over participating in prosocial actions they have higher levels of sustained motivation to act than when such choice or discretion is limited. In addition, some practices may have less impact on employees' self-construals because beneficiaries are more distant, which can undermine the meaning and pride that a person derives from beneficiary contact in prosocial actions. Keyes and Haidt (2003) also suggest that intense – rather than sporadic – involvement in prosocial behavior (i.e., several times a day rather than one day a month) is likely to have a greater impact on those who engage in such behavior.

Finally, future research needs to consider how other features of work organizations are likely to amplify or depress the impact of prosocial practices on positive work-related identities. For example, we know that an organization's leadership plays a significant role in shaping the meaning that individuals make of the work organizations they are a part of (Podolny, Khurana, & Hill-Popper, 2005). A leader's actions can reinforce the significance of acting in a prosocial way, and his or her actions can model appropriate actions that make it easier for employees to act prosocially. In organizations where leaders' actions are consistent with the purposes and values implied by the prosocial practices, there should be stronger links to the positive identities of employees. For example, an in-depth study of how one organization responded compassionately to harm incurred by its members provided evidence of this link (Dutton, Worline, Frost, & Lilius, 2006). A leader's symbolic actions made at a critical time amplified organizational members' awareness of acting in a caring way, speeding up and magnifying the prosocial (compassionate) response of individuals.

CONCLUSIONS

This chapter has begun to till the fertile ground in applied organizational psychology that asks: How do work organizations make a difference for employee flourishing? It has begun to address this question by considering how institutionalized programs and practices shape how employees define themselves. When organizational practices institutionalize ways of doing and being that involve helping, giving, and contributing to others (inside or outside the organization), then work organizations create the content and context for individuals to take on more positive work-related identities. Our hope is that work organizations can participate in improving society through a more mindful consideration of how the practices they deploy shape the identities that employees construct, and how these positive identities can be vital personal resources that contribute to flourishing at work and beyond.

In sum, our focus on the impacts of prosocial practices illuminates relationships between the three pillars of positive psychology: positive subjective experiences of the past, present, and future; positive individuals (i.e., a strengths-based conception of human nature); and positive institutions (Seligman, 2002; Seligman & Csikszentmihalyi, 2000). The third pillar – positive institutions – has received relatively less attention in the field of positive psychology compared to the study of positive emotion and individual strengths. This chapter develops work on positive institutions and illuminates one way in which positive institutions (prosocial practices) help to create more positive individuals (by facilitating positive identity construction), leading to more positive subjective experiences (employees flourish at work).

ACKNOWLEDGMENT

Thanks to Adam Grant for comments on an earlier version of this chapter.

REFERENCES

Antonacopoulou, E. P. (2006). The relationship between individual and organizational learning: New evidence from managerial learning practices. *Management Learning*, 37, 454–473.

Aristotle (1984). *The complete works of Aristotle*. Princeton, NJ: Princeton University Press.

Ashforth, B., & Kreiner, G. (1999). How can you do it? Dirty work and the challenge of constructing a positive identity. *Academy of Management Review*, 24, 413–434.

Ashforth, B., & Mael, F. (1989). Social identity theory and the organization. *Academy of Management Review*, 14, 20–39.

Barley, S. R. (1986). Technology as an occasion for structuring: Evidence from observations of CT scanners and the social order of radiology departments. *Administrative Science Quarterly*, 31, 78–108.

Bartel, C. A. (2001). Social comparisons in boundary-spanning work: Effects of community outreach on members' organizational identity and identification. *Administrative Science Quarterly*, 46, 379–414.

Baumeister, R. F. (1999). The self. In D. T. Gilbert, S. T. Fiske, & G. Lindzey (Eds.), *The handbook of social psychology* (4th ed., pp. 680–740). Boston: McGraw-Hill.

Bem, D. J. (1972). Self perception theory. In L. Berkowitz (Ed.), *Advances in experimental social psychology* (Vol. 6, pp. 1–62). New York: Academic Press.

Branscombe, N. R., Ellemers, N., Spears, R., & Doosje, B. (1999). The context and content of social identity threat. In N. Ellemers & R. Spears (Eds.), *Social identity: Context, commitment, content* (pp. 35–58). Oxford, UK: Blackwell.

Cameron, K. (2008). *Positive leadership: Strategies for extraordinary performance.* San Francisco: Berrett-Koehler.

Cameron, K., Mora, C., & Leutscher, T. (2009). *Effects of positive practices on organizational effectiveness.* Working paper, University of Michigan.

Carlsen, A. (2006). Organizational becoming as dialogic imagination of practice: The case of the indomitable Gauls. *Organization Science, 17*, 132–149.

Cascio, W. F. (2003). Changes in workers, work, and organizations. In W. Borman, R. Klimoski, & D. Ilgen (Eds.), *Handbook of psychology: Industrial and organizational psychology* (Vol. 12, pp. 401–422). New York: John Wiley & Sons.

Crocker, J. (2008). *From egosystem to ecosystem: Implications for learning, relationships, and well-being.* Washington, DC: American Psychological Association.

Crocker, J., & Canevello, A. (2008). Creating and undermining social support in communal relationships: The role of compassionate self-image goals. *Journal of Personality and Social Psychology, 95*, 555–575.

Dahlsgaard, K., Peterson, C., & Seligman, M. (2005). Shared virtue: The convergence of valued human strengths across culture and history. *Review of General Psychology, 9*, 202–213.

Dukerich, J. M., Golden, B. R., & Shortell, S. M. (2002). Beauty is in the eye of the beholder: The impact of organizational identification, identity, and image on the cooperative behaviors of physicians. *Administrative Science Quarterly, 47*, 507–533.

Dutton, J. E., & Dukerich, J. M. (1991). Keeping an eye on the mirror: Image and identity in organizational adaptation. *Academy of Management Journal, 34*, 517–554.

Dutton, J. E., Dukerich, J. M., & Harquail, C. V. (1994). Organizational images and member identification. *Administrative Science Quarterly, 39*, 239–263.

Dutton, J. E., Roberts, L. M., & Bednar, J. S. (2010). Pathways for positive identity construction at work: Four types of positive identity and the building of social resources. *Academy of Management Review, 35*, 265–293.

Dutton, J. E., Worline, M. C., Frost, P. J., & Lilius, J. (2006). Explaining compassion organizing. *Administrative Science Quarterly, 51*, 59–96.

Elsbach, K., & Kramer, R. (1996). Members' responses to organizational identity threats: Encountering and countering the business week rankings. *Administrative Science Quarterly, 41*, 442–476.

Feldman, M. S. (2004). Resources in emerging structures and processes of change. *Organization Science, 15*, 295–309.

Feldman, M. S., & Pentland, B. T. (2003). Reconceptualizing organizational routines as a source of flexibility and change. *Administrative Science Quarterly, 48*, 94–118.

Fine, G. A. (1996). Justifying work: Occupational rhetorics as resources in restaurant kitchens. *Administrative Science Quarterly, 41*, 90–115.

Fredrickson, B. L. (1998). What good are positive emotions. *Review of General Psychology, 2*, 300–319.

Fredrickson, B. L. (2009). *Positivity.* New York: Crown.

Gecas, V. (1982). The self-concept. *Annual Review of Sociology, 8*, 1–33.

Gherardi, S. (2006). *Organizational knowledge: The texture of organizing.* Oxford, UK: Blackwell.

Gini, A. (1998). Work, identity and self: How we are formed by the work we do. *Journal of Business Ethics, 17*, 707–714.

Gittell, J. H. (2003). *The Southwest Airlines way: Using the power of relationships to achieve high performance.* New York: McGraw-Hill.

Goodstein, J. (1995). Employer involvement in eldercare: An organizational adaptation perspective. *Academy of Management Journal, 38*, 1657–1671.

Grant, A. M. (2007). Relational job design and the motivation to make a prosocial difference. *Academy of Management Review, 32*, 393–417.

Grant, A. M. (2008a). Does intrinsic motivation fuel the prosocial fire? Motivational synergy in predicting persistence, performance, and productivity. *Journal of Applied Psychology, 93*, 48–58.

Grant, A. M. (2008b). The significance of task significance: Job performance effects, relational mechanisms, and boundary conditions. *Journal of Applied Psychology, 93*, 108–124.

Grant, A. M., Campbell, E. M., Chen, G., Cottone, K., Lapedis, D., & Lee, K. (2007). Impact and the art of motivation maintenance: The effects of contact with beneficiaries on persistence behavior. *Organizational Behavior and Human Decision Processes, 103*, 53–67.

Grant, A. M., Dutton, J. E., & Rosso, B. D. (2008). Giving commitment: Employee support programs and the prosocial sensemaking process. *Academy of Management Journal, 51*, 898–918.

Grant, A. M., & Mayer, D. M. (2009). Good soldiers and good actors: Prosocial and impression management motives as interactive predictors of affiliative citizenship behavior. *Journal of Applied Psychology, 94*, 900–912.

Grant, A. M., Molinsky, A., Margolis, J., Kamin, M., & Schiano, W. (2009). The performer's reactions to procedural injustice: When prosocial identity reduces prosocial behavior. *Journal of Applied Social Psychology, 39*, 319–349.

Hakanen, J. J., Perhoniemi, R., & Toppinen-Tanner, S. (2008). Positive gain spirals at work: From job resources to work engagement, personal initiative and work-unit innovativeness. *Journal of Vocational Behavior, 73*, 78–91.

Harter, J., Schmidt, F., & Keyes, C. (2003). Well-being in the workplace and its relationship to business outcomes: A review of the Gallup Studies. In C. Keyes & J. Haidt (Eds.), *Flourishing: Positive psychology and the life well lived* (pp. 205–224). Washington, DC: American Psychological Association.

Hochschild, A. (1997). *The time bind.* New York: Henry Holt & Co.

Hogg, M. A., & Terry, D. J. (2001). Social identity theory and organizational processes. In M. A. Hogg & D. J. Terry (Eds.), *Social identity processes in organizational contexts* (pp. 1–12). Philadelphia: Psychology Press.

Ibarra, H. (2003). *Working identity: Uncoventional strategies for reinventing.* Cambridge, MA: Harvard Business School Press.

Jarzabkowski, P. (2004). Strategy as practice: Recursiveness, adaptation, and practices-in-use. *Organization Studies, 25*, 529–560.

Keyes, C. (1998). Social well-being. *Social Psychology Quarterly, 61*, 121–140.

Keyes, C., & Haidt, J. (2003). *Flourishing: Positive psychology and the life well lived.* Washington, DC: American Psychological Assocation.

Kreiner, G., Ashforth, B., & Sluss, D. (2006). Identity dynamics in occupational dirty work: Integrating social identity and system justification perspectives. *Organization Science, 17*, 619–636.

Losey, M., Meisinger, S., & Ulrich, D. (2005). *The future of human resource management.* Hoboken, NJ: John Wiley & Sons.

Lyubomirsky, S. (2007). *The how of happiness: A scientific approach to getting the life you want*. New York: Penguin Press.

MacIntyre, A. (1981). *After virtue*. South Bend, IN: Notre Dame Press.

Markus, H., & Kunda, Z. (1986). Stability and malleability of the self-concept. *Journal of Personality and Social Psychology, 51*, 858–866.

Mauno, S., Kinnunen, U., & Ruokolainen, M. (2007). Job demands and resources as antecedents of work engagement: A longitudinal study. *Journal of Vocational Behavior, 70*, 149–171.

Michel, A. A. (2007). A distributed cognition perspective on newcomers' change processes: The management of cognitive uncertainty in two investment banks. *Administrative Science Quarterly, 52*, 507–557.

Newman, S., Vasudev, J., & Onawola, R. (1985). Older volunteers' perceptions of impacts of volunteering on their psychological well-being. *Journal of Applied Gerontology, 4*, 123–134.

Orlikowski, W. (2002). Knowing in practice: Enacting a collective capability in distributed organizing. *Organization Science, 13*, 249–273.

Perry-Smith, J. E., & Blum, T. C. (2000). Work–family human resource bundles and perceived organizational performance. *Academy of Management Journal, 43*, 1107–1117.

Peterson, C., & Seligman, M. (2004). *Character strengths and virtues: A handbook and classification*. Washington, DC: American Psychological Association.

Pierce, J. L., & Gardner, D. G. (2004). Self-esteem within the work and organizational context: A review of the organization-based self-esteem literature. *Journal of Management, 30*, 591–622.

Piliavin, J. (2003). Doing well by doing good: Benefits for the benefactor. In C. Keyes & J. Haidt (Eds.), *Flourishing: Positive psychology and the life well lived* (pp. 227–247). Washington, DC: American Psychological Association.

Podolny, J., Khurana, R., & Hill-Popper, M. (2005). Revisiting the meaning of leadership. *Research Organizational Behavior, 26*, 1–36.

Pratt, M. G. (2000). The good, the bad, and the ambivalent: Managing identification among Amway distributors. *Administrative Science Quarterly, 45*, 456–493.

Ragins, B., & Kram, K. (2007). *The handbook of mentoring at work. Theory, research and practice*. Thousand Oaks, CA: Sage Publications.

Reed II, A., & Aquino, K. F. (2003). Moral identity and the expanding circle of moral regard toward out-groups. *Journal of Personality and Social Psychology, 84*, 1270–1286.

Roberts, L. M., & Dutton, J. E. (2009). *Exploring positive identities and organizations: Building a theoretical and research foundation*. New York: Psychology Press.

Roberts, L. M., Dutton, J. E., Spreitzer, G. M., Heaphy, E. D., & Quinn, R. E. (2005). Composing the reflected best-self portrait: Building pathways for becoming extraordinary in work organizations. *Academy of Management Review, 30*, 712–736.

Ryff, C. D., & Keyes, C. L. M. (1995). The structure of psychological well-being revisited. *Journal of Personality and Social Psychology, 69*, 719–727.

Seligman, M. (2002). *Authentic happiness: Using the new positive psychology to realize your potential for lasting fulfillment*. New York: Free Press.

Seligman, M., & Csikszentmihalyi, M. (2000). Positive psychology: An introduction. *American Psychologist, 55*, 5–14.

Trice, H. M., & Beyer, J. M. (1984). Employee assistance programs: Blending performance-oriented and humanitarian ideologies to assist emotionally disturbed employees. *Research in Community and Mental Health, 4*, 245–297.

Turner, J. C. (1982). Toward a cognitive redefinition of the social group. In H. Tajfel (Ed.), *Social identity and intergroup relations* (pp. 15–40). Cambridge, UK: Cambridge University Press.

Ulrich, D., & Brockbank, W. (2005). *The HR value proposition*. Cambridge, MA: Harvard Business School Press.

Van Maanen, J., & Schein, E. H. (1979). Towards a theory of organizational socialization. In B. M. Staw (Ed.), *Research in organizational behavior* (pp. 209–264). Greenwich, CT: JAI Press.

Xanthopoulou, D., Bakker, A. B., Demerouti, E., & Schaufeli, W. B. (2009). Work engagement and financial returns: A diary study on the role of job and personal resources. *Journal of Occupational and Organizational Psychology, 82,* 183–200.

11

Effects of Virtuous Leadership on Organizational Performance

I became interested in Positive Organizational Scholarship (POS) as a result of studying organizational downsizing in the USA during the 1980s and 1990s. In those research projects, I discovered that a large majority of organizations that abolished jobs, eliminated employment, consolidated activities, and retrenched operations also experienced 12 negative, dysfunctional outcomes. I referred to them as "the dirty dozen," and they included factors such as increased conflict, restricted communication, escalating politicking, scapegoating leaders, the threat-rigidity response, destruction of trust, worsening morale, and so forth. As you would expect, the emergence of these factors produced declining performance in the vast majority of downsizing organizations.

A key finding from those research projects was not surprising – almost all organizations deteriorate in performance after downsizing. On the other hand, I observed a few organizations that thrived. Despite the fact that employees were involuntarily terminated, that the organization experienced contraction and consolidation, and that unpleasant decisions were made by senior executives, these organizations flourished. Whereas I had little empirical data to back up my hunch at the time, I began forming an impression that the organizations that flourished after a downsizing experience were characterized by virtuousness – institutionalized compassion, forgiveness, gratitude, trustworthiness, optimism, integrity, and so forth.

This hunch was one of the factors that eventually led me and some of my colleagues at the University of Michigan to form a research center focused on what we now refer to as Positive Organizational Scholarship (POS). The title of the center was carefully selected, so that the three terms – *positive, organizational,* and *scholarship* – have specific meaning. The term "organizational" is not very controversial because it refers to investigations of organizational dynamics – the context in which positive phenomena occur. "Scholarship" is also well-understood to mean empirical, rigorous, theoretically based academic work on positive topics.

The term "positive," however, has created controversy as well as ambiguity among scholars, so I want to highlight the aspects of "positive" that I associate with POS.

POS currently has at least three areas of focus, as illustrated in Figure 11.1. One is a focus on affirmative phenomena in organizations – for example, on strengths rather than weaknesses, on flourishing rather than languishing, on abundance gaps rather than deficit gaps. Problems, difficulties, and obstacles are not ignored, of course, because flourishing often occurs as a result of responses to negativity in the form of difficulties, obstacles, and challenges. POS is unapologetic, however, about having a distinctive affirmative bias in organizations. The positive takes priority over the negative. Another area of focus is on virtuousness. This means an emphasis on the best of the human condition, or on the highest aspirations that humankind holds for itself. In music a virtuoso is the most inspiring performer, and uplifting music is often characterized by virtuosity. The original Greek word *eudaemonism* captures the essence of virtuousness – an inspirational level of excellence. POS is also unapologetic about studying the best of the human condition and its relationship to performance.

The third area of focus in POS is on positively deviant performance in organizations. This means that POS examines extraordinarily successful performance and tries to explain why it occurred – what are the enablers, what are the indicators, and what are the explanatory factors when spectacular and unexpectedly positive performance occurs?

To illustrate what I mean by positively deviant performance, consider the line in Figure 11.2 as representing a deviance continuum. In English, the term *deviance* normally has a negative connotation, so if a person is labeled a deviant, it is usually a criticism. But deviance is really just an aberration from the norm or from expected performance, so we can think of negatively deviant activities or we can think about positively deviant activities. Think of the left-hand point of the line as representing negative deviance, the middle representing normal or expected performance, and the right-hand point representing positive deviance. These points are not so much a continuum as they are qualitatively different states.

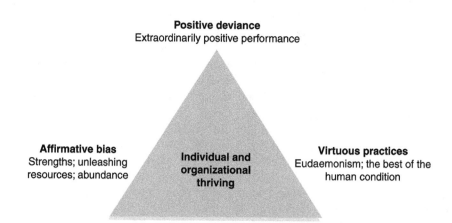

Positive deviance
Extraordinarily positive performance

Affirmative bias
Strengths; unleashing resources; abundance

Individual and organizational thriving

Virtuous practices
Eudaemonism; the best of the human condition

FIGURE 11.1   Three areas of investigation in POS.

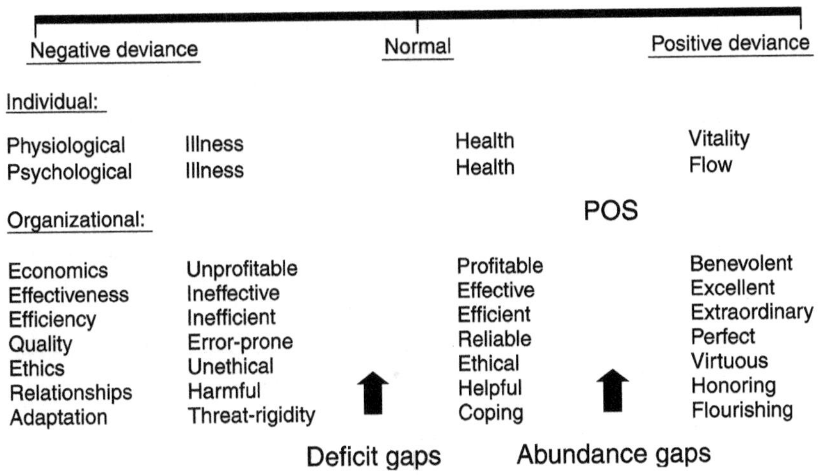

Negative deviance		Normal	Positive deviance

Individual:

Physiological	Illness	Health	Vitality
Psychological	Illness	Health	Flow

Organizational: **POS**

Economics	Unprofitable	Profitable	Benevolent
Effectiveness	Ineffective	Effective	Excellent
Efficiency	Inefficient	Efficient	Extraordinary
Quality	Error-prone	Reliable	Perfect
Ethics	Unethical	Ethical	Virtuous
Relationships	Harmful	Helpful	Honoring
Adaptation	Threat-rigidity	Coping	Flourishing

Deficit gaps   Abundance gaps

FIGURE 11.2   A deviance continuum (from Cameron, 2003).

One important implication becomes clear when we use this continuum to explain positive deviance. The implication is that all organizations exist, by definition, to eliminate deviance. The reason we organize is to abolish unexpected, chaotic, abnormal, unpredictable behavior. For example, if we have a group of people engaged in a project, say building a Habitat for Humanity house, the first thing we do is organize. If we don't, the resulting activity is chaotic, unpredictable, and full of deviance. Organizing, by definition, eliminates deviance – usually negative deviance. The trouble is, organizing also eliminates positive deviance. Organizing, by definition, eliminates unexpectedly extraordinary, spectacular, or positively deviant performance. To achieve positive deviance, a conscious strategy must be put in place that overcomes the natural tendency in organized activity toward emphasizing standard or expected performance.

Another implication of this continuum in Figure 11.2 is that one side receives much more scholarly attention than the other. We know much more about the left side of the continuum than the right side. About 90% of medical research focuses on the gap between the left-hand point (illness) and the middle point (basic health), that is, the National Institute of Health spends a great deal of money sponsoring studies of diabetes, heart disease, the common cold, cancer, and so on. Once normal or expected health is achieved and once disease is eliminated, much less scientific attention is paid. Yet, we know that on the right-hand end of the continuum exists a condition of positively deviant health. This might be represented by Olympic fitness levels, the ability to do 400 push-ups, or 5% body fat for men and 15% body fat for women. Unfortunately, much less scientific attention is paid to positively deviant health and how to achieve it than how to overcome illness.

Psychologically speaking, Marty Seligman and Mike Csikszentmihalyi were among the first to publish the fact that well over 90% of all psychological research since the end of World War II focuses on the gap between negative deviance on the left and the middle point of the continuum. They were the first to ask questions about the gap between normal psychological functioning and positive deviance – for example, a state of psychological flow. This is the condition where brains function at peak performance, thinking patterns are at their highest levels of efficiency, and emotional well-being is extraordinary. Some recent scientific attention has been paid to this phenomenon, but not much yet.

Organizational scholarship is not quite as biased, but it is similar. That is, when a person is educated in the traditional business school, a large part of the information learned comes through a case method. Typically, an instructor assigns a case study, and students are challenged to identify the threats, the potential mistakes, the challenges, the obstacles, or the problems. They mainly focus on making recommendations regarding how to cope with threats and problems. Most of the focus is on the left-hand side of the continuum.

The right-hand side of the continuum, on the other hand, is qualitatively different. I refer to it as a positively deviant, or a virtuous, condition. The terms we use to represent this positively deviant state are not well-developed – terms such as benevolence, flourishing, honor, virtue, and compassion are examples – and they are often dismissed or denigrated by critics as saccharine, naïve, or substanceless.

The divergence between the left-hand point and the middle point is referred to as a deficit gap. The gap between the right-hand point and the middle point is referred to as an abundance gap. POS doesn't ignore the left-hand side, but the focus – because so little work has been conducted – is on abundance gaps.

My observations about flourishing in organizations after downsizing led me to pursue investigations embedded in POS. The research questions in which I have been interested for the past several years have to do with identifying, measuring, and predicting abundance gaps. For example, how do I know positive deviance when I see it in organizations? What are the attributes? What are the predictors of positively deviant performance? What are the effects of virtuous practices in organizations? Are organizations more or less effective when they focus on abundance gaps and virtuous practices?

I will summarize several of my own studies that have addressed these kinds of questions. I will not describe the research designs and statistical procedures, but I will highlight findings from investigations across a variety of industries (from airlines to financial services) and a variety of sectors (including government, not-for-profit, and private sector organizations). The initial studies were quite simple and exploratory, merely trying to determine whether or not positivity and virtuousness are related at all to organizational performance. Later studies explored these questions in somewhat more depth. Unfortunately, more research questions are yet to be answered than have been verified to date.

One of my early studies was aimed at merely trying to answer the question: "Does a relationship exist between virtuousness – as measured by organizational practices that emphasize compassion, forgiveness, gratitude, trustworthiness, optimism, and integrity – and indicators of organizational performance – as measured by profitability, productivity, quality, innovation, customer satisfaction, and employee engagement?" The study assessed seven organizations in the same industry using correlational analyses.

A survey instrument was developed to assess the virtuous practices in organizations. For example, items assessing forgiveness asked respondents to rate the extent to which – when downsizing was implemented, when harm occurred, or when people were really damaged by the organization – employees hold grudges. Did the organization develop the negative and defensive attributes that usually accompany downsizing and deterioration, or was there an institutionalized way to look forward optimistically, to learn, to forgive mistakes, and to progress toward a positive future? Each of the six dimensions of virtuousness used in this study was measured with several survey items across a sample of organization members. We were especially interested in the questions: "Do these virtuous practices exist in the organization?" and "What are the relationships between these practices and the six indicators of performance?" This particular study only used panel data, so results are merely suggestive of a relationship and no causality can be attributed. As indicated in Figure 11.3, the regression line appears to support the idea that this relationship may exist.

Given this preliminary support, a second investigation expanded the sample to include organizations across 16 different industries – profit and not-for-profit organizations as well as large and small firms. Organizations included large firms such as General Electric, National City Bank, and OfficeMax, as well as small and not-for-profit firms such as the YMCA, hospitals, and educational organizations. The question being investigated was whether the first study's findings were merely an aberration or a generalizable finding.

We measured the same dimensions of virtuousness as well as multiple outcomes, including objective indicators such as profitability and productivity, and subjective indicators such as morale and engagement. Once again, strong and statistically significant relationships emerged across these various organizations ($p < .01$). Organizations that implemented positive practices were significantly more effective than organizations that did not. These findings led us to conclude that this relationship was worth pursuing. That is, if outcomes that organizations espouse as their primary objectives – such as profitability, productivity, and quality – are affected by virtuousness, then we had better become more precise about understanding what is going on.

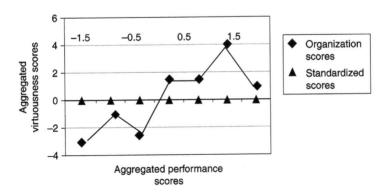

FIGURE 11.3   Organizational virtuousness and performance.

A third study added further support to the relationship between positive practices and improvement in performance. This study looked in depth at two organizations that consciously tried to implement positive practices after suffering through downsizing and deterioration in outcomes. Figure 11.4 illustrates the results.

These two organizations were struggling financially, and they had engaged in at least one major downsizing as a result. They approached us and asked for some assistance. In essence they said: "We have learned about positive organizational scholarship. We have heard about the material relating to an abundance culture.

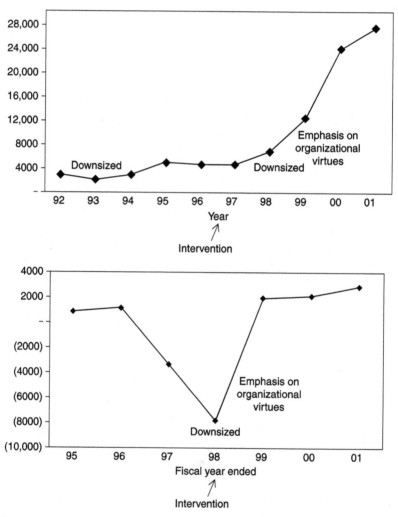

FIGURE 11.4 Culture change. Interventions included: Reflected best-self feedback, positive energy networks, Personal Management Interview program, Everest goals, reciprocity networks, engagement practices, empowerment, supportive communication, and teambuilding.

Help us implement some principles that may make a positive difference in our organization."

Several interventions occurred that were directed at trying to change the organizations' practices and culture. Figure 11.4 shows some of those tools and techniques, as well as the change in performance that occurred. Again, we could not prove that the positive practices caused the performance improvements, but again the trends certainly seem suggestive.

Another study added even more credibility to this conclusion. This investigation was conducted in the US airline industry after the tragedy of September 11, 2001. We all know that as soon as the World Trade Center towers came down, people stopped flying in airplanes. It was against the law to fly for two or three days. When the airlines were allowed to fly again, ridership topped out at 80% of previous ridership levels. The problem is, the economic model of the US airline industry at the time was based on an 86% seat-fill rate. All of the airlines had at least 20% too much capacity and costs. Seven of these companies filed for bankruptcy relatively quickly. The two airlines that were hurt the worst were the short-haul carriers, or the companies highly dependent on short routes. U.S. Airways had an average flight of less than 500 miles. Southwest Airlines had an average flight of less than 400 miles.

U.S. Airways responded by downsizing more than 20% and by declaring financial exigency. This means that they could lay off employees with no benefits and no severance. Southwest Airlines, on the other hand, laid off no one!

Why would Southwest Airlines adopt this stance when it was suffering more than the industry average? The Chief Executive Officer (CEO) said: "Look, we can't continue to do this indefinitely. We are losing millions of dollars a day. But, we are willing to suffer some damage, even to our stock price, to protect the jobs of our people." In my book, that represents a very virtuous approach to employee well-being. But the question arises, why would he adopt that stance? Isn't it foolhardy business practice? He responded: "You want to show your people that you value them, and that you're not going to hurt them just to get a little more money in the short run. Not furloughing people breeds loyalty. It breeds a sense of security. It breeds a sense of trust." His statement reflects the virtuous culture that was being perpetuated at Southwest Airlines.

Some skeptics dismiss this virtuous motive by pointing out that Southwest Airlines hedged fuel prices and that they simply had more money in the bank than most airlines. That is true. But the CEO explained: "Everybody hedges fuel prices. I mean, fuel prices go up and down every day. You can't change the price of a ticket every day. All airlines hedge. We are not unusual." Moreover, Southwest Airlines is more unionized than the industry average, so this approach is not a matter of being non-unionized. Here is the explanation: "We have money in the bank because we want enough financial resources so that, if something like this happens, we have sufficient slack to pay our people." The virtuousness of the culture is reflected consistently, even in Southwest Airlines' financial strategy.

But, here is the problem: Wall Street doesn't care. Stockholders and investors are impervious to how employees are treated. They do not care if the firm has layoffs or not. They simply require a return on investment. Wall Street may be among the least virtuous places on the planet, because the goal is clear: "Show me the money."

In this study we differentiated among ten US airline companies in terms of the virtuousness of their approach to downsizing. All firms downsized (except Southwest and Alaska), but some did so in a way that preserved the dignity, financial support, and safety nets of employees. Others did not. Some were more virtuous than others in implementing this strategy. As is illustrated in Figure 11.5, the correlation between stock price return or financial investment in these companies in the following 12 months and the virtuousness of the downsizing strategy is .86. Firms that approached downsizing virtuously made more money. Virtuous firms recovered more quickly. Wall Street investment followed virtuousness.

When is the last time you found a .86 correlation with anything? This is remarkably strong, practical support for the relationship between virtuous practices and organizational outcomes.

The published article that described these results reported the airline companies' performance through to the end of 2006, and the correlation only declined to .79. Obviously, there remained a very strong correlation between virtuousness and financial return over an entire five-year period of time.

As mentioned, financial service organizations are one of the least likely places to find an emphasis on virtuous practices. Shareholder value and financial return dominate the espoused objectives. We conducted research in this industry, there-

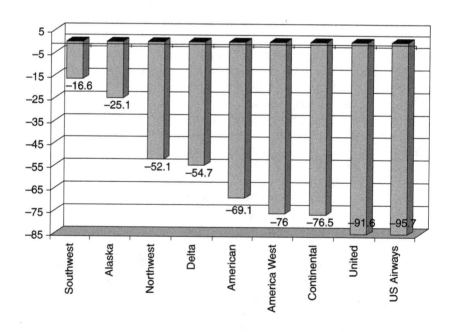

FIGURE 11.5   Stock values – September 2001 to September 2002.

fore, to see if the relationship between virtuousness and performance held up in financial services. If we could find an impact of virtuousness on financial service organization performance, we surmised that we could find it anywhere.

The study included 40 different organizations. Most of them were explicit in wanting to improve their performance, generally defined as financial performance. We exposed all of these organizations to the idea of positively deviant performance and to information about the association between performance and virtuous practices. One organization actually said: "We want this to become our competitive strategy. We may never be the largest in the industry, but becoming a virtuous organization will attract the best employees, more investors, and better leaders. We can become the best company in the industry."

By measuring virtuous practices as well as six measures of financial performance in these companies, we discovered that the correlation between virtuous practices and financial performance is .49, which is a surprisingly strong positive relationship. More importantly, we looked at change scores in these organizations between 2005 and 2006. The question of interest was: "If a firm improves in virtuousness scores, what happens to financial performance in the following year?" This begins to address the causality question of whether virtuous practices actually produce desired outcomes. Sure enough, evidence emerged that by improving virtuous practices the financial performance goes up. The size of the R^2 statistic was astounding. It was .45, which means that almost half the variance in financial performance could be accounted for by improvement in positive practices in these financial services firms.

Taken together, these studies began to make a reasonably compelling case that virtuousness in organizations has a strong positive relationship with performance. But one additional study helps to solidify this conclusion: an in-depth investigation of the Rocky Flats Nuclear Arsenal, located 16 miles west of Denver, Colorado.

This facility produced most of the nuclear triggers found in the US arsenal. During the Cold War, the Soviet Union was stockpiling nuclear weapons, and so the USA also had to stockpile nuclear weapons to keep the world safe for democracy. Balance of power was crucial at the time. Starting in 1951, this site handled the most dangerous materials known to mankind – plutonium, enriched uranium, acids of various kinds – the types of materials that you don't want terrorists to get hold of.

Over a period of 40 years, this facility had become the best on the planet at what it did – producing the explosive devices for nuclear weapons. Of necessity, the facility maintained extremely tight security and secrecy. Neither the surrounding communities, the State of Colorado, nor the federal government knew how well safety and pollution were being scrutinized. Monitoring by external agencies, such as the Environmental Protection Agency (EPA), was not present inasmuch as the EPA did not have jurisdiction over Rocky Flats. If EPA monitors came on site, they had to be blindfolded because of the top secret nature of the activity. The citizenry in the communities surrounding Rocky Flats (Denver, Boulder, Golden, and others) were skeptical and fearful that cancer-causing pollution was being emitted, or that groundwater and airborne pollutants were contaminating the entire region. ABC *Nightline* produced a television special on Rocky

Flats in 1994 entitled "The Most Dangerous Building in America" – the most polluted, hazardous buildings on the continent.

The EPA sued in the federal courts to obtain jurisdiction over Rocky Flats in order to determine how much, if any, radioactive pollution was being emitted into the air, the surrounding soil, and the groundwater. The EPA finally obtained partial jurisdiction over the site and in 1989 showed up with the FBI. They essentially said to employees: "Step back from the equipment. Do not touch anything. Prove to us that the soil is okay, the water is okay, and the air is okay. You may do no work until the contamination studies have been completed."

The trouble is, the Rocky Flats' employees were engineers, production personnel, steel workers, construction workers, and security guards. They were not soil samplers. They essentially lost their mission with the arrival of the FBI. They were changed overnight from patriotic heroes to accused environmental criminals. Consequently, for six years nothing was done – no production work, no clean-up, no progress – except paper studies of pollution levels. The problem is, the cost of operating the facilities (running air conditioning, keeping the water on, maintaining security, and so forth) was $700 million per year. This was essentially a maximum security facility. You can't just walk away or let terrorists get access to the site. The half-life of plutonium is 26,000 years, so the dangerous materials are not going anywhere for a very long time. Over the six-year period, more than $6 billion was spent to keep the lights on but with no production work or clean-up occurring at all.

Finally, the U.S. Department of Energy put together a Blue Ribbon Commission and charged them to do an analysis of the Rocky Flats site and about a dozen other Atomic Energy sites in the USA. The task was to figure out how long it would take, and at what cost, to clean up and close these facilities. For Rocky Flats, the estimate was 70 years with a budget of $36 billion. The 70-year time-frame was claimed by some of the experts to be a gross underestimate. They assumed that it would take 200 years to finish the job, but they couldn't send out an RFP (Request for Proposal) specifying 200 years. What firm would bid on that long a duration? So, 70 years was the timeframe selected for the project, and the allocation was set at $36 billion.

In 1995, a company competed for and won the contract to close and clean up the Rocky Flats facility. Here is what they found in 1995: 21 tons of nuclear grade material was present, enough to blow up the world several times over; more than 100 tons of high-content plutonium residues existed on site, with no treatment or disposal path; 30,000 liters of plutonium and enriched uranium solutions were in tanks and pipes, some of them leaking; more than 258,000 cubic meters of low-level radioactive waste and nearly 15,000 cubic meters of transuranic waste (some of this radioactive material was stored in barrels buried in pits, so it wasn't clear where all the dangerous materials and acids were located); pollution in the form of dust and micro-pollutants was in many of the buildings, including in the furnishings, equipment, concrete, duct work, and fixtures, so workers had to strip the concrete, scour the duct work, and clean every square inch of the facilities and every piece of equipment that had been in them; and finally, more than 1500 glove-boxes (in which plutonium was handled) existed on site and in the normal maintenance schedule it took approximately one year to tear apart a glove-box, so the challenge of dismantling and cleaning 1500 glove-boxes was overwhelming.

More than 800 buildings existed on 358 acres of production area, surrounded by 6000 acres of buffer area. Nobody really knew how to clean up a nuclear arsenal because no entity had ever done it before. Environmentalists, community organizations, state regulatory agencies, and most of the surrounding communities hated the place, and it is not difficult to imagine that many protests and demonstrations were frequently being staged at the site. Security was incredibly tight and, by necessity, limited access to the site had to be maintained. A siege mentality existed as the workforce were inclined to protect themselves against what they viewed as false and unfair stereotyping, and by 1995 more than 900 grievances had been formally filed against management.

Now, what is the relevance of this story? What does Rocky Flats have to do with virtuous practices and performance? Here is the reason.

The firm that won the contract to clean up and close Rocky Flats finished the job 60 years early, at a cost $30 billion under budget. Most amazingly, the result was 13 times cleaner than required by federal standards. Adversaries and antagonists became advocates and lobbyists. The president of the steel workers' union stated: "This is the best labor relations I've ever seen in my 35 year career, and they're laying off people as fast as they can." Unions are designed to keep jobs, of course, not eliminate them, so how did they get unions to enthusiastically work themselves out of a job as fast as possible? How did they get environmentalists to become supporters and promoters? How did they get government entities to encourage rather than block innovative activities? How did they get the surrounding community members to become promoters? How did they overcome the resistance faced by other nuclear sites in the country that are on-time and on-budget?

Figure 11.6 shows how the Rocky Flats site looked at full production and how it looked upon closure in October of 2005. You can tell there is nothing there. It is now a wildlife refuge, and there have been antelope and buffalo brought in so that people can picnic and play in the area. This is one of the most dramatic success stories I have ever heard. It represents a quintessential example of positive deviance in organizational performance. It is difficult to imagine more spectacular performance, especially when most other sites are on-schedule.

FIGURE 11.6   Rocky Flats in full production and in 2005.

We began studying this facility and the clean-up and closure process in 2001, so four years before completion we were gathering data on what was being done rather than asking people to provide retrospective sense-making and rationalization after the project was completed. What we discovered was the presence of virtuousness and positive practices throughout the entire facility. We wrote a book, *Making the Impossible Possible*, to document the 21 leadership lessons learned. At the very core was a culture that emphasized abundance gaps, virtuousness, and positivity. The way they hired people, the way they compensated people, the way they promoted people, the way they tore down buildings, the way they organized the workforce, the way they contracted with the government, the way they replaced leaders, the way they downsized, the way they interacted with the local media, and the way they coordinated with citizen groups all represented an abundance mentality. Focusing on the gap between expected and effective performance and positively deviant performance – extraordinary, spectacular, and almost unimaginable performance – made all the difference. Identifying the strategies and organizational processes used to achieve this level of performance was the subject of the study.

The conclusion of this stream of research has become quite compelling: virtuous practices in organizations are associated with, and may even produce, desired performance in organizations, even when the outcomes are traditional performance indicators such as profitability, productivity, quality, customer satisfaction, and employee engagement. Of course, the significance of virtuousness does not require that it be associated with other outcomes in organizations. Almost all of humankind believes that there is inherent value in virtuousness, or in reaching the highest aspirations that human beings hold for themselves. Fostering virtuousness is inherently good even if no other organizational outcomes are achieved. But when faced with stockholder demands for measurable results, when trying to help organizations improve their mandated outputs, or when trying to lead an organization through trying times, an emphasis on abundance gaps and virtuous practices provides an important and frequently neglected opportunity to flourish.

FURTHER READING

Bright, D. S., Cameron, K. S., & Caza, A. (2006). The amplifying and buffering effects of virtuousness in downsized organizations. *Journal of Business Ethics, 64*, 249–269.

Cameron, K. S. (1994). Strategies for successful organizational downsizing. *Human Resource Management Journal, 33*, 89–112.

Cameron, K. S. (1998). Strategic organizational downsizing: An extreme case. *Research in Organizational Behavior, 20*, 185–229.

Cameron, K. S. (2003). Organizational virtuousness and performance. In K. S. Cameron, J. E. Dutton, & R. E. Quinn (Eds.), *Positive organizational scholarship: Foundations of a new discipline* (pp. 48–65). San Francisco: Berrett-Koehler.

Cameron, K. S. (2008). Positively deviant organizational performance and the role of leadership values. *Journal of Values Based Leadership, 1*, 67–83.

Cameron, K. S. (2008). *Positive leadership*. San Francisco: Berrett-Koehler.

Cameron, K. S., Bright, D., & Caza, A. (2004). Exploring the relationships between organizational virtuousness and performance. *American Behavioral Scientist*, 47, 766–790.

Cameron, K. S., & Lavine, M. (2006). *Making the impossible possible: Leading extraordinary performance – the Rocky Flats story*. San Francisco: Berrett-Koehler.

Gittell, J. H., Cameron, K. S., Lim, S., & Rivas, V. (2006). Relationships, layoffs, and organizational resilience. *Journal of Applied Behavioral Science*, 42, 300–328.

12

Contexts of Positive Adult Development

JEANNE NAKAMURA

It is perhaps surprising that so much of the study of human development has been the study of normal progress and its derailment, without nearly as much attention to flourishing. When it comes to infancy and childhood, the normative developmental achievements such as walking, talking, and taking another's perspective strike us as just that – remarkable achievements. (I would nevertheless suggest that an emphasis on flourishing needs to be brought to bear on the study of early life, as the emerging field of positive education is richly illustrating.) But is normalcy and its disruption an adequate way to conceive development beyond childhood? Currently, efforts to bring a focus on flourishing to developmental psychology are most visible in the studies of adolescence and aging, the two areas that were traditionally viewed primarily through a pathology lens – *sturm und drang* (storm and stress) and delinquency, and disease and decline, respectively. Development during the half-century or more of life between adolescence and old age, however, has continued to be viewed in recent decades to a large extent in terms of normative roles and transitions, with greater emphasis on the management of stress, strain, and conflict than on flourishing. Meanwhile, despite important exceptions, the recent work in positive psychology on adult goals, purpose, meaning, and engagement, and other topics central to an understanding of the life well lived, has not tended to be examined from a developmental perspective. That is, researchers have not explored how phenomena are affected by, or specific to, a person's place in the life course or how processes of gain, loss, and transformation can be understood through the lens of developmental theory. This chapter will first present some general observations about positive psychology. These provide the rationale and framework for a discussion of the constructive role of context in adult development, which I illustrate with the case of mentoring during professional training and the early career.

THE POSITIVE, AGENCY, AND CONTEXT: UNIFYING THEMES IN POSITIVE PSYCHOLOGY

What, if anything, do positive psychologists have in common? Elsewhere, I have suggested that positive psychology began by erecting a "big tent" and inviting all comers (Nakamura, 2005). It was not, and is not, characterized by a single unifying theory of psychological functioning. What, then, unites it? The obvious commonality, of course, is a focus on the positive. I will return to this and what it means.

A second, perhaps less obvious candidate is a focus on intentional action. This has a strong form in that, in some research traditions important to positive psychology, human agency stands front and center. Two leading examples are Bandura's (2006) work on agency and Ryan and Deci's (2000) self-determination theory. Within lifespan developmental psychology, Lerner's (1982) notion of individuals as producers of their development, Baltes and Baltes' (1990) model of selection, optimization, and compensation, and Brandstadter's (2006) work on self-regulatory processes are influential examples.

More generally, a shared premise in positive psychology is that individuals possess a measure of control over their own flourishing. The assumption – in sharp contrast to all forms of determinism – underlies the science of positive functioning: for example, the investigation of engagement, creativity, wisdom, and the formation and pursuit of purpose. In the applied sphere, it underlies the stances that one can learn optimism (Seligman, 1991), cultivate character (Park & Peterson, 2008), find flow (Csikszentmihalyi, 1997), craft meaningful work (Wrzesniewski & Dutton, 2001), and, most boldly and broadly put, work toward getting the life you want (Lyubomirsky, 2008). The examples could be multiplied many times over.

Given the latter thrust of positive psychology up until now, when we ask where applied positive psychology is headed, one obvious answer is continued efforts to increase the well-being of individuals through the building of their personal resources – in other words, directly. But the environments in which we live exert their own powerful influences. Thus, a second possibility is an expansion of attention to the way in which *contexts* can increase the well-being of individuals – indeed, populations – indirectly. This would comprise an applied positive psychology of homes, schools, and workplaces, and of relationships, communities, and societies. Less often discussed, it would be a positive psychology of plazas and parks, streets and subways, and of the natural, built, and virtual environments. Despite a slower start, there is promising work underway on good schools, complex families, virtuous organizations, aligned professions, gross national well-being, and a happy planet. It is the integration of this second possibility with the first, more familiar one – of context with agency – that will occupy the present chapter.

First, however, let us return to the other common denominator in positive psychology, which seems so obvious and definitional as to go without saying: a focus on the psychologically positive. At the outset of positive psychology, it was the field of psychology's focus on the many negative aspects of human functioning in urgent need of attention – deficits and disorders, risk factors, negative moods and emotions, intrapsychic and interpersonal conflict – that inspired a call for greater attention to the positive aspects of human functioning (Gable & Haidt,

2005; Seligman & Csikszentmihalyi, 2000). Positive psychology trained a spotlight on what had been some comparatively neglected, marginalized, and in some cases almost entirely unconceptualized topics (e.g., elevation, gratitude) and increased the attention to others (e.g., hope/optimism, positive emotions, meaning, flow). In this role, positive psychology has been corrective: it notes the study of pessimism, depression, character weaknesses, toxic relationships, and sick institutions, and aims to introduce a study of optimism, happiness, character strengths, positive relationships, and healthy institutions (see Figure 12.1).

But a compartmentalization of psychological phenomena into "the positive" and "the negative" would oversimplify matters in a variety of ways, and in fact current positive psychology already offers more differentiated and more integrated understandings of positive, negative, and the relations between them. To take one very simple example of a more differentiated view, in some areas positive psychology can be seen as encompassing (1) what we think, and find, to be negative; (2) what we think, and find, to be positive; (3) the negative in what we think of as positive; and (4) the positive in what we think of as negative. For example, we might think of pessimism as negative and optimism as positive. In fact, the picture is more complex if we distinguish between expected and unexpected impacts on well-being. Research differentiates between *strategic or realistic* optimism and *naïve or unrealistic* optimism (Schneider, 2001). Whereas we expect optimism to positively affect well-being, the case of naïve or unrealistic optimism shows that it can also have negative impacts on well-being. Similarly, research distinguishes between *dispositional* pessimism and strategic or *defensive* pessimism (Norem & Chang, 2002). While we expect pessimism to have negative impacts, and dispositional pessimism does, the case of defensive pessimism shows that it also can have a positive impact on well-being under some conditions (see Figure 12.2).

Optimism/pessimism is not an isolated example of the more nuanced analysis of positive and negative. Abundant choice (Schwartz, 2004) and "the goods life" (Kasser, 2004) are two other phenomena discussed in positive psychology where positive outcomes might be expected but negative outcomes emerge. And the

Study of the "negative"	Study of the "positive"
Pessimism, depression, character weaknesses, toxic relationships, sick institutions	Optimism, happiness, character strengths, positive relationships, positive institutions

FIGURE 12.1   The "positive" as a complement to the "negative" in psychological science.

Unexpected impact on well-being	Expected impact on well-being	
	Negative	Positive
Positive	Defensive pessimism	Strategic/realistic optimism
Negative	Dispositional pessimism	Naïve/unrealistic optimism

FIGURE 12.2   Differentiating further the "positive" from the "negative."

emotion of regret provides an additional example of a phenomenon wherein negative outcomes might be expected but positive outcomes can be found (King & Hicks, 2007; Saffrey, Summerville, & Roese, 2008).

For a dynamic relating of positive and negative possibilities it is instructive to turn to the field of developmental psychology, which adopts an integrated perspective on the phenomena that it studies, in the sense of identifying and analyzing the multiple developmental trajectories or pathways that individuals traverse. In most basic terms (see Figure 12.3), it does not merely restrict attention to simple deterministic pathways in which (1) limiting or negative conditions lead to poor or negative functioning (e.g., the contribution of risk factors to later interpersonal problems) or (2) positive conditions lead to positive functioning (e.g., the contribution of rich family resources to later academic success). In addition to these pathways, developmental psychology considers (3) how positive conditions can be followed by poor or negative functioning (Csikszentmihalyi & Schneider, 2000) and (4) how limiting or negative conditions can be followed by positive functioning

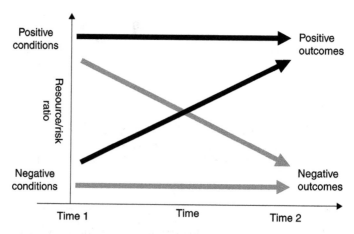

FIGURE 12.3   Types of developmental pathways.

(Masten & Reed, 2002). With respect to the latter, intervening experiences can be transformative; experiences in early adulthood as divergent as military service (e.g., Elder, 1986) and a felicitous marriage (Quinton, Pickles, Maughan, & Rutter, 1993) may provide pathways out of delinquency. Rewarding leisure experiences and marital happiness during midlife may lead to a satisfying retirement despite significant childhood disadvantage (Vaillant, DiRago, & Mukamal, 2006). Moreover, the negative can give rise to the positive, as when disability is a resource (Delle Fave & Massimini, 2003) or trauma leads not to dysfunction or derailment but to meaning and growth (Joseph & Linley, 2008; Nolen-Hoeksema & Davis, 2002); and it can be integrated within a more complex positive condition, as in the mature capacity to acknowledge lost possible selves rather than denying or being defined by them (King & Hicks, 2007).

As these examples illustrate, the positive and its relations to the negative are complex. Science and its application will benefit as models in the field of positive psychology increasingly capture this complexity, further differentiating the understanding of the positive and integrating it with the negative. The examples also show that in the dynamics of optimal functioning both agency and positive context play important roles. Agency plays a central role in processes such as strategically using pessimism and finding meaning in loss, as well as in such familiar forms of positive functioning as (realistic) optimism. And positive contexts, such as a strong marriage, can play crucial roles in processes such as moving from delinquency to thriving or disadvantage to well-being, as well as supporting such processes as enhanced learning in the case of abundant resources in the childhood home. The next section continues these themes with special attention to adult development.

A POSITIVE PSYCHOLOGY OF DEVELOPMENT

In various quarters of developmental psychology, many already mentioned, there is increasing interest in the study of positive development – a focus on flourishing, thriving, and an increase of complexity over the lifespan. As in positive psychology, there are currently multiple views of the nature of positive development, both in terms of optimal processes over the life course and the forms of functioning toward which people optimally move.

In general, however, it is common in developmental psychology to think in terms of the developmental *challenges* encountered at each phase of life and to think of positive development in terms of the mobilization of developmental *supports* for engaging these challenges in ways that contribute to flourishing. The challenges include the expected developmental tasks that are encountered over the life course, such as crystallizing a psychosocial identity in late adolescence or early adulthood and finding a satisfying way at midlife to use accumulated experience for the benefit of future generations (Erikson, 1950). They also include the unexpected or idiosyncratic (non-normative) problems, and opportunities for action, that shape lives and may be experienced differently depending on one's place in the life course (Baltes & Smith, 2004). The supports include *individual resources* – such as one's own agency or initiative, discussed above as a unifying theme in positive psychology, as well as other assets and strengths. In addition, they include environmental or *contextual resources*, which are one instance of the positive contexts whose study stands to advance positive psychology. The interplay of challenges and supports features importantly in numerous developmental models, including those noted here.

In investigating how human beings recruit and deploy resources to optimally engage the challenges and opportunities they encounter across the life course, a positive perspective on human development is necessarily concerned with context. Recognizing that development takes place through the reciprocal interaction of multiple systems, contemporary models of human development are biopsycho-social, cultural, and ecological rather than narrowly psychological (e.g., Baltes & Smith, 2004; Bronfenbrenner, 2000; Elder, 1998; Lerner, 2006; Massimini & Delle Fave, 2000; Neugarten, 1996; Shweder, Goodnow, Hatano, LeVine, Markus, & Miller, 2006). We study the person in context and examine the relations among interacting systems. It follows that to fully understand flourishing or thriving over the life course, it is necessary to study positive contexts of development. Positive contexts have the potential to facilitate optimal development across the life course. This is well recognized with respect to childhood and increasingly adolescence; it underlies longstanding attention to such contextual factors as parenting well, enriching the early home environment, and more recently providing out-of-school settings that allow the identification and development of strengths. With respect to adulthood, however, development in general has received less attention and the same is true of the role of positive contexts in supporting development.

One important passage in adult development is the process through which a young person prepares for and enters full-time working life (Levinson, 1978; Vaillant, 2003). In the professions, for example, during professional education and the early career a young adult begins to be one kind of physician, teacher, or scien-tist rather than another, mastering one set of practices and adopting one set of guiding values and priorities rather than others. He or she may become, for example, a doctor dedicated to developing virtuoso technique, or communicating with patients clearly and compassionately, or maximizing the number of office visits accrued per day. We can think of professional formation as a developmental challenge and ask how a young adult engages it, drawing on individual resources (such as individual agency) and contextual resources (such as the relationships that the young person forms) in order to navigate this challenge well. With respect to extra-individual resources, one's relationships with others comprise a series of critical developmental contexts across the life course. Relationships that are positive can be key catalysts of optimal development and flourishing. In the study of young adults' professional formation, for example, well before the advent of positive psychology much attention already was being devoted to the positive developmental context provided by supportive relationships with more experi-enced professionals (Kram, 1985; Levinson, 1978). This, then, is a natural focus for a psychology of positive adult development.

As suggested at the outset, one promising future direction for positive psychology is to gain a better understanding of contexts that support human flour-ishing. However, also raised was the possibility that the most promising work within positive psychology not only considers the positive in an area of psychological functioning but situates it within the wider terrain, including positive and negative. Thus, part of the power of Fredrickson's analysis of positive emotions is her juxtaposition of this analysis with the pre-existing theory of negative emotions, with both positive and negative understood in terms of their evolutionary significance. Similarly, part of the power of Csikszentmihalyi's account of flow is his analysis of its conditioning by a balance between high challenges and high skills, with other relationships between challenge and skill levels giving rise instead to negative states of anxiety and apathy/boredom. What does this mean for a positive psychology approach to developmental relationships during young adult professional formation? To address this question, I illustrate, with qualitative data from the GoodWork Project, a series of interview studies conducted between 1996 and 2006 to understand the nature and conditions of good work in the USA in different professions (Gardner, Csikszentmihalyi, & Damon, 2001).

In an interview study of about 70 active American scientists, many of them eminent and most at mid-career or beyond, one set of interview questions concerned people who had been formative influences. From the recollections elicited, here are three scientists' accounts of significant influences:

> "I feel he's responsible for my career . . . helping me get started."

> He "got me motivated, inspired me, was interested in what I wanted to do . . ."

> They "pushed me to the limit . . . challenged me. . . . But I always knew that they cared."

Without going into detail, these scientists are describing one type of positive context for adult development: a relationship with a more experienced member of the profession during training and/or the early career that has a significant, positive impact on the young adult's professional formation. The term typically applied to the more seasoned professional in relationships of this type is *mentor*.

Interestingly, an abundant literature in organizational psychology has the opposite of the imbalance that positive psychology articulated and has sought to address; as others have noted (Eby, McManus, Simon, & Russell, 2000), for most of its history it has focused almost exclusively on the *positive* role of experienced professionals in novices' lives. However, to follow the earlier line of argument, an understanding of developmental relationships during professional formation is enriched by considering both positive and negative influences. The case of the sciences is helpful in this regard. In the sciences, professional formation takes place by apprenticeship during graduate and postgraduate education. As a result, every young scientist has an advisor and thus has a developmental relationship that may be positive and/or negative. This allows us to put mentoring in its broader context. From the same study, then, here are three scientists' accounts of the advisor/advisee relationship as a starkly negative interpersonal context:

> "He would start screaming at me about how lousy the work was, that I was doing."

"He said, 'It doesn't matter what you do, you won't impress me.' "

"She actively tried to undercut [her students'] careers. . . . I've seen the anti-Christ and she was it."

The scientists sharing these recollections went on to successful careers so they were not derailed by the encounters described – indeed, knowledge and skills may even have been gained – but it is evident that the relationships left a scar. I borrow a label for this category of developmental relationship from colleague Howard Gardner of the GoodWork Project: *Tormentor*.

As with optimism/pessimism, and with developmental pathways, however, it is possible to productively differentiate the typology of developmental relationships further. Distinguishing between the intended and actual outcomes of a more experienced professional's actions yields two other ideal types. First, there is the potential that positive behavior on the part of a veteran professional inadvertently may have a negative impact on the novice. Developmentally, in early adulthood and particularly in training for a career as an independent research scientist, a mentor with all of the best intentions might, for example, provide an advisee with too much support, hobbling development and encouraging dependence – too much of a good thing, in short; here we might speak not of a Tormentor but a *Too*-mentor.

Second, there is the potential that negative behavior on the part of a veteran professional may have an unintended positive impact. As in post-traumatic growth or defensive pessimism, in this case the young adult does not suffer passively but rather actively makes use of disagreeable experience. Negative behaviors are instructive because by seeing concretely what he or she does *not* want to be, the young person clarifies the kind of professional he or she *does* want to become, and solidifies a commitment to doing so. The role of agency is apparent. As a clinician-scientist put it: "They were people who I saw and said, 'I definitely don't want to be doing things the way they're doing them. . . . Very paternalistic in their approach to patients. Very hierarchical in their approach to colleagues. . . . Very much feeling that they were somehow above other people.' " Here we can speak of an *Anti-mentor*.

There are many ways to increase the complexity of our understandings of positive, negative, and the relations between them; I have suggested that doing so represents a promising direction for positive psychology. In the example offered here, distinguishing between behavior and its impact produces a more complex understanding of positive and negative developmental relationships (Figure 12.4). These are ideal types, of course; most actual relationships include both positive and negative aspects and understanding the interaction of the two is another important task.

With this taxonomy as a frame of reference, we can turn to a fuller discussion of the ways in which good mentoring creates a positive context for development during early adulthood – and simultaneously, the ways in which development depends on the young person's initiative or agency. But before going further, I should say a little more about the "Good Work" perspective and its relevance for an applied positive psychology.

Impact on novice	Behavior toward novice	
	Negative	Positive
Positive	Anti-mentor	Good-mentor
Negative	Tormentor	Too-mentor

FIGURE 12.4   Four types of developmental relationship.

GOOD WORK AND GOOD MENTORING

The study of working life has been to a great extent the study of organizational life. The positive psychology of work correspondingly has been for the most part a positive organizational scholarship, foregrounding the organization when examining the role of context. It asks: How can we create organizations in which workers will flourish, and in which these workers will help the organizations thrive?

The positive psychology of work is expanded by research on professionals – physicians, engineers, teachers, attorneys, architects, clergy, nurses, and other workers who traditionally have oriented themselves toward their professions and the professions' aims, as much as toward the particular organizations that may employ them. The notion of work as a calling is related: In the professions and beyond, one typically speaks of being called to a line of work rather than to work for a specific organization. The concept of *good work* (Gardner et al., 2001) was developed in an effort to capture what workers in the professions traditionally have aspired to, in their doctoring, teaching, and so on: (1) excellence by the standards of their field; (2) ethical conduct or responsibility to the profession's defining aims; and (3) personal engagement with the work undertaken. In short, good work unites the concern for societal goods toward which positive psychology has been moving and the concern for individual well-being that has been the primary impetus behind positive psychology so far. Creating contexts that enable good work, and identifying and promoting societal conditions that support it, would seem to have a critical place in any applied positive psychology.

How does the notion of good work expand our view of mentoring? Researchers have tended to ask how mentoring benefits the young person, as we have been doing in this chapter so far. As understandings of mentoring have evolved over the past few decades, its potential to benefit the mentor has also come to be studied (Bozionelos, 2004). In the case of workplace relationships, attention has been drawn to mentoring's potential contribution to the dyad's firm or organization as well (Wilson & Elman, 1990). What the mainstream mentoring literature considers much less often is the significance of these developmental relationships (both positive *and* negative) for the well-being of the profession, and therefore indirectly for the populations that the profession serves. How we train the next generation of doctors and teachers today will affect the health of medicine and teaching as professions 25 years from now, and the quality of the medical care and education that our great-grandchildren will enjoy. In this respect, the fates of individual and society are yoked. To return to the framework of positive adult development, one could say that we need to examine if and how good mentoring supports individual well-being, and also the perpetuation of good work, by providing a positive developmental context in which the novice learns what it means to do good work and how to do it.

GOOD MENTORING AND THE ROLE OF CONTEXT IN POSITIVE DEVELOPMENT

There are many contexts that foster positive development in adulthood: colleges and universities that immerse students in a clear and compelling ethos; families that provide stimulation, stability, and support; workplaces that challenge and fulfill; neighborhoods that bestow a sense of safety, opportunity, and connection. Like each of these, good mentors create a context in which development is supported. For example, examining a qualitative study of graduate training in science (Nakamura, Shernoff, & Hooker, 2009) from this perspective suggests at least three distinct developmental contexts created by outstanding scientists who mentor well: the interpersonal, cultural, and social. These are: (1) the interpersonal relationship itself; (2) the subset of the cultural "meme pool" that the mentor embodies and communicates; and (3) the community – in this case, the research laboratory – that the mentor oversees. We now consider each of these forms of positive context, as illustrated by findings from this study of good mentoring in science.

The Interpersonal Context

The interpersonal relationship that is established and sustained between novice and mentor is the first and most obvious respect in which mentoring comprises a developmental context, or a setting that fosters development. The mentor–novice relationship is one of multiple interpersonal contexts over the lifespan, beginning with the infant–caretaker dyad, which may contribute to development depending on the quality of the bond formed, the nature of interactions, the interplay with the individual's other social contexts, and so on, and of course the needs of the individual at the point in the life course when the relationship occurs.

Much of what is known about mentoring concerns the relationship context, and our research too suggested characteristics of the dyad that foster development. For example, in the sciences and many other lines of work, novices learn by doing. We concluded that for young-adult scientists, the mentor–novice relationship fosters development when an appropriate balance is struck between guidance and freedom. In contrast, either contextual provision might be perceived as a deficiency without the other: a great deal of guidance but not much freedom might be experienced as controlling; a great deal of freedom but scant guidance might be experienced as neglect. Moreover, different students have different needs. What one student experiences as welcome independence, another might experience as abandonment; good mentoring requires that the mentor pay attention to individual differences. In addition, each student's needs change as factors such as competence and self-efficacy change; apprentices tend to benefit from more guidance early in the educational career and more freedom later; more guidance when they have hit a wall and more freedom when work is going smoothly. As an interpersonal context, good mentoring thus also requires that the mentor be aware of a student's evolving and fluctuating needs in order to recognize when a period of useful struggle is threatening to become extended floundering. More generally, in terms of key features of the interpersonal context we found that good mentors were remembered as having provided valuable feedback and counsel, and being accessible when needed even if not continually available.

The Meme Pool

A second, less obvious way in which mentoring creates a context for development is by exposing the novice to what might be called the mentor's meme pool – the part of the culture, in particular the culture of the profession, that is "carried" by the mentor. That is, culture can be conceptualized as the body of symbolically encoded information that survives from one generation to the next in a society, encompassing a host of specific *domains*: medicine and the other professions, as well as cooking, music, meteorology, navigation, and so on. This information includes knowledge, practice, and the tools (broadly defined) that they require, as well as values, norms, goals, and standards. The most basic unit of cultural information was dubbed a *meme* by the biologist Richard Dawkins (1976) to highlight the fact that, much like genes in the biological realm, these elements of culture – theories and procedures, tunes and stories, beliefs and prescriptions – all undergo a process of variation and selective survival across generations.

When viewed through this lens, a profession consists of one such domain plus the *field* or community of individuals who practice, teach, preserve, and transform it (Csikszentmihalyi, 1988; Gardner et al., 2001). In a mentor–student relationship, the newcomer to the field is exposed to the mentor's set of work-related memes: professional orientations, values, practices, ideas, et cetera. Some of these the mentor actively attempts to transmit; others might make an impression even though the mentor does not try to pass them on. From this perspective, mentoring creates a second kind of developmental context alongside the relational matrix: a cultural or memetic context. It might be manifested in many ways: the mentor's words and actions; the tacit and explicit rules of the laboratory; the material that the student is asked to study; and the tools with which the mentor furnishes the laboratory. At the same time, the mentor's meme pool is selective and many memes in the wider professional culture are not available to the student in the particular cultural context afforded by the mentor. In our research, we were specifically interested in whether professionals say they absorbed memes that characterize good work if they have had mentors who have trained a lot of students and also are perceived as doing good work by members of their field.

In case studies of three senior scientists fitting this criterion, former students reported absorbing some memes that are characteristic of good work in all professions: honesty and integrity in professional practice; fairness and equity in the treatment of other members of the field; and an approach to the practice of mentoring itself. Students often were chosen by mentors because of affinities of orientation, and none recounted "conversion" experiences (i.e., wholesale rejection of a prior set of values after exposure to a mentor's meme pool); yet the reported role of the memetic context in these cases was very significant. Although honesty and fairness seem self-evident, in fact it may not be at all clear, even to the best intentioned novice, how to translate these values into specific professional practices. Through instruction and especially through example, a mentor may show what it means to report research results honestly or handle credit for work fairly.

Alongside these "good-work" memes, many scientists also reported absorbing distinctive memes from a mentor's meme pool – that is, characteristics of a mentor's approach to work, such as breadth of interest or the close integration of research and application, that distinguish it from the work of others in the same profession. One is reminded here of positive psychology's concept of individual's signature strengths (Peterson & Seligman, 2004). These are memes that may create a sense of pride about being part of a lineage known for a particular kind of good work – signature memes for the mentor and his or her lineage, if you will.

Table 12.1 shows the transmission of "good-work" memes and "lineage-signature" memes within the three senior scientists' lineages (see Nakamura et al., 2009). We interviewed members of the three lineages drawn from multiple generations: the senior scientists themselves, several of each one's former students, and several of these mentees' former students – the senior scientists' professional grandchildren, so to speak. Of 25 memes that the scientists said they possessed, those in Table 12.1 stood out. One subset could be viewed as "good-work" memes. They were affected by mentors equally often across lineages. Their transmission suggests that mentors can play a role in the perpetuation of good work across generations. These mentor-influenced memes include an approach to one's work and work relationships in general (honesty and integrity, fairness and equality) and, unexpectedly, an approach to mentoring specifically (provision of freedom and guidance, creation of a fruitful learning/working environment). A second subset could be seen as "lineage-signature" memes, more frequently absorbed in one lineage than in the others, supporting the view that each mentor to some extent creates a distinctive meme pool or memetic context for novices' professional development.

The Community

Finally, in addition to the dyadic relationship and the subset of the culture to which the novice is exposed by the mentor, the latter may deliberately shape the environment – the laboratory, in the case of a scientist – so that it is a positive developmental context. In the sciences, graduate education immerses students in

TABLE 12.1 Reported transmission of memes: Number of lineage members inheriting each meme from mentor

Meme	Lineage 1 (n = 12)	Lineage 2 (n = 11)	Lineage 3 (n = 13)	X^2
"Good-work" memes				
Science ethics (honesty, integrity)	8	7	8	n.s.
Interpersonal equality and fairness	7	5	5	n.s.
Intellectual freedom and guidance	4	5	6	n.s.
Facilitative laboratory structure	8	—[a]	8	n.s.
"Lineage-signature" memes				
Anti-careerism	4	0	1	6.0°
Effort-based authorship credit	6	1	3	5.0†
Humanitarianism	0	7	1	15.9°°°
Research–practice integration	0	6	0	16.4°°°
Intrinsic motivational orientation	1	3	7	6.2°
Scientific breadth	0	0	7	15.4°°°

Source: Adapted from Nakamura and Shernoff (2006).
[a] Not laboratory-based.
° † $p < 0.10$; $p < 0.05$; °°° $p < 0.001$.

the life of a laboratory for many hours a day over a number of years. The laboratory is thus at least as constant an influence on each student as is the relationship with the mentor. Of course, not all scientists work to make the laboratory a positive context for student development. Some highly successful and thus attractive laboratories are designed instead to maximize the advisor's productivity; students are reduced to being "extra hands" in the advisor's work. In the cases we studied closely, however, the scientists sought to make the laboratory a positive developmental context. The physical environment, the ethos, and in particular the social organization were all deliberately shaped by the mentor; the resulting community served as an extension of the mentor's own direct influence.

Just as there are different ways of doing good work in a profession, with signature memes alongside a core of common values and practices, the case studies suggest that there are different ways of deliberately creating an environment that introduces novices to good work through immersion in a model microcosm of the professional community. Over time, the laboratory's ethos and relationships among its members come to reinforce (echo) and/or complement (fill gaps in) the mentor's influence: "step-ahead" peers are carriers of the mentor's core values and practices, and they introduce novices to more basic skills and knowledge. By maintaining an active if not continual presence in the laboratory, the mentor can intervene if things go wrong.

It is instructive to compare two laboratories remembered with great satisfaction by most alumni. Both good mentors worked to fill their laboratories with ample resources, including stimulating peers and rich material resources, and strove to make the laboratory a safe and welcoming environment. In the first laboratory, however, students were selected with an eye toward their love of research; in the second, their maturity. In the first, the tenor of the laboratory tended to be respectful and harmonious; in the second, challenging and vigorous. In the first, the advisor made sure each student chose a project that did not overlap with others in the laboratory, which minimized rivalry and fostered willing cooperation; in the second, the advisor maintained a low profile and students forged collaborative projects and fluid study groups on their own. In the first, students pursued quiet, focused work at the laboratory bench, encouraged by the example of the mentor. In the second, students talked and debated long into the night around a big table in a common room that the mentor had designed to encourage interaction. The two laboratories illustrate that there are variations on the theme of good work and good mentoring.

As researchers, we need to understand better each of these aspects of mentoring as a developmental context: the interpersonal relationship, the meme pool, and the larger learning environment created by the mentor. Practitioners – both a profession's potential mentors and others responsible for the character of professional education – can use this knowledge in their efforts to provide good mentoring.

THE ROLE OF AGENCY IN GOOD MENTORING

I have offered the example of good mentors, and provided some detail about three respects in which they create a milieu for development, in order to illustrate the importance of context. Alongside and integrally related to the role of the mentor, however, is the role played by the novice in his or her formation as a professional. The two, context and agency, interact to foster development. Research needs to articulate how agency enters into the developmental process, just as we need to understand the multiple ways in which context matters. Graduate and professional education may constitute something like a sensitive period in the process of professional formation, when novices are actively constructing an approach and identity, for the first time defining their practices and priorities as professionals. In this process, individuals differ. Personal agency and self-formation may be primary for some individuals; their approach to work is experienced as being largely a reflection of their own temperament, personality, earlier life history, and conscious choices, while mentors and others in the environment are perceived as playing little or no role. However, in general the process of professional formation is one of interaction between agency and context. Young adults may be particularly receptive to external influences – and they also may invest considerable energy in actively seeking out and selectively learning from models and guides.

In the cases under discussion, both the mentors and their former students emphasized three specific means by which the mentor had an impact within the graduate apprenticeship as opposed to the classroom: (1) modeling, (2) informal exchanges, and (3) deliberate structuring of the laboratory context as a learning environment. However, the novices who reported being positively influenced by their mentors played an active role in each instance. Moreover, the novices did more than help make effective what the mentors deliberately offered them; they also played active roles in other aspects of their professional formation.

Because apprenticeship is a matter of learning by doing, it depends by definition on the effort of the student. A resistant or reluctant apprentice may be successfully prodded or coerced into learning. However, the apprentices we studied, who had gone on to successful careers, recalled being ambitious to learn, active, and selective. They needed to be; their efforts to learn were monitored and encouraged but they worked under conditions of considerable freedom.

In terms of modeling, the mere presence of a model did not by itself account for its impact; instead, motivated by keen admiration, the novices closely observed and actively emulated the mentor. One is reminded of martial arts training; traditional instructors demonstrate but don't explain the intricacies they have mastered and the avid student learns by "stealing with the eyes." In addition, while learning also occurs outside of awareness, students were selective, emulating some values, practices, and even personal qualities while actively rejecting others. In terms of informal exchanges, the mentors in this case were senior and busy; to a significant extent, they expected students to initiate interactions as needed, and the more satisfied students were those who took the initiative and did so. Finally, the students also played an active, selective role in gaining from and participating in the laboratory community. They formed relationships with peers who became co-learners; they sought out more experienced members of the laboratory who could teach them technical skills; and they watched step-ahead peers grapple with problems that the mentors themselves, with their greater expertise, adroitly avoided encountering at all.

The novices played an active role in determining the impact of senior scientists on their professional development in other respects as well. Advanced training in the sciences today exposes most novices to multiple senior practitioners because most students will work in a series of laboratories over the course of their training and/or on multi-laboratory teams. In this respect, it is like many other contemporary careers. They need to decide how, and how much, to draw on these multiple influences as they form an approach to work and a way of balancing work with the rest of life. In addition, to return to the earlier study of scientists and the taxonomy it suggested, the scientist-in-training may need to learn how to avoid being derailed by a tormentor – or a "too" mentor – and how to draw out constructive "negative" lessons from the example of senior practitioners whom the novice does not admire – to find a way to turn what could otherwise be tormentors into anti-mentors. The critical processes involved are not yet well understood.

CONCLUSION

Good mentoring is recognized as a rich context of adult development for both of the individuals involved: it facilitates the young person's navigation of the transition to adulthood and allows the more experienced adult to contribute to the welfare of rising generations by sharing the lessons of longer experience. The GoodWork Project also highlights the contribution of good mentoring to the well-being of the profession in which younger and older adults work, and thus indirectly to the flourishing of those served by the profession and those who may work in it in the future. In this chapter, I examined how the relationship with more experienced adults can be a context for professional formation for the young adult, with effects both negative (e.g., tormentors and too-mentors) and positive (e.g., good mentors and anti-mentors). To develop more concretely how good mentoring is a context for positive development in early adulthood – and also a potential contributor to the evolution of good work in the professions – I then discussed lessons learned from a study of the lineages associated with professionals who exemplify good work. It remains for future research to determine how widely the analysis generalizes. Based on these cases (Nakamura et al., 2009), I suggested that good mentors provide a positive context for development in at least three respects: first, and most familiar, the interpersonal relationship between mentor and student; second, and perhaps least familiar, the memetic context or meme pool to which the mentor exposes the student; and third, the community in which the mentor situates the student, which is particularly important in fields where working and learning occur communally.

Via this extended example, the chapter has focused on the study of positive adult development and, through it, has made a case for a positive psychology – or, more precisely, a positive social science – that integrates positive with negative, and agency with context. First, in considering the nature of the positive, I have suggested that a picture more differentiated than "negative versus positive" is possible; positive psychology seems to be moving toward it, and this is a fruitful direction for the field. In the subdiscipline of human development prior to positive psychology per se, some researchers were already integrating positive and negative developmental pathways, and gain and loss, within a single frame of reference. Much work remains to be done, however. Second, alongside positive psychology's assumption of agency and the field's legitimate interest in how individuals can and do cultivate their own flourishing, I have suggested (congruent with the theme of this volume and the conference that inspired it) that positive psychology could beneficially study – as the mentoring field already does – how the various contexts of daily life can be shaped so that they are resources for, rather than obstacles to, flourishing.

REFERENCES

Baltes, P. B., & Baltes, M. M. (1990). Psychological perspectives on successful aging: The model of selective optimization with compensation. In P. B. Baltes & M. M. Baltes (Eds.), *Successful aging* (pp. 1–34). Cambridge, UK: Cambridge University Press.

Baltes, P. B., & Smith, J. (2004). Lifespan psychology: From developmental contextualism to developmental biocultural co-constructivism. *Research in Human Development, 1*, 123–144.

Bandura, A. (2006). Toward a psychology of human agency. *Perspectives on Psychological Sciences, 1*, 164–180.

Bozionelos, N. (2004). Mentoring provided: Relation to mentor's career success, personality, and mentoring received. *Journal of Vocational Behavior, 64*, 24–46.

Brandtstadter, J. (2006). Action perspectives on human development. In R. M. Lerner (Ed.), *Handbook of child psychology: Vol. 1. Theoretical models of human development* (pp. 516–568). Hoboken, NJ: John Wiley & Sons.

Bronfenbrenner, U. (2000). Ecological systems theory. In A. E. Kazdin (Ed.), *Encyclopedia of psychology* (Vol. 3, pp. 129–133). Washington, DC: American Psychological Association.

Csikszentmihalyi, M. (1988). Society, culture, and person: A systems view of creativity. In R. J. Sternberg (Ed.), *The nature of creativity* (pp. 325–339). New York: Cambridge University Press.

Csikszentmihalyi, M. (1997). *Finding flow*. New York: Basic Books.

Csikszentmihalyi, M., & Schneider, B. (2000). *Becoming adult*. New York: Basic Books.

Dawkins, R. (1976). *The selfish gene*. New York: Oxford University Press.

Delle Fave, A., & Massimini, F. (2003). Making disability into a resource. *The Psychologist, 16*, 133–134.

Eby, L. T., McManus, S. E., Simon, S. A., & Russell, J. E. A. (2000). The protégé's perspective regarding negative mentoring experiences: The development of a taxonomy. *Journal of Vocational Behavior, 57*, 1–21.

Elder, G. H. (1986). Military times and turning points in men's lives. *Developmental Psychology, 22*, 233–245.

Elder, G. H. (1998). The life course as developmental theory. *Child Development, 69*, 1–12.

Erikson, E. H. (1950). *Childhood and society*. New York: Norton.

Gable, S. L., & Haidt, J. (2005). What (and why) is positive psychology? *Review of General Psychology, 9*, 103–110.

Gardner, H., Csikszentmihalyi, M., & Damon, W. (2001). *Good work*. New York: Basic Books.

Joseph, S., & Linley, A. P. (2008). *Trauma, recovery, and growth: Positive psychological perspectives on posttraumatic stress*. New York: John Wiley & Sons.

Kasser, T. (2004). The good life or the goods life? Positive psychology and personal well-being in the culture of consumption. In P. A. Linley & S. Joseph (Eds.), *Positive psychology in practice* (pp. 55–67). New York: John Wiley & Sons.

King, L. A., & Hicks, J. A. (2007). Whatever happened to "what might have been"? Regrets, happiness, and maturity. *American Psychologist, 62*, 625–636.

Kram, K. (1985). *Mentoring at work*. Glenview, IL: Scott Foresman.

Lerner, R. M. (1982). Children and adolescents as producers of their own development. *Developmental Review, 2*, 342–370.

Lerner, R. M. (2006). Developmental science, developmental systems, and contemporary theories of human development. In R. M. Lerner (Ed.), *Handbook of child psychology* (Vol. 1, pp. 1–17). New York: John Wiley & Sons.

Levinson, D. J. (1978). *Seasons of a man's life*. New York: Knopf.

Lyubomirsky, S. (2008). *The how of happiness: A scientific approach to getting the life you want*. New York: Penguin Press.

Massimini, F., & Delle Fave, A. (2000). Individual development in a bio-cultural perspective. *American Psychologist, 55*, 24–33.

Masten, A. S., & Reed, M. J. (2002). Resilience in development. In C. R. Snyder & S. Lopez (Eds.), *Handbook of positive psychology* (pp. 74–88). New York: Oxford University Press.

Nakamura, J. (2005, June 22). Under the big tent. *PsycCRITIQUES – Contemporary Psychology: APA Review of Books, 50*.

Nakamura, J., & Shernoff, D. (2006). *If good mentoring isn't taught, how is it learned?* Paper presented at the American Educational Research Association Meeting, San Francisco, CA.

Nakamura, J., Shernoff, D., & Hooker, C. (2009). *Good mentoring*. San Francisco: Jossey-Bass.

Neugarten, D. A. (1996). *The meanings of age: Selected papers of Bernice L. Neugarten*. Chicago: University of Chicago Press.

Nolen-Hoeksema, S., & Davis, C. G. (2002). Positive responses to loss: Perceiving benefits and growth. In C. R. Snyder & S. Lopez (Eds.), *Handbook of positive psychology* (pp. 598–607). New York: Oxford University Press.

Norem, J. K., & Chang, E. C. (2002). The positive psychology of negative thinking. *Journal of Clinical Psychology, 58*, 993–1001.

Park, N., & Peterson, C. (2008). The cultivation of character strengths. In M. Ferrari & G. Potworowski (Eds.), *Teaching for wisdom* (pp. 59–77). Dordrecht, The Netherlands: Springer.

Peterson, C., & Seligman, M. E. P. (2004). *Character strengths and virtues: A handbook and classification*. Washington, DC: APA Press.

Quinton, D., Pickles, A., Maughan, B., & Rutter, M. (1993). Partners, peers and pathways: Assortative pairing and continuities and conduct disorder. *Development and Psychopathology, 5*, 763–783.

Ryan, R., & Deci, E. (2000). Self-determination theory and the facilitation of intrinsic motivation, social development, and well-being. *American Psychologist, 55*, 68–78.

Saffrey, C., Summerville, A., & Roese, N. J. (2008). Praise for regret: People value regret above other negative emotions. *Motivation and Emotion, 32*, 46–54.

Schneider, S. L. (2001). In search of realistic optimism: Meaning, knowledge, and warm fuzziness. *American Psychologist, 56*, 250–263.

Schwartz, B. (2004). *The paradox of choice*. New York: HarperCollins.

Seligman, M. E. P. (1991). *Learned optimism*. New York: Knopf.

Seligman, M. E. P., & Csikszentmihalyi, M. (2000). Positive psychology: An introduction. *American Psychologist, 55*, 5–14.

Shweder, R. A., Goodnow, J. J., Hatano, G., LeVine, R. A., Markus, H. R., & Miller, P. J. (2006). The cultural psychology of development: One mind, many mentalities. In R. M. Lerner (Ed.), *Handbook of child psychology* (Vol. 1, pp. 716–792). New York: John Wiley & Sons.

Vaillant, G. E. (2003). Mental health. *American Journal of Psychiatry, 160*, 1373–1384.

Vaillant, G. E., DiRago, A. C., & Mukamal, K. (2006). Natural history of male psychological health, XV: Retirement satisfaction. *American Journal of Psychiatry, 163*, 682–688.

Wilson, J. A., & Elman, N. S. (1990). Organizational benefits of mentoring. *Academy of Management Executive, 4*, 88–94.

Wrzesniewski, A., & Dutton, J. E. (2001). Crafting a job: Revisioning employees as active crafters of their work. *Academy of Management Review, 26*, 179–201.

Part V

Future Directions for Applying the Science of Positive Psychology

13

Positive Psychology and a Positive World-View: New Hope for the Future of Humankind

MIHALY CSIKSZENTMIHALYI

The other chapters collected in this volume suggest the broad scope of issues that can be addressed from the perspective of positive psychology. They deal with concrete issues that can be measured without too much trouble, and that have clear applications with important consequences for societal, as well as individual, well-being.

What I will try to discuss in this chapter is a much less concrete and clear set of issues – and yet I will argue that they are no less important for collective or individual well-being than other, better defined topics such as character strengths, satisfaction with work, or the geographical distribution of happiness. What I will focus on is the intangible and almost invisible difference that positive psychology is likely to make to our understanding of what it means to be human. We are about to change – I shall argue – our vision of the human condition from one of dismal pessimism to a vision that foregrounds what is good about women and men and provides ideas and processes that will nurture, cultivate, and increase what is good about us and our actions. And this change is likely to pay dividends in many areas of life, from the economy to the arts, and from politics to religion.

THE HUMAN SELF-IMAGE: A BRIEF HISTORY

Any organism with a brain that is complex enough to reflect on itself must eventually also develop a mental image of itself. Sooner or later all human groups come to grips with the fundamental questions of existence: What am I? Why am I alive? What will happen to me after I die? And, of these, perhaps the most basic question is the first: What – or who – am I? (See Table 13.1 for an extremely schematic and abbreviated summary of how the perception of human nature has changed over time.)

Anthropologists have reported a bewildering array of answers to this basic question. In some cultures people believe they are descended from gods. In others,

TABLE 13.1   Major milestones in the evolution of the image of man

1,000,000 BCE	• Information processed mainly in terms of built-in stimulus–response pathways • Some information interpreted based on direct personal experience – *learning*
100,000 BCE	*Presumably self-image is taken for granted. Existential questions are unlikely* • Shared experience within the family/household – emergence of *memes* • Experience transmitted by proto-language within the tribe • Technological knowledge mediated by simple tools
50,000 BCE	*Notions of individuality vs. collectivity develop. Memes begin to shape behavior* • Evolution of language • Expanded importance of memes as sources of information • Myths and religions start to influence self-image
10,000 BCE	*Man's relationship to cosmic forces begins to influence his identity* • First urban revolution – information shared across occupations and ethnic groups
5000 BCE	*Comparison of world-views brings with it critical reflection* • Information coded extra-somatically and memes are codified • Writing, proto-science, farming, and tools become important • Mathematics (Pythagoras, 500 BCE; Euclid, 300 BCE)
	Humans begin to realize their special nature – start of the idea of progress • Appearance of the great world religions Moses, 1391 BCE Confucius, 551 BCE Siddhartha Gautama (Buddha), 563 BCE Jesus of Nazareth, 0 CE Muhammad Ibn Abdullah, 570 CE
1400–1600	*Men begin to forge bridges to the Supreme Power – start of the belief in human primacy on the planet* • The Renaissance brings to Europe new self-confidence • Scientific experiments begin • René Descartes provides grounds for belief in the supremacy of reason
1900	• Western science, economy, and political systems seem destined to triumph over nature and over other cultures
1900–2000	*Apogee of the belief in human supremacy* • Two senseless world wars, an economic depression, and the rise of irrational ideologies bring into question the supremacy of Western science, economics, culture, and political institutions • Darwin demonstrates our descent from earlier species • Marx demonstrates the power of class identity in shaping thought and behavior • Freud questions the rationality of human behaviors
	Human self-image is undermined, leading to a pervasive sense of nihilism and despair . . .

they believe that they are weak beings at the mercy of supernatural forces that need to be placated with sacrifices lest their wrath becomes destructive. Some cultures teach that men are bad, some that they are good, and still others that they are malleable: they are good to begin with but get corrupted, or, vice versa, that they are bad but salvageable.

Even a single religion, Western Christianity, holds all these beliefs in a single vision of who we are as human beings. And as centuries follow one another, the image of humankind has changed from one end of the continuum to another.

Just to stay within the well-documented Western tradition, we know that Plato in the 6th century before Christ saw himself at the end of an era – a time when men, in his opinion, were passing from a long-past age of gold, and then of silver, into an age of base iron. Much has been written about why Plato had a downbeat view of the men of his age. It makes sense that, as a descendant of the early warrior aristocracy of Greece, he felt that the democratic changes ushered in by the new commercial plutocracy were sad signs of decay.

Like Plato's world-view, that of entire generations may reflect the external changes (political, economic, religious) that infringe on them at any given time. In periods of prosperity it should be easier to believe that men are good and the destiny of humankind is rosy. When there is hunger, war, or oppression, on the other hand, the belief in goodness suffers. And when a majority of people come to believe that they are nothing but specks of dust floating in a cold, uncaring universe, it is difficult to face one's life with equanimity.

Of course history is too complex to be told in such a simple, linear fashion. For instance, Christianity arose at a time when the Roman Empire, while riddled with decay, was still relatively wealthy and powerful.

The early Christians were poor and persecuted, yet they held to the belief that the Lord of creation had sent his son to die for the sins of mankind, thus opening the possibility for humans to join God as pure spirits after the dissolution of their material lives. For many centuries in Europe people believed that they were born as sinners, but could redeem themselves; and that life was brutish and short, but the after-life could be eternally sweet.

As the hardships of the Middle Ages were turning into the more stable and comfortable epoch we now call the Renaissance, a new perception of what men were and what they could do began to emerge. Secular humanism started in the more prosperous regions of Italy, and soon moved to The Netherlands, France, England, and Southern Germany. Its founders were often agnostic as to where men come from or what happened to them after death. Instead, they believed that humans had a choice to be what they could make of themselves; with learning and discipline they could increasingly improve themselves and the world they lived in.

One of the most influential thinkers of the last 500 years, one whose image of mankind still informs much of our institutions and our world-view, was the French polymath René Descartes. Basically, Descartes convinced European intellectuals that reason was the most precious human endowment; with its help, we can objectively resolve any predicament in life. Cartesian logic, coupled with the scientific experimentation begun by Galileo and others at about the same time – the beginning of the 17th century – portended that with the use of the brain humans could finally achieve almost god-like status.

The optimism of the Renaissance was tested by many catastrophic events, by plagues and stubborn wars, by famines and schisms, but basically the view of men as flexible and on an upward trajectory was also compatible and synergistic with the technological advances that started occurring in Europe in the 18th century and onward. Material progress was obvious; was it not likely that this meant that progress in other aspects was also inevitable, that better morals and a better quality of life were just around the corner? During the Victorian era, at the end of the 19th century, and especially in the countries most blessed by technological progress, a basically very upbeat self-image emerged. Humans believed that they were the pinnacle of creation and had solved the riddle of existence once and for all. But this optimism turned out to be short-lived.

By the start of the 20th century some storm clouds were gathering, due to scientists' second thoughts and the historical evidence about human fallibility. One of the first scientific challenges to the belief in linear progress came from the most technologically and economically advanced country of the times – England. Charles Darwin's work not only argued that we descended from apes, but also implied that whatever superiority humans had achieved could well be a temporary one, because evolution was basically fickle, now selecting for one trait, now for another, depending on what trait made survival in a given environment more likely. Although Darwin himself does not seem to have believed a reversal even remotely likely, the principles of evolution that he discovered opened up a Pandora's Box of possible *de*volutionary scenarios.

Descartes' belief in the infallibility of reason suffered a series of severe blows roughly at the same time. The gravest of these came from a Viennese physician who, extrapolating from how the minds of neurotics worked, came to the conclusion that even the healthiest minds were simply trying to satisfy basic instincts of the kind that were banned from the conversation of polite society. Freud certainly was not the first to recognize that men and women were driven by libidinal drives, and that they often covered up their animal cravings with a veneer of rationality and hypocritical moralizing. Yet Freud's insistence, supported by the trappings of science, that this is what the nature of man was like, tipped the scales in favor of a negative image of humankind. And his conclusions were reinforced by the visionary philosophical arguments of Friedrich Nietzsche and Arthur Schopenhauer, and by thousands of scientists who felt liberated by the notion that "God is Dead!" – thus allowing professional scientists to take over his mantle. But the flowering of science did not necessarily help to restore the stature of humankind to its former glory. By the time the Nobel-Prize-winning French biochemist Jacques Monod described our existence on earth as living in a "frozen universe of solitude" (Monod, 1971), few laymen could take pride in the image of man that science had created.

Of course, scientists and intellectuals had not been thinking about these issues in a vacuum. They, as well as the population as a whole, were being influenced by the course of events in the last 100 years: The two World Wars that resulted in millions of deaths, the Great Depression, the horrors perpetrated by ideological fanatics in countries that had created some of the greatest works of science, art, and literature, the poisoning of so much of the planet by the bounty of chemistry, and the greedy disregard of the haves for the misery of the have-nots have all contributed to a re-evaluation of the role of reason and morality in human affairs. No thinking person can avoid having deep doubts about who we are and what the sources of our actions are. Yet, as the scholar of contemporary history John Lukács has noted, the liberal Western Democracies may have overestimated human nature at first, but that mistake was infinitely better than the opposite mistake which is threatening us now – giving up on human nature.

THE CONTRIBUTIONS OF PSYCHOLOGY TO THE IMAGE OF MAN

Academic psychology, modeled on the hard sciences that contributed initially so much to the privileged positions that humankind believed it had attained, did not help stay "the discounting of human nature." Instead, informed by what wags have called *physics envy*, it refused to give credit to the better instincts of humankind, or recognize those elements of human nature that were beyond the capacity for measurement available to 19th century psycho-physicists. Even more recently, the cognitivist revolution resulted in seeing human reason as following programs set down by inherited biological instructions without much personal intervention; it is no wonder that we so easily accepted the analogy of the computer as a model for human thought (see Table 13.2).

What psychology has dealt with hardly at all are the results of the last phases of human evolution, which seem to have taken place between about 10,000 and 1000 BC (the psychologist James Jaynes dates the transition at the very end of this period, between the writing of the *Iliad* and the *Odyssey*; see Jaynes, 1977).

Although we know nothing directly about what happened to the human mind during this period, it is clear that, partly as a result of biological transformations in the prefrontal cortex and partly as a result of cumulative experiences with tools and other memes invented by successive generations, our ancestors developed what we now call *reflective consciousness* – an awareness of oneself as a thinking and feeling entity separate from, yet connected to, other human beings who presumably have the same capacity to think and feel.

TABLE 13.2   Some milestones in the evolution of scientific psychology

Laboratory experimentation
       Wilhelm Wundt, 1832–1920 (Leipzig)
       Human nature and behavior considered in purely bio-mechanical terms

Learning theory (behaviorism)
       John B. Watson, 1878–1958 (Chicago)
       Human behavior, like that of other living things, is purely the result of "learning" (i.e., of mechanical reactions to positive or negative stimuli)

Psychoanalysis
       Sigmund Freud, 1856–1939 (Vienna)
       Human behavior is governed by unconscious processes activated by the need to repress instinctual cravings

Cognitivism
       Jean Piaget (Geneva), Ulric Neisser (Cornell), and Noam Chomsky (Boston), 1950–2000
       Human behavior is based on the unfolding of neuronal templates. The reigning metaphor for human behavior becomes the computer

While few psychologists would deny the existence of reflective consciousness, even fewer dared to take its existence seriously enough to try to integrate it with a scientific approach to human behavior, or to reflect on its consequences. For instance, when reflection allowed humans to invent the idea of "freedom," this notion began to act as a cause of behavior, regardless of whether freedom really exists or not as an ontological entity. Certainly non-human animals also suffer when prevented from exercising their biological endowment – from moving where they want when they want, to explore a varied environment, to provide for themselves as their natures incline them to do. So did our distant ancestors also suffer?

But with reflective consciousness the *meme* of freedom was abstracted from experience, and so it became a powerful goal – a source of well-being when present but a source of psychological pain when absent. The implication of this evolutionary development is that while "free choice" may not exist in a physical sense, it exists psychologically because it is the cause of emotional states, a cause of behavior no less potent than food is to the hungry, or than electric shocks. And human behavior, much as it owes to the instructions coded in genes, is also constantly following the instructions of memes such as *freedom, love, honesty*, and *democracy*, just to mention a few (for the definition of memes, and arguments about the evolution of consciousness, see Csikszentmihalyi, 1993).

Of course not all memes are "good" in the sense of programming us to exhibit behavior that will result in desirable consequences to us or to others. Mussolini, enamored of a self-image based on the meme of ancient Roman emperors, did not foresee that this would lead his nation to a ruinous war, or to himself being shot and then being hung by his feet on a post at a service station. Similarly, the source of the millions of murders committed by Hitler, Stalin, or Pol Pot can be sought in the murderers' genes, but would they have been carried out without the memes that supported them, the ideology that provided them with an attractive excuse?

And this brings us to the most important point concerning evolution and psychology. We do have a choice about which memes will survive and which will not. While genetic instructions are selected by the environment, memetic instructions are selected by *us*. It is we who are responsible for what cultural instructions will rule our lives and that of our descendants.

Although we have little choice whether we inherit "good" or "bad" genes, we do have a choice about whether our consciousness contains "good" or "bad" memes. Our choice is restricted by the fact that the cultural environment may have a bias towards one or the other but, as the Great Naturalistic Experiment of the last century has shown, even children who had never been exposed to freedom, democracy, or public decency during the long night of Communist rule eventually followed their own personal experiences and rejected those memes that were blatantly in conflict with their self-interest (broadly understood). For children growing up in the affluent West, the question is: Will they be able to reject the steady dose of commercially sold "entertainment" and consumer goals for the sake of more meaningful memes?

But these kinds of questions have been, by and large, beyond the pale of academic psychology. By trying to be objective and scientific, all so-called "value-issues" were banned because they could be open to mystification introduced by personal advantage, prejudice, or, at best, nostalgia for past traditions. This stance is understandable up to a point, but when carried to an extreme it is reminiscent of the old adage of "throwing the baby out with the bathwater."

Positive psychology was started, in part, as an attempt to redress this reigning image of what it is to be human, by focusing attention on ideas and kinds of behavior that people had found desirable and valuable in most cultures. Some critics worry that such an approach is unscientific, because it introduces values into what should be an "objective" scientific endeavor. However, if the scientific credentials of an oncologist are not diminished by the fact that she wants to prevent cancer cells from spreading, or if the reputation of an engineer is not tarnished by his insistence to build bridges that will not collapse, then it is hard to understand why a psychologist should be castigated for studying the conditions that help people lead satisfying and meaningful lives. Striving to keep cells healthy and bridges sturdy is no more value-free than striving to make lives happy.

The view of humankind suggested by positive psychology has at least three important methodological implications. The first is that any explanation of human behavior is incomplete unless one takes into account the most recent developments in the evolution of the brain: self-reflective consciousness. This is the seat of the *psyche*, that unique human ability to transcend the instructions of the genes, of society, of powers outside itself, and follow its own counsel (see Table 13.3).

The second implication concerns the issue of value neutrality. This will not be an easy task to resolve successfully, but it seems evident that without a well-founded agreement as to what is good or bad for humans and humankind we are going to be clueless about how to help improve present conditions and prepare for an even better future.

The third implication is to take seriously the wisdom our ancestors have drawn from their own life experiences. An evolutionary perspective suggests that if an organ of the body or a behavior of the organism persists over time and space, it is likely to be of enduring utility – barring severe environmental change. The reason why most animals keep being born with eyes is that seeing gives a huge survival advantage. The same argument can be made about memes: they endure over time because they provide some advantage (Csikszentmihalyi & Rathunde, 1990). It would be *hubris* – the overweening pride that the gods send to those they wish to destroy – for a science of man to ignore the discoveries of past generations.

TABLE 13.3   How positive psychology can help provide an emergent image of humankind

---

- By using the knowledge and techniques that psychology has developed so far but at the same time taking into account that human consciousness is a new phenomenon, with its *sui generis* organization and possibilities, therefore non-reductionistic explanations are necessary to understand human behavior
- By realizing that the future will depend on the decisions we are making in the present, therefore psychology cannot be neutral about the consequences of human action
- By taking seriously the best of the past, for example, the experience of earlier generations codified in older sources of wisdom

---

In this respect, positive psychology has already gone quite far. The Values in Action (VIA) dictionary of strengths, for example (Peterson & Seligman, 2004), takes into account a wide variety of virtues that religions and philosophies of the past had considered valuable. It recognizes, for example, that gratitude, kindness, fairness, and honesty are as important for the well-being of a community as strong foundations are for the solidity of a bridge; or that zest, hope, curiosity, and self-regulation are as important to the well-being of a person as good nutrition is.

Table 13.4 lists three representative formulations of what good conduct consists of. The first is the well-known advice that St. Paul gave, and which has left such a pervasive legacy on Western cultures as well as on the VIA classification. The second are the tenets of Zoroastrianism, less known in the West but eloquently summarized by Massimini and Delle Fave (1991). The relevance of these spiritual instructions has become increasingly evident with the need to develop a planetary consciousness, and could serve as an inspiration to conservation psychology. Finally the Eightfold Path of Buddhism formulates one of the most influential prescriptions for how an individual can create a good life by mastering attention.

Of course, none of these "how to" suggestions should be taken as final – or even as being relatively useful. The task of science is to put propositions to test, and this is where positive psychology can be of great service to humankind. It is strange, in fact, that with the enormous accumulation of knowledge in the past centuries humanity has not attempted to do what positive psychology has now begun to envision: integrate systematically and scientifically what has been found across time and space to be best about men and women and what constitutes a good life.

In summary, the opportunities that the new image of humanity presents to positive psychology are listed in Table 13.5. This short list, simple as it seems, is fraught with enormous difficulties but, as we know, the ability to match high

TABLE 13.4 Some sources of past wisdom that inform positive psychology

Christian theological virtues (1. Corinthians 13:13)
- Hope (refraining from despair)
- Faith (steadfastness in belief)
- Charity (selfless, voluntary loving-kindness)

Zoroastrianism
- Order and disorder are in constant conflict in the universe. Each individual needs to actively participate in life through good thoughts, good words, and good deeds to ensure happiness and keep chaos at bay. This *active* participation is a central element in Zoroaster's concept of free will.
- Responsibility for the environment: Zoroastrians prayed each evening to express their gratitude to the air, the water, the plants, and the earth, and asked forgiveness from each for the harm that the person might have done during the day to each of them (conservation psychology)

Buddhism
- Control of attention – mindfulness, savoring
- Eightfold path:

(1) Right view	(5) Right lifestyle
(2) Right intention	(6) Right effort
(3) Right speech	(7) Right mindfulness
(4) Right action	(8) Right concentration

TABLE 13.5   Some of the questions that positive psychology might choose to consider in the future based on the new image of what it means to be human

---

We are responsible for our lives, so:
How can we learn to live happier and more meaningful lives?

We are the shapers of our future, so:
In which directions should we help steer evolution?

We are the stewards of our world, so:
How can we achieve sustainable harmony on the planet?

---

challenges with one's skills provides some of the most rewarding experiences in life. Therefore, by definition, this new perspective in psychology should guarantee a rewarding life to those who choose to pursue it.

REFERENCES

Csikszentmihalyi, M. (1993). *The evolving self.* New York: HarperCollins.

Csikszentmihalyi, M., & Rathunde, K. (1990). The psychology of wisdom: An evolutionary interpretation. In R. J. Sternberg (Ed.), *Wisdom: Its nature, origins, and development* (pp. 25–51). New York: Cambridge University Press.

Jaynes, J. (1977). *The origin of consciousness in the breakdown of the bicameral mind.* Boston: Houghton Mifflin.

Massimini, F., & Delle Fave, A. (1991). Religion and cultural evolution. *Zygon: Journal of Religion and Science, 16,* 27–48.

Monod, J. (1971). *Chance and necessity.* New York: Random House.

Peterson, C., & Seligman, M. E. P. (2004). *Character strengths and virtues: A handbook of classification.* New York: Oxford University Press/Washington, DC: American Psychological Association.

Epilog: A Practitioner's Guide for Applying the Science of Positive Psychology

STEWART I. DONALDSON

"If you want truly to understand something, try to change it."
"No research without action, *no action without research.*"

Kurt Lewin

These two famous quotes by psychologist and action researcher Kurt Lewin capture the spirit of what I would like to convey in this Epilog. First, psychological research is often concerned with snapshots of naturally occurring behavior at limited (often one) points in time and based on measures of association. Applying the science of positive psychology requires more, including an understanding of the dynamics of planned interventions designed to create positive change in society. As Lewin suggests, one needs a much deeper understanding of the phenomena of interest when the goal is to change human experience and behavior. It is my view that efforts to change human behavior for the purpose of social betterment are most likely to succeed when they are based on sound scientific evidence, and when research and evaluation procedures are used to develop, guide, and improve planned change efforts (Donaldson, 2007; Donaldson & Lipsey, 2006).

In this volume, leading positive psychologists have shared with us their research and views about how to use the science of positive psychology to improve public policies, health and healthcare, schools and educational systems, organizations, and the quality of work environments. This diverse set of chapters presents us with a wealth of positive psychology research, and illustrates possibilities for using this emerging evidence base to think differently about societal challenges and the interventions we might mount to overcome those challenges.

The authors were charged with helping us understand what works (or what might work) if we attempt to use theories, principles, and research from positive psychology to improve aspects of society. I submit they have done a nice job of fulfilling their charge. Keep in mind, they were not asked to critique the research or the positive psychology movement in general within their presentations or chapters. Fortunately, other scholars and popular writers have done a nice job of raising concerns, issuing warnings, and suggesting the limits of positive psychology (e.g., Ehrenreich, 2009; Fineman, 2006a, 2006b; Hackman, 2009a, 2009b; Hedges, 2009; Lazarus, 2003a, 2003b). I will briefly highlight a few of these challenges and cautions about positive psychology below, encouraging practitioners to seek disconfirming views and evidence. Finally, I will provide a few suggestions as to how practitioners might consider using positive psychology and evidence to guide their work.

CAREFULLY EXAMINING THE OTHER SIDE OF THE STORY

The chapter authors in this volume have presented a compelling case for the value of positive psychology and its potential applications for improving the human condition. However, in my view, practitioners should seek out and carefully consider the critiques of the positive psychology movement before deciding to adopt aspects of it for the purpose of improving their practice. Applied social psychologist and social problem-solver Donald Campbell taught us of the benefits of fostering what he called *"disputatious* communities of *truth seekers"* (Chen, Donaldson, & Mark, in press). I believe that positive psychology has been very fortunate in this respect, as a number of leading scholars have passionately debated and challenged the purpose, basic foundations, conceptual clarity, and methodological soundness of the positive psychology movement and the research it has produced to date (e.g., see Fineman, 2006a, 2006b; Hackman, 2009a, 2009b; Lazarus, 2003a, 2003b). These challenges promise to improve the development of the field, as well as provide cautions, encourage critical thinking, and possibly prevent practitioners from moving too quickly to application in some areas.

For example, Lazarus (2003a) asked the question: "Does the positive psychology movement have legs?" In his view, positive psychology is likely to be just another one of the many fads that come and go. He believes that the movement makes the spurious claim of being new, as many of the topics now put under the positive psychology umbrella have been studied for decades. Lazarus challenged the notion of focusing research on only the positive side of life. He asserted that it creates a false dichotomy out of positive and negative instead of integrating them, and that you can't separate them and make good sense out of most topics in psychology. Lazarus also argued that many of the claims of positive psychology are naïve and misleading, the field lacks conceptual clarity, and that serious measurement and methodological problems are not being faced. He concluded his response to rebuttals of his target article (Lazarus, 2003b, p. 188) with:

> I hope that some of the young people who are being led down the garden path of simplistic thought and weak research methods will read and give serious thought to what I have said.

Five years later, Miller (2008) repeated and extended Lazarus' arguments about the limits of the positive psychology movement. He asserted that the science of positive psychology is founded on a whole series of fallacious arguments. These arguments are believed to involve circular reasoning, tautology, failure to clearly define or properly apply terms, the identification of causal relations where none exist, and unjustified generalization.

Similar critiques have emerged in the literature on positive organizational behavior and scholarship. For example, Hackman (2009a) outlines the "perils of positivity." He acknowledged that this work is an outgrowth of the positive psychology movement and that the passion and productivity in this area are impressive. However, he implied that the research is accumulating so rapidly that it may be producing a wobbly structure on top of a shaky foundation. For example, he challenged this emerging literature by pointing out that work organizations are not sick patients, that positive organizational scholarship is curiously ahistorical, that there are too many constructs and not enough evidence of validity, that too few methods are being used, that making the best of a bad situation is not enough, and that new paradigms such as positive organizational behavior are seductive and should be critically examined. Hackman's critique was preceded by similar critiques in the management literature, such as Fineman's (2006a) work "On being positive: Concerns and counterpoints."

Sales of popular books that have attacked the positive psychology movement also appear to be doing very well. For example, Ehrenreich (2009) goes after the positive psychology movement in her book entitled *Bright-Sided: How the Relentless Promotion of Positive Thinking has Undermined America*. She argues that claims about positive thinking are often exaggerated and used in the relentless pursuit of profit. She warns her readers about practitioners of positive thinking and psychology, such as sects, cults, faith healers, coaches, preachers, and gurus of various sorts.

Perhaps most relevant to this volume is the work of Chris Hedges: *Empire of Illusion: The End of Literacy and the Triumph of Spectacle*. Mr. Hedges was invited to our symposium and attended as our guest. He used this opportunity to write a chapter in his book called "The illusion of happiness." The chapter is essentially a mockery of the entire event and, by extension, this volume. His main thesis seems to be that positive psychology is the ideology of the corporate state, suggesting that fulfillment in life can only be found in complete and total conformity. He makes the claim:

> Positive psychology is to the corporate state what eugenics was to the Nazis. Positive psychology – at least, as applied so broadly and unquestionably to corporate relations – is a quack science. It throws a smokescreen over corporate domination, abuse, and greed. Those who preach it serve the corporate leviathan.
>
> (Hedges, 2009, pp. 117–118)

In addition to his substantive concerns, he personally attacked some of our presenters, painting them in a very demeaning light to his readers. For example:

> David Cooperrider, a professor from Case Western Reserve University, is a plump, balding man in a shapeless black suit and checkered tie. He stands in the center of the stage in the high-ceilinged lecture hall of Claremont Graduate University before some 600 people. The spotlight illuminates his head.
>
> (Hedges, 2009, p. 115)

While Hedges' critique may go well beyond what Donald Campbell had in mind when he encouraged cultivating a community of constructive critics, it is very important to read and reflect upon his work as we consider applying the ideas put forth by the authors in this volume. We must thank him for his time and contributions to the dialogue.

The presenters and chapter authors have spent much time and effort providing us with their best thoughts on how to use the science of positive psychology to improve society. Other positive psychologists and scholars have spent their time responding to critiques such as those described above (e.g., Csikszentmihalyi, 2003; Luthans & Avolio, 2009a, 2009b; Lyubomirsky & Abbe, 2003; Peterson & Park, 2003; Roberts, 2006; Ryff, 2003). The main point I'm trying to make in this section is that practitioners would be well advised to use these chapters as the starting point toward considering application. It is also important in my view to carefully read and consider the critiques of positive psychology (and responses to them) before adopting or developing applications. That is, don't rely on the views of positive psychologists alone, as many of the issues raised by the critics are not going away any time soon. So read diverse perspectives, make up your own mind, take a stand, and enter the fray.

USING EVIDENCE TO GUIDE APPLICATION

If in the end you do decide to join forces with those conducting research and/or applying the science of positive psychology, let me suggest that you consider the value of credible and actionable evidence to guide your work (Donaldson, Christie, & Mark, 2008). Going back to the wisdom of Kurt Lewin, creating successful and sustained positive changes in the various aspects of society that were discussed in this volume is not a "high probability of success" endeavor. In fact, it is damn hard to create lasting positive changes in people's lives no matter how positive or well-intentioned one may be. Lewin advises us that as we intervene in society (in people's lives) we should not do so lightheartedly or without the investment of rigorous research. I will extend his argument below to include the importance of both research and evaluation in our efforts to use positive psychology to improve society.

First, I can imagine many situations where practitioners need to make decisions in a very timely manner. That is, I don't want to come across as out of touch with the reality of working in government organizations, healthcare, schools, work organizations, and the like. And I do realize that very often decisions must be made in the absence of credible and actionable evidence. Under these conditions, logic and reason must carry the day. You may find a good reading and awareness of the

ideas and principles presented in this volume, and the positive psychology literature in general, to be very helpful for decision-making in a range of practice
contexts and situations.

However, when at all possible, I urge you to carefully examine the empirical
literature related to the topic in positive psychology that you are interested in
using. This review should not only consider findings, but also the quality of research
that the findings are based on. For many topics, if you look hard enough, you will
find conflicting evidence or fatal flaws in individual studies, and it will be your job
to sort through the puzzle. Knowing the quality of empirical evidence supporting
your work is a good first step toward successful application.

Next, though, you must answer the question: Does the evidence you have
examined apply to your application and context? External validity concerns are
paramount when practitioners transition from research evidence into designing an
intervention. Gargani and Donaldson (in press) outline a range of issues that need
to be considered when one uses evidence from a research study to design a new
intervention in new and/or multiple settings. They also point out that the common
main effects-type question of "what works" is often too limiting in real-world
settings. Instead, they advise applied researchers and evaluators to design studies
to answer questions such as what works for whom, where, why, for what, and
when?

Once you have the evidence you need to feel confident about moving forward
with the design of a new intervention, it is time to consider the research or evaluation approach that is most likely to lead to success. Donaldson (2007) outlines a
range of applied research and evaluation strategies that are helpful for increasing
the success of interventions. In short, one objective to his theory-driven approach
is to tailor the applied research or evaluation design to meet the challenges of the
specific application. A key part of the tailoring process is determining what questions need to be addressed, taking into account time and resource constraints – for
example, questions about the need, design, theory, process, implementation,
outcome, impact, or cost-effectiveness of the intervention. The research or evaluation design is then tailored to provide credible and actionable evidence to answer
the questions of most interest.

Much of the intervention research to date in positive psychology is referred to
as efficacy evaluation in Donaldson's (2007) framework. This type of work deter-
mines if interventions work under ideal or research-like conditions. The value of
this work is to determine if interventions are efficacious under ideal conditions
before they are unleashed on society. The work on interventions designed to treat
depression (described in Chapter 6) provides an example of high-quality work in
this domain. The limitation of these types of studies is that they don't indicate
whether the same effects would occur in real world settings (more work needs to
be done), and some may question their objectivity given that the evaluator/
researcher often has a vested interest in finding positive results.

Effectiveness evaluation and research, on the other hand, answers questions
related to whether an intervention makes a difference out in society. This
work typically evaluates the interventions being implemented for clients, service
recipients, or consumers in real-world school, healthcare, organizational, and

community settings. A formative evaluation design, or using timely evidence from an evaluation to guide the successful development and implementation of an intervention, is often used as part of this strategy to increase the chances of an intervention succeeding. Again, whether an effectiveness evaluation focuses on formative or summative evaluation questions depends on the context and constraints of the application. An obvious limitation of effectiveness evaluations is that the investigator has much less control of the design and data collection than in a typical efficacy research or evaluation situation.

The profession of applied research and evaluation has grown tremendously over the past two decades. There is now a wide range of tools, techniques, guiding principles, and quality standards that can be used to help practitioners design and implement effective interventions (Donaldson & Christie, 2006). Practitioners who choose to use the theories, principles, and findings of positive psychology to improve society may benefit greatly from partnering with objective professional evaluators – evaluators equipped to provide credible and actionable evidence to help increase the success of positive psychology interventions, as well as to determine their success or failure in real-world settings.

CONCLUSION

Ruark (2009) describes positive psychology as an intellectual movement for the masses. She points out that while most scholars labor in obscurity, positive psychologists and their research are in incredibly high demand. Some of the most successful scholars and leaders in this new field participated in the 2009 Stauffer Symposium in Claremont, and most followed up by contributing a chapter to this volume. The ideas for improving the human condition and the society they have left us with are informative and inspiring. With the benefits of the wisdom of our authors and the critics of positive psychology, an emerging research literature, and the tools and techniques of professional evaluation, applied positive psychology is poised for a productive future. It is my hope that the passion and optimism expressed throughout this volume have inspired you to become involved in rigorous, systematic efforts to further the science and practice of positive psychology.

REFERENCES

Chen, H. T., Donaldson, S. I., & Mark, M. M. (in press). Validity frameworks for outcome evaluation. In H. T. Chen, S. I. Donaldson, & M. M. Mark (Eds.), *Advancing validity in outcome evaluation: Theory and practice. New Directions for Evaluation.*
Csikszentmihalyi, M. (2003). Legs or wings? A reply to R. S. Lazarus. *Psychological Inquiry,* 14, 113–115.
Donaldson, S. I. (2007). *Program theory-driven evaluation science: Strategies and applications.* Mahwah, NJ: Lawrence Erlbaum Associates, Inc.
Donaldson, S. I., & Christie, C. A. (2006). Emerging career opportunities in the transdiscipline of evaluation science. In S. I. Donaldson, D. E. Berger, & K. Pezdek (Eds.),

Applied psychology: New frontiers and rewarding careers (pp. 243–259). Mahwah, NJ: Lawrence Erlbaum Associates, Inc.

Donaldson, S. I., Christie, C. A., & Mark, M. M. (2008). *What counts as credible evidence in applied research and evaluation practice?* Newbury Park, CA: Sage Publications.

Donaldson, S. I., & Lipsey, M.W. (2006). Roles for theory in contemporary evaluation practice: Developing practical knowledge. In I. Shaw, J. C. Greene, & M. M. Mark (Eds.), *The handbook of evaluation: Policies, programs, and practices* (pp. 56–75). London: Sage Publications.

Ehrenreich, B. (2009). *Bright-sided: How the relentless promotion of positive thinking has undermined America.* New York: Metropolitan Books.

Fineman, S. (2006a). On being positive: Concerns and counterpoints. *Academy of Management Review, 31,* 270–291.

Fineman, S. (2006b). Accentuating the positive? *Academy of Management Review, 31,* 306–308.

Gargani, J., & S. I. Donaldson (in press). What works for whom, where, why, for what, and when?: Answering important questions in contemporary evaluation practice. In H. T. Chen, S. I. Donaldson, & M. Mark (Eds.), *Advancing validity in outcome evaluation: Theory and practice. New Directions for Evaluation.*

Hackman, J. R. (2009a). The perils of positivity. *Journal of Organizational Behavior, 30,* 209–319.

Hackman, J. R. (2009b). The point of POB: Rejoinder. *Journal of Organizational Behavior, 30,* 321–322.

Hedges, C. (2009). *Empire of illusion: The end of literacy and the triumph of spectacle.* New York: Nation Books.

Lazarus, R. S. (2003a). Does the positive psychology movement have legs? *Psychological Inquiry, 14,* 93–109.

Lazarus, R. S. (2003b). The Lazarus manifesto for positive psychology and psychology in general. *Psychological Inquiry, 14,* 173–189.

Luthans, F., & Avolio, B. J. (2009a). The "point" of positive organizational behavior. *Journal of Organizational Behavior, 30,* 291–307.

Luthans, F., & Avolio, B. J. (2009b). Inquiry unplugged: Building on Hackman's potential perils of POB. *Journal of Organizational Behavior, 30,* 323–328.

Lyubomirsky, S., & Abbe, A. (2003). Positive psychology's legs. *Psychological Inquiry, 14,* 132–136.

Miller, M. (2008). A critique of positive psychology – or "the new science of happiness". *Journal of Philosophy of Education, 42,* 591–608.

Peterson, C., & Park, N. (2003). Positive psychology as the evenhanded positive psychologist views it. *Psychological Inquiry, 14,* 143–147.

Roberts, L. M. (2006). Shifting the lens on organizational life: The added value of positive scholarship. *Academy of Management Review, 31,* 292–305.

Ruark, J. (2009, August 3). An intellectual movement for the masses: 10 years after its founding, positive psychology struggles with its own success. *Chronicles of Higher Education.* Retrieved June 10, 2009, from http://chronicle.com/article/An-Intellectual-Movement-for/47500/

Ryff, C. D. (2003). Corners of myopia in the positive psychology parade. *Psychological Inquiry, 14,* 153–159.

Author Index

Subject Index

CPSIA information can be obtained
at www.ICGtesting.com
Printed in the USA
FSHW011958160120
66190FS